Understanding
Hypertext
Concepts and Applications

NOTICES

AmandaStories™	Amanda Goodenough
AppleLink™	Apple Computer, Inc.
AskSam™	AskSam Systems
AutoCAD®	Autodesk
BlackMagic™	NTERGAID
ComputorEdge®	Byte Buyer
DOSHelp™	Flambeaux Software
EMPOWERment™	Seyer Associates
Eyecons™	Heizer Software
FANATAVISION™	Broderbund Software
Fluency-building™	Precision Teaching and Management Systems, Inc.
Guide™	Owl International
HotShot Graphics™	Symsoft
HyperArrays™	Clear Lake Research
HyperBase™	Cogent Software
HyperBASIC™	Teknosys, Inc.
HyperCard™	Apple Computer, Inc.
Hyperdoc™	Hyperdoc, Inc.
HyperNotes™	Saucer Computer Systems
HyperPAD™	Brightbill-Roberts & Company, Ltd.
HyperRez™	MaxThink
HyperSprint™	Seyer Associates
HyperTalk™	Apple Computer, Inc.
HyperTIES™	Cognetics Corp.
HyperTSR™	Seyer Associates
HyperTutor™	Channelmark Corp.
HyperWriter™	NTERGAID
IBM PC®	IBM, Inc.
Ize™	Persoft
KeyPilot™	Blaise Computing
KnowledgePro™	Knowledge Garden
KPWIN™	Knowledge Garden
LOGiiX®	Owl International, Inc.
OpenScript®	Asymetrix Corp.
PADtalk®	Brightbill-Roberts & Company, Ltd.
PC-Browse™	QuickSoft, Inc.
Persoft®	Persoft, Inc.
Quattro®	Borland International
QuickBASIC™	Microsoft
ScanMan™	LogiTech, Inc.
SPEECH THING®	COVOX, Inc.
VOICE MASTER®	COVOX, Inc.
StackPaks™	Educorp
SuperText™	Zortech Inc.
ToolBook™	Asymetrix Corp.
TransText™	MaxThink
Traveler's Guilde: Japanese™	GuildWare, Inc.
Traveler's Guild™	GuildWare, Inc.
VIMAGER™	Aitech International Corp.
Xhelp™	Exwells Software Co.
XTC™	Flambeaux Software

Understanding

Hypertext

Concepts and Applications

Philip Seyer

FIRST EDITION
FIRST PRINTING

© 1991 by **Windcrest Books**, an imprint of TAB Books.
TAB Books is a division of McGraw-Hill, Inc.
The name ''Windcrest'' is a registered trademark of TAB Books.

Library of Congress Cataloging-in-Publication Data

Seyer, Philip C., 1941—
    Understanding hypertext : concepts and applications / by Philip
Seyer.
        p.   cm.
    Includes index.
    ISBN 0-8306-9108-1 (hard)   ISBN 0-8306-3308-1 (pbk.)
    1. Hypertext systems.   I. Title.
QA76.76.H94S48   1991
005.75'4—dc20   90-28582
                                                       CIP

TAB Books offers software for sale. For information and a catalog, please contact
TAB Software Department, Blue Ridge Summit, PA 17294-0850.

Questions regarding the content of this book should be addressed to:

Reader Inquiry Branch
Windcrest Books
Blue Ridge Summit, PA 17294-0850

Acquisitions Editor: Stephen-Moore
Technical Editor: Patti McCarty
Production: Katherine G. Brown
Book Design: Jaclyn J. Boone

Contents

Acknowledgments   *ix*

Introduction   *xi*

1 Introduction to hypertext   **1**

History of hypertext   *4*
Recent hypertext developments   *8*
PC hypertext systems   *9*
Hypertext concepts   *12*

2 Elements of hypertext   **13**

Nodes   *13*
DOS utilities and hypertext   *15*
Links and buttons   *18*
Editors   *23*
Navigation tools   *23*
Webs   *28*
Built-in programming languages   *30*
Summary   *30*

3 Hypertext nodes   **31**

Text nodes   *31*
Graphics nodes   *33*
Computer-animated nodes   *38*
Video nodes   *41*
Buttons on video displays   *43*
Musical nodes   *43*
Using macro scripts to refine commands   *45*
Digitized voice nodes   *47*
People as nodes   *47*
Faxable nodes   *48*

4   Buttons and links   **49**

Guide buttons   *50*
HyperSprint reference buttons   *55*
Reference buttons in EMPOWERment   *56*
LinkWay buttons and objects   *56*
HyperWriter buttons and links   *58*
Creating links from graphics   *60*
Command buttons   *64*
Linking with other computers   *73*
Advantage of command buttons   *73*
Date buttons   *74*
Automatic linking   *75*
Typed links   *79*
Summary   *80*

5   Why use hypertext?   **83**

Maintain continuity   *83*
Capture inspirational thoughts   *84*
Hypertext as a writing tool   *85*
Better organized, more creative documents   *86*
Project management   *88*
Hypertext help systems   *89*
If I don't want to switch   *92*

6   Issues in developing hypertext networks   **93**

Table of contents approach   *93*
Hierarchical approach   *95*
Hypermaps   *97*
Summary approach   *98*
Guided tour   *98*
Decision table approach   *99*
Empirical approach   *103*
Index approach   *103*
Combine the approaches   *104*
Authoring guidelines   *105*
Selecting a hypertext system   *118*
Summary   *119*

7   Hypertext applications   **121**

Improving personal productivity   *121*
Ensuring follow-through   *122*
Book development with hypertext   *124*
The Oxford English Dictionary   *125*
KAS (Knowledge Acquisition System)   *126*
Reg-In-A-Box   *128*

Dr. Dobb's Journal   *129*
ComputorEdge magazine   *130*
On-line help with HyperTSR   *133*
Hypertext and museums   *134*
A hyptertext simulation   *135*
Hypertext/expert systems   *135*
Hypertext tutorials   *136*
Summary   *141*

8   Programming hypertext   **143**

Scripting in HyperCard   *143*
Scripts and PC programs   *150*
Setting up memory-resident hypertext systems   *162*
Distributing your own hypertext systems   *175*
Developing original hypertext applications   *175*
Summary   *207*

9   Future developments   **209**

New pointing devices   *209*
New media   *209*
User seduction   *211*
Hypertext and telecommunication   *211*
The media lab   *211*
Hypertisements   *211*
Hypertext of the future   *212*
Ted Nelson's dream   *213*
Hypertext and world hunger   *213*
I invite your help   *213*

10   Hypertext sources and resources   **215**

Hypertext programming tools   *215*
Node design methodology   *217*
PC hypertext development systems   *218*
Macintosh hypertext systems and related programs   *230*
The "HyperCard" for the Apple II   *232*
Hypertext for the Amiga   *232*
Hypercard on the Atari   *233*
Hypertext applications   *233*
HyperCard applications on the Macintosh   *234*
Articles, magazines, newsletters   *238*
Books   *242*
Organizations and individuals   *244*
Graphics video, sound, and animation   *253*

Index   *259*

Acknowledgments

My thanks go to:

Kumiko Seyer for enduring the hypertext clutter that almost overwhelmed me during the writing of this book: multiple computers, diskettes, hypertext manuals, magazines, books, and more.

Dan Seyer for loaning me his AT laptop when I hurt my back and needed to work from a comfortable chair.

Kristina Seyer for sharing her knowledge of HyperCard and the U.C. MKSCRN program.

Ron Powers, Sandra Johnson, and Stephen Moore for helping to shape the purpose and focus of this book.

Safaa Hashim for many fine discussions and friendly, informative arguments on Prolog, AI, object-oriented programming, and hypertext.

Wally Wang of *ComputorEdge* magazine, San Diego for his helpful referrals.

The many companies who provided me with information and review copies of their hypertext products.

Introduction

Understanding Hypertext: Concepts and Applications will give you a solid grasp of the new emerging technology called hypertext. (Another term in common use is hypermedia. These two terms are used interchangeably in this book.) When you finish this book, you will be able to:

- Distinguish hype from hypertext.
- Identify the main features present or absent in a hypertext system.
- Ask key questions when evaluating a hypertext system. For example: "Does the system allow hypertext buttons to be embedded in graphical nodes?"
- Choose a hypertext system appropriate to your needs and interests.
- Identify suppliers of various hypertext systems.
- Get free or low-cost hypertext systems for your Macintosh, IBM PC, or ATARI ST.
- Find individuals and organizations that can help you develop special-purpose hypertext systems.
- Develop hypertext-based instructional materials.
- Envision hypertext systems of the future.

More than this, you will be able to use hypertext to:

- Boost your productivity.
- Get better organized.
- Increase your learning power.
- Follow through on important tasks.

No special computer programming knowledge is needed to benefit from this book, although, a knowledge of at least one language will help you get the most out of chapter 8, Programming hypertext.

I begin with a simple introduction to hypertext, which assumes that you know little, if anything, about it. Each following chapter goes into more depth about the features of hypertext introduced in the beginning chapters. You'll learn about such things as nodes, networks, autotours, hypertext editors, replacement buttons, reference buttons, links, typed links, link maps, intelligent hypertext, dynamic links, scripting, and principles of hypertext design. In addition, you will see how various organizations are using hypertext in a wide variety of situations: in government, business and education. You will also take a look at the future of hypertext. The final chapter identifies several products and publications, as well as several organizations that can help you make the best use of this emerging technology.

Special features

This book offers some special features that will be difficult to find in other books:

- The complete source code needed to compile a handy PC hypertext editor.
- The source code for adding hypertext to an existing commercial word processor.
- A comprehensive, annotated hypertext bibliography that lists hypertext systems, books, magazines, articles, companies, add-on software, and helpful individuals and organizations. Complete addresses and phone numbers are provided for your convenience.
- Multiple illustrations along with explanations that show many different hypertext systems in action.

Through special arrangement with TAB Books, two PC hypertext products: EMPOWERment and HyperTSR are offered to readers at a discount. For details, see the order form in the back of this book.

1
Introduction to hypertext

Although the term "hypertext" is relatively new to many of us, it was actually coined in 1965 and an article predicting hypertext was published in 1945. I'll say more on these early developments later in this chapter, but first let's define hypertext. Quite simply, *hypertext* is nonlinear, or nonsequential, text. That is, the text is organized so you can easily jump around from topic to topic. You do not need to read the text in a fixed sequence. Although hypertext is probably best brought to life on a computer, you can find hypertext in simple paper documents.

Consider two examples of text: a paperback novel and the front page of a newspaper. Which of these would you say is hypertext? I would say the newspaper page is hypertext because you can easily jump from topic to topic; if you want more depth on any one topic you can turn to the appropriate page. The novel, on the flip side, does not encourage you to skip around. The novelist assumes you will be reading in a fixed sequence—that you will read one page right after another. Of course, we don't always do this. But the point is that a novel does not provide any structured way for us to "skip to the good parts."

When hypertext is implemented on a computer system, there is potential for giving readers more flexibility in jumping around from topic to topic. The text for each topic may be stored in a special area of computer memory and then easily accessed. In the hypertext literature these "areas of computer memory" are referred to as "notecards," "cards" or "nodes." (Some writers use other names as well.) *Hypertext*, using this terminology, is an approach to information management where you store information in a network of nodes and connect the nodes with links. A *node* is usually a small collection of data organized around a single topic.

In the early days of hypertext, nodes contained only textual data. Now nodes can contain various kinds of data: graphics, audio, video, computer-animated images, film clips of animated scenes, digital sound or other kinds of information. Some people use the term *hypermedia* when referring to systems that include a wide variety of node types. Following the current practice, I use the term hypertext interchangeably with hypermedia.

The word "hyper" in hypertext has the meaning of "extending into another dimension" as in hyperspace, hypersphere, or hyperdimensional. If you haven't experienced hypertext before, imagine this: you are listening to a fine performance of Beethoven's Fifth

Symphony. As you listen, the musical score is displayed on your screen. When you press the Spacebar, a description of orchestra and conductor appears. At the bottom of the screen you see:

Other recordings
Books
Articles

These words appear in yellow on your color monitor, whereas the rest of the text is white on blue. This indicates to you that these highlighted words are hyperwords. By moving the cursor to Other recordings and pressing, say, F10, you zoom off to a list of all of the other published recordings of this piece. After selecting a specific recording, your PC immediately begins to display the score and play that recording. When you press an appropriate key (for example Esc), you return to the previous node. In the same way, you can get a list of all published documents that refer to or discuss the current musical selection. Then by selecting any particular document, you can immediately zoom into it. Think of how enjoyable it would be to use such a system to listen and compare the work of various artists and writers. That's hypertext. Although we can't yet access all published documents related to a single topic from a hypertext program—we are moving in that direction in the 1990s.

Hypertext is now being used in more and more areas. Educators are making good use of hypertext and making learning difficult subjects more and more accessible. Imagine you are reading instructional material on a computer screen. Several technical terms on the screen are highlighted—shown in a different color, say, yellow letters on a green background or black letters on a white background. Imagine that you can instantly branch off to a new window of information—a definition or elaboration of any of these highlighted words. Think of how comfortable learning with a well-designed hypertext system is! If you don't know the meaning of a word, just point to it and press a key—shzamm! An explanation will appear. In this way you can go on exploring and learning in your own way until you are ready to return to the original node.

Examples of this kind of hypertext are available now. Figure 1-1 shows an example: a PC hypertext tutorial on musical composition taken from a course called "What Makes Music Work" developed with a program called HyperWriter. In this example the tutorial is testing the student's ability to create what is known as a "sequence variation." The user can get help by clicking the mouse button with the mouse pointer on the phrase sequence variation. When the user clicks the mouse button, an explanation pops up in a separate window as you can see in Fig. 1-2.

Also, notice that certain words are marked in the pop-up window with little triangles. By clicking on these words with the left mouse button, the user can pop up even more information. Each time the user selects a highlighted word, the program jumps to a new node. To return a previous node, the user can press Esc or click the right mouse button.

Many hypertext reference guides and tutorials are now becoming available on a wide range of topics as you will see in chapter 7 and chapter 10.

In Fig. 1-2, the user branched to a new node by clicking a mouse. But how you branch varies from system to system; usually you can do it by moving the cursor over a highlighted word and pressing a key or clicking a mouse button. See Fig. 1-3, which illustrates the concept of hypertext.

COMPOSING VARIATIONS

Introduction   In this exercise you will get some guided practice
in composing variations. All of the variations
will be based on this ◄motive►:

Exercise   First, let's create a ◄sequence variation► . Write
your answer on your music score paper.▶ When you're
to check your answer, click on the "Next page"
button.

◄<---Previous page►   ◄Next page --->►

Fig. 1-1 Hypertext tutorial on musical composition.

Introduction   In this   A sequence is a series of notes that have the
same melodic contour as the previous notes. The
in compo ◄intervals► in the sequence are kept the same as
will be   the original, but the sequence starts on a
different ◄degree► of the ◄scale►.

Exercise   First, let's create a ◄sequence variation► . Write
your answer on your music score paper. When you're
to check your answer, click on the "Next page"
button.

◄<---Previous page►   ◄Next page --->►

Fig. 1-2 Definition of "sequence" in a pop-up node.

Figure 1-3 illustrates how I used hypertext to help me manage some of my writing
activities. In this figure you can see the name of three nodes. When I select 12-01-88.1, the
contents of second node (Article On Hypertext) appears on the screen. Article On Hypertext
is a node that I used to help me manage the writing of an article on hypertext for a professional society I belong to called the National Society for Performance and Instruction
(NSPI). (More on NSPI in chapter 3.)

Within the Article On Hypertext node you can see links to several other nodes. If I were
to select thiagi.adr, the third node would appear, which contains the address of the editor
to whom I needed to submit the article. When I select a highlighted word I am, in effect,

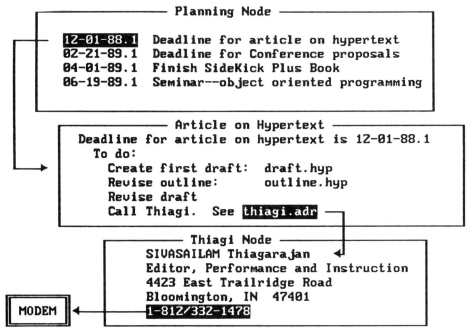

Fig. 1-3 A simple hypertext model.

accessing a different node in the network. The third node might, in turn, contain links to other nodes. I can go off exploring on my own, jumping from node to node until I am satisfied that I'm ready to return to the original starting place. In some hypertext systems you can press a "home" key and return to where you started your branching.

NOTE: One of the possible difficulties with hypertext, is that users may become disoriented and lost in the network of nodes. We'll discuss this issue in more detail in chapter 6 and give some suggestions how to avoid this problem.

Hypertext is a distinct computer technology, which is continuing to mature and develop. Some see it as one of the next major application types for the 1990s. Our existing application types include databases, spreadsheets, desk top publishing, telecommunication. But hypertext can help us make better use of the application types that already exist. Although hypertext is just now coming into its own, it has been around for a long time! Let's consider the early days of hypertext.

History of hypertext

Hypertext has a fascinating history. Although Ted Nelson coined the term "hypertext" in 1965, Vannevar Bush was probably the first to discuss the concept in print—20 years earlier!

Bush was one of America's early computer scientists. He built an analog computer at MIT in the 1930s. During World War II, Bush was the director of the Office of Research and Development; he managed some 6,000 U.S. scientists. He saw that the methods of sharing and reviewing information in 1945 were "totally inadequate." He noted that the means for threading through the maze of scientific publications had not changed for nearly 200 years. Bush, however, saw that a change was coming. Even before the invention of the first transistor he observed: "The world has arrived at an age of cheap complex devices of great reliability; and something is bound to come of it."

Bush imagined a device that he called the "memex," a powerful device that a person could use to store all of his information: books, pictures, records, letters, and so on. Most importantly, Bush imagined that the user of the memex could consult the information with "exceeding speed and flexibility" in an associative way—the way the mind works in jumping from thought to thought. In Bush's time, of course, this was just a dream. In his words: "Selection by association, rather than indexing, may yet be mechanized."

Bush stressed that the main contribution of the "memex" would be its capability to link two things together:

> "It affords an immediate step . . . to associative indexing, the basic idea of which is a provision whereby any item may be caused at will to select immediately and automatically another. This is the essential feature of the memex. The process of tying two items together is the important thing."

After Bush's visionary article appeared in 1945, not much happened for about 14 years. Then in the 1950s, researcher Doug Engelbart began thinking about the interaction of humans and computers. Engelbart had read Bush's article and was inspired to implement a hypertext system. In 1959 he began a research project called "Augmenting Human Intellect" at the Stanford Research Institute. The goal of Engelbart's research has been to develop computer systems that help us think—rather than just record and retrieve data and automate work. Said another way, Doug has focused on finding ways to use the computer to approach and solve complex problems. He believes that our use of traditional computer systems for this purpose just barely taps the surface.

Eighteen years after Bush's article was published, Engelbart published his ideas under the title: "A Conceptual Framework for the Augmentation of Man's Intellect." In 1968, Engelbart, in connection with the Stanford Research Institute, gave an impressive demonstration of a hypertext system at a conference of computer scientists.

His demonstration in 1968 involved the use of his "Augment" system to create a hypertext document with a colleague 500 miles away. This Augment system has evolved over the years and is now a well-developed system used at McDonnell Douglas for internal projects. Today, the main purpose of Augment is to support communication among software engineers. It's interesting to note that it was Engelbart who invented the mouse. He invented it so users of his system could branch off to different nodes simply by "pointing" at highlighted words. Engelbart is also credited with inventing multiple-window screens, outline processing, idea processing, and composite text-graphic files. Some even say he invented hypertext.

But others contributed to hypertext as well. Remember, the concept of hypertext was published in 1945 by Vannevar Bush and Engelbart had read Bush's article. As I mentioned earlier, Ted Nelson coined the term hypertext in the 1960s. Nelson was a seventh-grade drop out (now with a Master's degree!) and a self-proclaimed social critic, rogue intellectual, and designer.

Let's take a brief look at how Nelson came upon the idea of hypertext. In 1960, he was taking a course in computer programming in the second year of graduate school.

(Although Nelson left school in seventh grade, apparently he was somehow pushed back into it.) Prior to taking the computer course, Nelson had started to collect notes on file cards for the purpose of writing various college papers. But the note card system proved inadequate. The cards got "out of hand." In his book *Literary Machines* Nelson explains:

> "Every file card wanted to be many places at once, many needed to be pasted in the middle of several different documents and separately reworked, but needed to stay connected between documents as well. All methods of paper were wholly inadequate and imposed connective restrictions that masked the true structure of the ideas."

When Nelson took the computer programming course in 1960, he thought that perhaps the computer could offer a better way of handling note cards. In his programming course, Nelson studied machine language and assembly language. As a result he learned to dig into the belly of the computer. He's still glad that this course didn't deal with a language like Fortran, which would have shielded him from what was really happening in the machine.

As part of his programming class, Nelson had to do a term project. He announced that it would be a writing system. This proposed system would let you store your manuscripts in the computer, edit them, and then print them out. He called this process "text handling." It wasn't until years later that this idea was commercialized and called "word processing." But Nelson's project went further than simple "text handling." He wanted a user to be able to carefully compare ideas by bringing up two versions of something side-by-side. He also included in his design historical backtracking and "revision by outline." The only system available at that time was a gigantic 7090 IBM computer that worked with punch cards. Nelson didn't finish the project on time and got an incomplete for the course. He did, however, receive a Master's degree—"only a Master's degree," as he describes it.

Nelson's first design was basically word processing with intercomparison of alternative versions with historical backtracking capability. In the early 1960s there was a lot of government money supporting CAI (Computer-Assisted Instruction). Nelson was in favor of CAI at first, but then he discovered that its primary focus was on helping teachers deliver tightly controlled curriculum. Nelson's goal, instead, was to help students break away from highly structured and predefined learning outcomes.

Nelson, however, benefited greatly from talking to CAI researchers at Cambridge. CAI at that time emphasized the branching capability of the computer—the ability to branch to different instructional materials on the basis of student's responses. All this talk about branching inspired Nelson to conceive of what he finally called hypertext. Many of the elements of hypertext were present in the early CAI programs, but in those CAI programs users could not branch freely. The branching that was allowed was tightly controlled by the program to ensure that the student would stick to the prescribed curriculum.

About this time Nelson conceived of his second design for hypertext: "chunk-style" hypertext. *Chunk-style hypertext* is hypertext in which the user reads a chunk of text and then decides which chunk to be read next. Nelson became excited about getting into the computer field. But in those days the prevailing attitude was that computers were "mathematical." Because Nelson felt he was mathematically incompetent, he was unable to get a job in the computer field. (The California school system still holds the archaic view that computers are primarily mathematical. You can't teach computer programming in California public high schools without a credential to teach mathematics.)

In 1965 Nelson came up with a third design for hypertext. This design combined his original concept of side-by-side editing and comparison of documents with his ideas about nonsequential writing. About this time Nelson started to make headway in convincing others that his ideas might actually work. But at that time people had computer screens; they did their work on punchcard machines and read printouts from teletype machines. So the idea of being able to branch by selecting a "hyperword" on a screen seemed a bit far-fetched to many people. They lost interest in Nelson's ideas and called it "arm waving" and "blue sky." (A government intelligence agency did contact Nelson and suggest that they might be willing to provide money to support his research. But it turned out that this was just "empty" talk.)

Then in the late 1960s Nelson was invited to cooperate on a project at Brown University. The people at Brown University told him their objective was to try out some of his ideas. For several years he consulted at Brown and helped them develop a hypertext editing system. Nelson kept pushing for more elaborate hypertext features, but the boss there, Andries van Dam, was focusing on paper output at the time. Nelson claims that this early focus on paper output may have set progress on hypertext back considerably.

Through the years Nelson has continued to work on his hypertext system despite a constant lack of funds. While at a large book firm, he came up with the name Xanadu for his developing hypertext system. The name comes from the mysterious palace in Coleridge's poem "Kublai Khan." Over time, Nelson and his cohorts have developed and refined a number of secret algorithms that reportedly enable their hypertext system to maintain and quickly access alternative versions of hypertext documents. In the late 1980s Nelson landed a job at Autodesk, the firm that created the famous AutoCad that engineers love so much. It now appears that the long awaited Xanadu hypertext will actually be released soon to the general public. Many are skeptical, but my sources indicate that by the time you read this, a Xanadu system will be operating on a Sun workstation. Still it will probably be five more years before Xanadu will be on most people's kitchen table. (See chapter 10 for information on Xanadu.)

Besides Xanadu, development of a number of other hypertext systems began after Engelbart's demonstration in 1968. All of this early work, of course, was done by computer specialists on large computer systems—because microcomputers had not yet been invented. Some of the early hypertext systems were:

    ZOG—Carnegie-Mellon University
    INTERMEDIA—Brown University
    NOTECARDS—Xerox PARC
    DOCUMENT EXAMINER—SYMBOLICS
    NEPTUNE—Tektronix
    WE—University of North Carolina
    Xanadu—Ted Nelson
    Boxer—DiSessa (diSessa, 1985)

Most of these early systems are still evolving. For example, the Xanadu Operating Company (funded by Autodesk) is marketing Ted Nelson's Xanadu system as "industrial strength'' hypertext. It runs on in a local area network with a Sun workstation as a server. (See chapter 10 for details.) Brown University is continuing to expand and develop INTERMEDIA to the delight of both faculty and students. For more details on the early history of hypertext, see Lee Conklin's excellent survey of hypertext. (Conklin, 1987.) The October, 1988 issue of *Byte* magazine also offers some good information about the history of hypertext.

Recent hypertext developments

Even though hypertext research and development accelerated after Doug Engelbart's demonstration in 1968, hypertext, like certain ancient truths, has been a well-kept secret. In the past, hypertext was largely known only to computer scientists. But within the past two years interest in hypertext has skyrocketed:

- A new publication called *HyperMedia* appeared.
- Several universities now have laboratories devoted to research on hypertext.
- A recent issue of *Byte* magazine and *Communications of ACM* have focused on hypertext.
- A special Mix publication devoted to hypermedia appeared in the summer of 1988.
- New companies that specialize in developing *hyperware* are forming. (Hyperware is a special kind of software that works with a hypertext program. See chapter 7, Hypertext Applications.)

In 1987 Conklin reported that the first (and only known) Ph.D thesis on hypertext was written by Randall Trigg. Trigg describes a hypertext system designed for literary criticism and document analysis. Undoubtedly many other dissertations on hypertext are now under preparation. For example, Safaa Hashim, a Ph.D candidate at the University of California, is doing his dissertation on hypertext and developing a hypertext system designed to support a group decision-making process called Issue-Based Information Systems (IBIS). IBIS was conceived originally by Horst Rittel. Hashim is authoring PC software and has written a Windcrest book on this subject called *Exploring Hypertext Programming: Writing Knowledge Representation and Problem-Solving Programs* (No. 3208).

More recently a number of hypertext systems have appeared on microcomputers. The most widely known is probably HyperCard, which Apple Computer distributes free with its Macintosh computer. HyperCard really popularized hypertext and many people think that hypertext was invented by the HyperCard developers. As you've seen, however, the concept of hypertext is more general and existed decades before HyperCard.

Many instructional developers are finding HyperCard especially useful for storyboarding as well as for developing CBT (Computer-Based Training). A *storyboard* in the past was a large board on which a developer would tack up cards. Each card would contain a rough sketch of the primary graphic image to be displayed. Also on the card would be notes about the camera angle, music, dissolves (a gradual superimposing of one motion-picture or television shot upon another on the screen), as well as narration. Now with a hypertext system that has graphics capability, it is faster and more convenient to put each card into a hypertext node. The nodes can easily be viewed in miniature from a "browser node"—a node that gives you a bird's-eye view of all of the nodes that are related and which lets you easily browse among them.

Developers are researching ways to use HyperCard to enhance distance education offered through America Online, of Quantum Computer Services, Inc. (America Online is a telecommunication service similar to CompuServe, but it works especially well with Apple computers.)

"What is distance education?" you ask. Well, it's a kind of structured, formal education that doesn't require you to attend a campus. An example of an old-fashioned form of distance education is a "correspondence course." Although correspondence courses were acceptable in the past, they will probably be largely replaced in the 1990s by courses offered through telecommunication. The mail service is just too slow for our fast-paced information age.

A good example of modern distance education is the Master of Business Administration program offered by Saint Mary's College in Orinda, California. You can complete the program at home, using your computer—you don't have to attend regular classes. In some of the telecommunications-based classes, students meet together in real time—but each student sits at home in front of his or her personal computer. The instructor can present tutorials and ask questions. All students can respond simultaneously—as they do, their answers immediately display on all screens that are netlinked. Although on-line hypertext is not yet available students can download hypertext documents and study them at their own pace. For more information about telecommunication-based distance education courses, you might want to write to America Online, Quantum Computer Services, Inc., 8619 Westwood Center Drive, Vienna, VA 22182.

HyperCard might be the best known microcomputer hypertext system because it is so widely available—everyone who buys a Macintosh gets HyperCard. Even though hypertext is becoming better known, many people still don't seem to understand that HyperCard is not synonymous with hypertext. Others seem to think that there just aren't any hypertext systems on anything but Macintoshes. Although HyperCard does dominate the Macintosh, it is not the only hypertext system available on that machine. Other Macintosh hypertext systems include Hypergate, SuperCard and Guide. Guide was available on the Mac even before HyperCard. The Guide developers had been working closely with Apple, but not as closely as they thought. They were quite surprised when Apple suddenly announced that HyperCard was going to be given away free to all new Macintosh owners. If you are interested in Macintosh hypertext, be sure to see the listings of systems and hypertext software in chapter 10.

PC hypertext systems

Macintosh hypertext systems are not the end of the world when it comes to personal computer hypertext systems. Although Macintosh hypertext systems excel in graphics, a wide range of hypertext systems exist that have many features and boast fast access time and quick development of hypertext networks. Here is a list of just some of these hypertext products. The manufacturer's name is given in parentheses. See chapter 10 for more details.

askSam A free-form information storage and retrieval system that allows you to store both text and numerical data. Besides having a kind of hypertext quality, askSam can produce reports. (askSam Systems)

BlackMagic An inexpensive hypertext word processor distributed as shareware. Version 1.4 of BlackMagic features text and graphics, report generation, graphics printing, and a variety of node types. A new commercial version of BlackMagic called HyperWriter offers several new features. (NTERGAID)

EMPOWERment A hypertext system designed to help individuals organize their work, schedule appointments, manage various projects and use human performance technology in a systematic way. It features an intelligent planning node and automatic node linking. You may also send nodes automatically to MCI Mail subscribers and fax nodes anywhere in the world via MCI Mail even without a fax board. (Seyer Associates)

Guide A professional hypertext system that can display text and graphics. As mentioned earlier, a version of Guide is also available for the Macintosh. Guide features several different kinds of hypertext nodes. A single document (called a *guideline*) can contain many "hidden nodes," which you can unfold. So you can easily prepare different versions of the same document for different audiences. (Owl International)

The Hypertext Editor (HE) A shareware hypertext editor that works with standard ASCII text files. It has many useful editing features. You can customize HE by using the complete source code for it in chapter 8 of this book.

Hyperbase A development system that allows you to create dynamic hypertext. The hypertext, itself, can change in response to the user's history. When the user goes to a node, the system reads and analyzes the text in the node, so nodes may contain "latent code"—code which gets executed each time the user reads the node. The code may even change itself. (Cogent Software)

HyperPAD A hypertext system that resembles HyperCard because it has its own programming language for structuring nodes. The language, PADtalk, allows you to create intelligent hypertext nodes. HyperPAD's main limitation is that it uses only character graphics. (Brightbill-Roberts)

HyperRez A simple but effective memory-resident hypertext system. Each node is stored in a separate file. (MaxThink)

HyperTIES Developed at the University of Maryland, allows small text nodes (50 to 1,000 words) and graphic images to be interconnected. (The "TIES" in HyperTIES stands for "The Interactive Encyclopedia System.")

Hyperdoc A powerful hypertext/hypermedia development tool from France. It supports many different external file formats and has five different internal formats. It has extensive support for linking to video disk players.

HyperTSR A memory-resident hypertext authoring system. It is specially useful for developing on-line help systems for other programs. HyperTSR allows all nodes in a network to be stored in a single file. (Seyer Associates)

IBM LinkWay A flexible hypertext system that comes with a text editor, a picture editor, desktop tools, and teacher tools. Teacher tools include a homework designer, flash card maker, and lesson planner. Like HyperPAD, IBM Linkway has its own built-in script language. You can use this language to control the actions that occur when a user selects a hypertext button. (IBM)

Ize A text-based management system. Its main attraction in the hypertext world is its ability to automatically create an outline based on keywords. You can define keywords for nodes or you can ask Ize to create the keywords automatically based on criteria that you specify. Once Ize has created an outline, you branch from the outline to individual text nodes. (Persoft Inc.)

Knowledge Acquisition System (KAS) On-line (memory resident) full-fledged dictionaries—not just spelling checkers—with hypertext capability. (Inductel Inc.)

KnowledgePro A powerful expert system shell. With it you can develop your own expert system without having to write detailed instructional programs. (An *expert system* is a computer program that tries to emulate the way a human expert solves problems.) But KnowledgePro also incorporates a hypertext development system so users can become more active in exploring concepts and information when using the expert system that runs under it. (Knowledge Garden)

PC-Browse A shareware memory-resident program that lets you bring up file directories and do a keyword search for ASCII text documents. Once you have identified the file you want, you can link it in hypertext fashion or paste it into another document. (Quick-Soft)

PC-Key Draw This program began purely as a graphics package for drawing, but now it has hypertext capability. Some users like to use it strictly as a graphics program, others make more use of its hypertext capabilities. (Oedware)

Plus This is touted as an upgrade to HyperCard. A version is available for Macintosh computers and IBM PCs that run under Windows or the OS/2 Presentation Manager. (Spinnaker)

Sprint A powerful PC word processor that comes with an extensive macro programming language. This language allows multiple user interfaces. Sprint can act like Word-Star, WordPerfect or any other word processor. With some programming knowledge you can transform Sprint into a flexible hypertext word processor. One such system already available is HyperSprint. Sprint and HyperSprint is discussed in more detail in chapter 7 when the focus is on hypertext applications and in chapter 8 when the focus is on programming considerations. (Sprint is from Borland International; the HyperSprint Interface is from Seyer Associates)

Thinker For the Amiga; this is a flexible program that combines elements of text processing, outline processing, and hypertext. Thinker can link documents to picture files, other documents, or other Amiga programs. (Poor Person Software)

The Window Book Technology A highly sophisticated PC hypertext system aimed at major corporations and publishers who want to do large-scale documentation, on-line reference, and context-sensitive help systems. (Box Company Inc.)

Xhelp   An on-line information manager with hypertext capability. It is super fast and requires little memory. You can pop it up over other text-based PC programs. (Exwells)

xText   Another tool for developing memory-resident PC hypertext. It comes with a special compiler that you can use to turn ordinary ASCII files into a compressed hypertext network. The publisher of xText also distributes DOS Help! and TECH Help!—stand-alone hypertext help systems that were developed using xText.

Hypertext concepts

Even though computer technology is still in its infancy, the field of hypertext has come a long way. Remember, Bush's article appeared in 1945, and working models of hypertext have been around for more than 20 years. Consequently many hypertext concepts have evolved. I've alluded to some of those concepts. In the coming chapters, I'll take a closer look at them.

2
Elements of hypertext

In this chapter you will get a quick overview of the basic elements of hypertext. You will learn about:

Nodes	Trails
Links	Navigational tools
Buttons	Built-in programming languages
Editors/Browsers	

As you read this chapter, remember, it's just an overview. In later chapters I will go into more detail.

Nodes

As stated earlier, hypertext is a network of nodes; a node is a collection of data organized around a specific topic. I like the term node because it suggests a collection of data that is related or linked to another body of information. In a network, each node is linked to some other node. In different hypertext systems, different terms are used for nodes. In Hyper-Card, a Card is a node. In HyperPAD, the node is a Pad. HyperWriter and xText talk about nodes as pages.

In many hypertext systems a node is a screenful of data. As you will see later, nodes can be categorized in different ways and there can be different kinds of nodes. Figure 2-1 shows an example of top-level control text node in the EMPOWERment system. It is considered a top-level node because it contains only references and pointers to other nodes. In this system, references to other nodes are always enclosed in braces. That is, each item in braces is a pointer to another node. By moving the cursor to an opening brace and pressing F10, the user can instantly branch to the corresponding node in the network.

The first node reference is {Advertisement Notes}. When the user presses F10 with the cursor on the left brace, {, the node shown in Fig. 2-2 appears.

The second level node in Fig. 2-2 also contains references to other nodes rather than content information. So in this case, it is also a *control node*—it only allows the users to

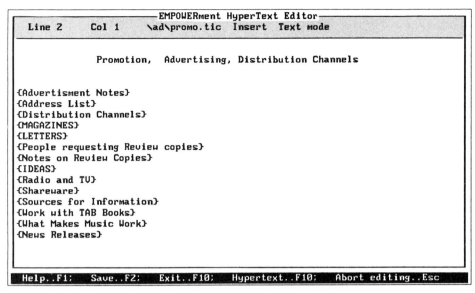

Fig. 2-1 Top level "control" node (from EMPOWERment).

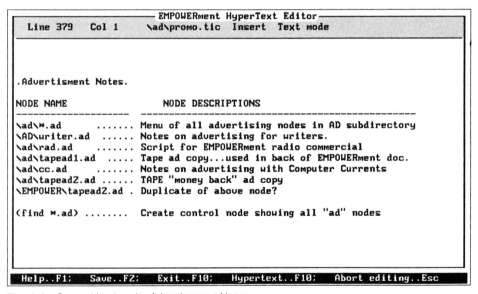

Fig. 2-2 Second level node: Advertisement Notes.

control their navigation through the network. (Control nodes may also be called *transitional nodes* or *navigational nodes*.) Notice that the node references in Fig. 2-2 are in the form of MS-DOS file names. Sometimes it is desirable to have node names that are not limited to the rigid requirements of DOS file names. For simplicity, however, I am using simple file names here.

When a user puts the cursor on a backslash and presses F10, EMPOWERment instantly displays the contents of that node. Here, each node is a separate text file. Figure 2-3 shows the contents of the node called \ad\tapead2.ad. If you look closely at Fig. 2-3, you will see that it contains some strange-looking IBM graphics characters: a smiling face, upside-down pyramids and some musical notes. These are actually word processing control codes—codes used by Borland's word processor: Sprint. That's because this node is a Sprint document file and EMPOWERment is accessing this node directly—without linking first into Sprint. Later you will see how EMPOWERment and other hypertext systems can use external programs, such as WordPerfect, Microsoft Word or Sprint to display such nodes.

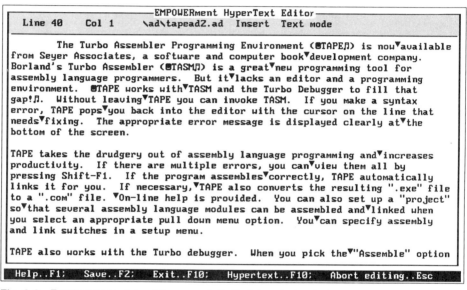

Fig. 2-3 Terminal node: Advertising copy (with Sprint control codes).

DOS utilities and hypertext

There are some DOS utilities that have hypertext-like qualities. For example, some DOS utilities let you view all the subdirectories on a hard disk. The RN utility available from *PC Magazine* is a good example. Using this utility you can view all subdirectories in alphabetical order. You can scroll a selection bar and highlight a subdirectory of interest. When you press F10, the RN program will activate another program called DR. DR will then show you all of the files in the subdirectory. You can now move the selection bar over a file name and press the Enter key to view the contents of the file. The name DR is based on the DOS command DIR. Both DR and DIR show the names of the files in a subdirectory. DR is much nicer than DIR because you can instantly view any file just by selecting it from a scrollable menu. The RN program is so named simply because it works with the DR. (You might have to think about that one for a while—Dr. stands for doctor and a Dr. usually works with an Rn.)

Although RN and DR have hypertext-like qualities, it's important to realize that they are missing an important element of hypertextness: they don't give you the ability to jump from one node to another or to forge links between nodes. For example, when using DR to examine files, you must first exit from a node and return to the main DR menu. Only then can you move the selection bar to a new file name and press the Return key to view it.

A number of application programs now have help systems that make use of hypertext functionality. A good example is Quattro Pro, a spreadsheet program. If you press F1 in Quattro, you will be presented with a help screen related to what you are currently working on. On this screen, several words will be highlighted, if you move the selection bar to a highlighted word you will jump into a new help node. For example, suppose you want to create a macro. If you press F1, the help screen shown in Fig. 2-4 will appear.

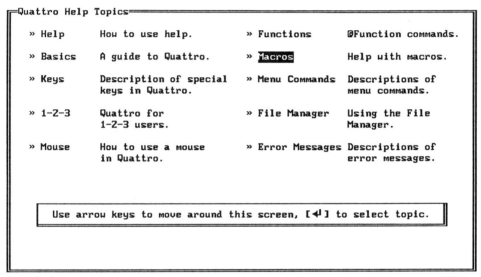

Fig. 2-4   Top level Quattro Pro hypertext help node.

Although you can't see it in Fig. 2-4, each of the help topics listed on this screen are highlighted because they appear in red. These red words are actually hypertext buttons. By using the arrow keys you can highlight different buttons. When you select a button, it appears in reverse video. In Fig. 2-4, I highlighted Macros. When I pressed Return, Quattro did a hypertext jump and displayed a help screen about macros (Fig. 2-5).

In Fig. 2-5 notice that there are seven additional hypertext buttons: Creating Macros, Macro Menu, Key Equivalents, Macro Commands, Menu-Equivalents, Help Topics, and Menu Topics. As you can see, I selected the Creating Macros button. Figure 2-6 shows the Creating Macros node that popped up when I selected this button.

Again, in Fig. 2-6 you can see additional buttons: Recording, Labels, Transcript, Help Topics, and Macro Topics. In Fig. 2-6 you can see that I've selected the Labels topic; consequently, if I pressed the Return key, I would jump to information about how to create macros as labels.

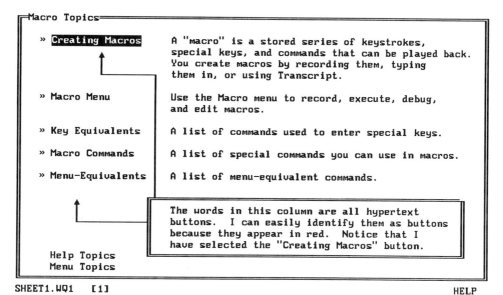

```
┌Macro Topics════════════════════════════════════════════════════════════
║  » Creating Macros     A "macro" is a stored series of keystrokes,
║                        special keys, and commands that can be played back.
║                        You create macros by recording them, typing
║                        them in, or using Transcript.
║
║  » Macro Menu          Use the Macro menu to record, execute, debug,
║                        and edit macros.
║
║  » Key Equivalents     A list of commands used to enter special keys.
║
║  » Macro Commands      A list of special commands you can use in macros.
║
║  » Menu-Equivalents    A list of menu-equivalent commands.
║
║                        ┌──────────────────────────────────────────────┐
║                        │ The words in this column are all hypertext   │
║                        │ buttons.  I can easily identify them as buttons│
║                        │ because they appear in red.  Notice that I   │
║                        │ have selected the "Creating Macros" button.  │
║                        └──────────────────────────────────────────────┘
║     Help Topics
║     Menu Topics
```

SHEET1.WQ1   [1]   HELP

Fig. 2-5   First macros Help node in Quattro Pro.

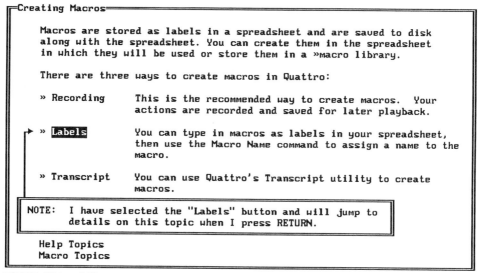

```
┌Creating Macros════════════════════════════════════════════════════════════
║  Macros are stored as labels in a spreadsheet and are saved to disk
║  along with the spreadsheet. You can create them in the spreadsheet
║  in which they will be used or store them in a »macro library.
║
║  There are three ways to create macros in Quattro:
║
║  » Recording      This is the recommended way to create macros.  Your
║                   actions are recorded and saved for later playback.
║
║  » Labels         You can type in macros as labels in your spreadsheet,
║                   then use the Macro Name command to assign a name to the
║                   macro.
║
║  » Transcript     You can use Quattro's Transcript utility to create
║                   macros.
║  ┌──────────────────────────────────────────────────────────────────┐
║  │ NOTE:  I have selected the "Labels" button and will jump to        │
║  │        details on this topic when I press RETURN.                  │
║  └──────────────────────────────────────────────────────────────────┘
║     Help Topics
║     Macro Topics
```

SHEET1.WQ1   [1]   HELP

Fig. 2-6   The Creating Macros node in Quattro Pro's hypertext Help.

The ability to return to a previous node is an important feature of a hypertext system. Can you do this in Quattro Pro? Absolutely. Just press the Backspace key and you will return to the node you were just reading. That is, if you pressed the Esc key while looking at the screen captured in Fig. 2-6, you would immediately return to the node shown in Fig. 2-5. To escape from the help system and return to your spreadsheet, you just press the Esc key. It's worth noting that Quattro Pro uses some useful labeling techniques to help the users keep their place. You might want to take another look at Figs. 2-4 through 2-6. Notice that each node is labeled in the upper left corner. Also, notice that Quattro Pro shows the current active hypertext network in the lower right corner of the screen. Similarly, Turbo C++ has an interesting hypertext-like feature. While writing or studying a program you can get help on any Turbo C command by putting the cursor on the command and pressing Ctrl-F1.

You learn about some other hypertext systems in chapter 7. For now, though, let's take a look at how nodes are linked together.

Links and buttons

Links   A link is information embedded in a node that connects it in some way to another node. Programmers implement links in different ways. A link might be just a file name or it might be a file name and certain numeric values. The numeric values might specify a record number or a byte offset value into the file. Other values might tell how many lines are in the node. In another system a link might be a string that a program must process and convert to a file name and offset values. Later, in chapter 8, Programming Hypertext, I'll go into detail and show you some specific examples of links and how to implement them.

Typed links   Links can be of different types. Consequently, different kinds of things can happen depending on the nature of the link. For example, a "wildcard" link might throw up a menu of ali nodes that match the link specification. Generally, the type of a link shows what kind of node will be accessed if you follow the link—or the link might tell the relationship of the destination node to the current node.

So besides just pointing to a node, a link may carry with it certain other kinds of information—information that the system may use to organize the network and process user queries.

For example, a user might ask the system to list all nodes that contain "refutation links." A refutation link might be a link that points to a node that contains information that disproves the contents of some *parent node*. The parent node, here, might be a *position node*, which contains someone's position on an issue that is being debated by a work group. The issue, in turn, might be contained within an *issue node*. Such a system of nodes is called *Issue-Based Information Systems* (IBIS). IBIS was invented by Horst Rittel at the University of California in Berkeley. The first IBIS system, interestingly enough, was developed on an Apple II with floppy disks. Safaa Hashim, who studied with Rittel, shows how to create an IBIS system on a PC with Turbo Prolog in his book: *Exploring Hypertext Programming: Writing Knowledge Representation and Problem-Solving Programs* (Windcrest book No. 3208). Hashim's book comes with the complete source code for an IBIS system. Figure 2-7 shows a screen from one of Hashim's programs, which presents part of an IBIS map.

There are several node types as well as link types. In this IBIS map, a node designated "I" is an *issue*, which is a controversial question. A node designated "P" is a *position*, which is an answer to a controversial question. A node designated with "A" is an *argument*, which may be for or against a position. A node designated "R" contains a reference to an issue; such a node usually provides background information on the issue.

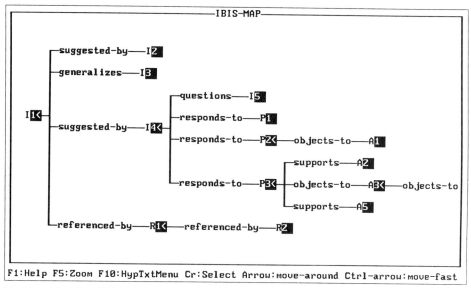

Fig. 2-7 An IBIS-MAP.

In the IBIS map in Fig. 2-7 notice that the relationship between each node is also shown. For example, you can see that node I2, which contains an issue, was suggested by node I1. You can also see that node P1, an answer or position, is responding to node I4 and that node A3 contains an argument that objects to the position in node P3.

At the far right of the screen in Fig. 2-7 you can see that an argument node is linked via an objects-to link to node A3, but you can't see the node itself. (There is an arrow pointing to A3, but you can't see the node attached to the arrow.) That's because the IBIS map is bigger than what could be presented on one screen. But the map is scrollable. To see the rest of the map, you just move the cursor to the far right. In addition to being able to scroll the map, you can also jump into any one of the nodes represented on it by moving the cursor onto a node designation and pressing the Return key. You can also link a node to an existing node by pressing F10. When you do that, IBIS gives you a menu of various options as you can see in Fig. 2-8.

If you choose the Relations option, IBIS displays a menu that lets you choose from the available link types. In this case only argument links are available so an Argument menu appears, as shown in Fig. 2-9. In this example, I chose the objects-to link type to show that I wanted to object to the discussion presented in node A5.

Figure 2-10 shows the revised IBIS map. Notice that I have scrolled to the right in the map window so you can see the new A6 node, which is connected to node A5 via an objects-to link.

In a personal discussion I had with Hashim, he pointed out that when IBIS is used by a group to study an issue, the map that represents the groups work on the issue grows. As the map grows it can provide more and more insights; individuals who study the map can gain a better understanding of the problem. The IBIS map then provides a tool that aids

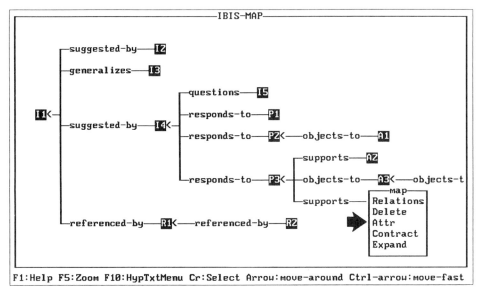

Fig. 2-8 IBIS-MAP menu.

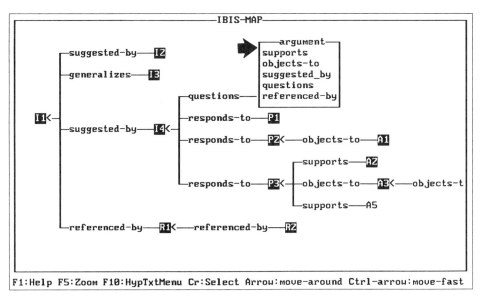

Fig. 2-9 The IBIS argument menu.

decision making. Just by visually inspecting the map you can gain a sense of what the group is thinking about the central issue. And even more important is that because the relationships of all the nodes in the hypertext network can be stored in a knowledge base, various kinds of interesting AI (artificial intelligence) programs can be developed to analyze the group process. For example, an AI program might analyze the IBIS knowledge

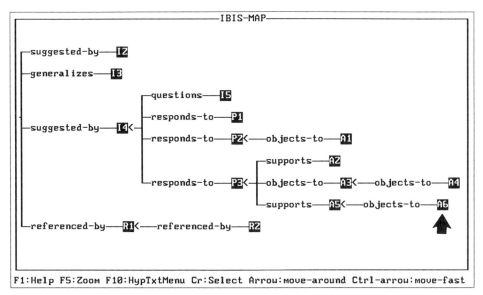

```
┌─────────────────────────IBIS-MAP──────────────────────────┐
│                                                            │
│   ┌suggested-by───I2                                       │
│   ┌generalizes───I3                                        │
│                    ┌questions───I5                         │
│   ┌suggested-by───I4<─┬responds-to───P1                    │
│                    ├responds-to───P2<───objects-to───A1    │
│                                    ┌supports───A2          │
│                    └responds-to───P3<─┬objects-to───A3<───objects-to───A4 │
│                                    └supports───A5<───objects-to───A6 │
│   └referenced-by───R1<───referenced-by───R2        ⬆      │
│                                                            │
│                                                            │
├────────────────────────────────────────────────────────────┤
│ F1:Help F5:Zoom F10:HypTxtMenu Cr:Select Arrow:move-around Ctrl-arrow:move-fast │
└────────────────────────────────────────────────────────────┘
```

Fig. 2-10 A revised IBIS-MAP.

base and try to answer questions such as:

- Is the group brainstorming solutions to the problem?
- Is there consensus on issue X?
- Is this a dangerous issue—one that might lead to group divisiveness?
- Are there individuals in the group who are acting as facilitators? Detractors? Flag waivers?

To my knowledge such AI programs do not yet exist; but there is plenty of room for exploration here.

Michael L. Begeman and Jeff Conklin have created a graphical version of IBIS, called gIBIS, in a system called the Design Journal. At the MCC Software Technology Program, in Austin Texas, the design team uses the Design Journal system to facilitate research thinking and design deliberation. William Horton, in his book *Designing and Writing Online Documentation* reports that the MCC group is developing programs to analyze an IBIS network to answer questions similar to the ones I suggested above.

Button Some writers use the terms button and link interchangeably. But there is a difference. A *button* is a visual cue in a node that alerts a user that a link exists. In other words, a button is a visual representation of a link in a node. By pressing a mouse button, or appropriate function key, the user can cause the system to activate a link to display a different node. Some literature describes a button as a "hot spot" on the screen—a spot that is sensitive. In Guide for example, if you move the cursor (or pointer) over a "hot spot," it will change shape indicating the type of button present.

Figure 2-11 shows a screen from NTERGAID's BlackMagic, a hypertext word processor. The buttons in BlackMagic appear in different colors on screen. There are different

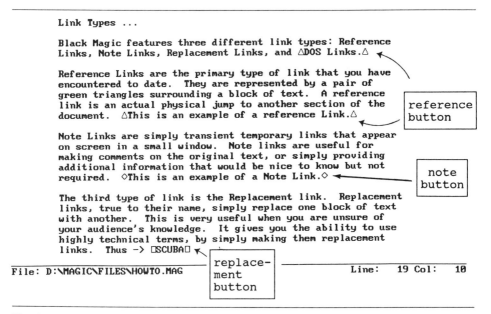

Fig. 2-11   BlackMagic screen with note button.

kinds of buttons and links. The different buttons are labeled in the annotated screen shown in Fig. 2-11.

In this discussion, the button includes the diamonds and the text in between the diamonds. When you move the cursor onto a diamond (or onto the text delimited by the diamonds) and press F1, a note node appears in a small window in the upper right corner of the screen, as shown in Fig. 2-12.

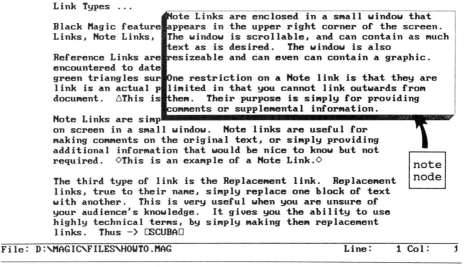

Fig. 2-12   BlackMagic screen with note node.

In BlackMagic note buttons are always indicated with diamond-shaped icons. If you read the text in Figs. 2-11 and 2-12 you might notice that the BlackMagic authors use the term "link" to refer in a general way to both buttons and nodes. This shows that hypertext terminology is still in flux and still evolving. BlackMagic has other kinds of buttons and nodes, discussed in detail in later chapters.

Editors

An editor is the part of the hypertext system that enables a user to create a node and link it into the network. Some hypertext systems are not distributed with an editor because they are intended as "presentation-only systems." For example, "Hypertext on Hypertext," distributed by the Association for Computing Machinery, is the July 1988 issue of *Communications of the ACM* in hypertext format, but it does not come with an editor. Hypertext editors are sometimes rather complicated beasts because they must deal with all of the usual text editing problems, as well as the problem of how you create and link nodes. Some hypertext editors are discussed, with source code, in chapter 8, Programming Hypertext.

Navigation tools

There are several different kinds of navigation tools available in a hypertext system and developers are inventing new ones all of the time. Here I'll discuss browsers, query systems, control nodes, trails, tours, and bookmarks.

Browsers

A hypertext *browser* is a program or subprogram that can display a diagram of a network of nodes. Few hypertext systems for personal computers currently have browsers.

The IBIS map shown earlier in Fig. 2-7 is actually a hierarchical browser. This browser shows a bird's-eye view of the network. In addition, you can jump into any node simply by moving the cursor to that node and pressing F10. It is called a *hierarchical browser* because some nodes are regarded as "parent" nodes which are at a higher level than nodes beneath them. They are sometimes regarded as "child" nodes.

In a hierarchical browser you can see each of the child nodes that are linked to each parent node. That is, you can see what child nodes spring from any given node. If the same child node is connected to two different parent nodes, the child node is repeated under each parent node. In a hypertext network, however, there may not be a hierarchical relationship among nodes. Nodes may be equal and just linked together. In such a case a network browser might be more appropriate. In a *network browser* each node would be designated only once and lines would be drawn to show all of the links between all of the nodes.

I said earlier that few hypertext systems for personal computers have browsers. One notable exception is the HyperWriter available from NTERGAID. HyperWriter is the new name given to an updated version of BlackMagic. (BlackMagic is shareware, whereas HyperWriter is not.) We'll look more closely at the HyperWriter in chapter 4.

Query systems

The usual way to find information in a hypertext network, is to first consult a control node or index node, one that gives you an overview of the entire system. You gradually narrow down your search by stepping down through a series of nodes. This doesn't always work as well as one would like it to as hypertext users have discovered. But my experience is that it is sometimes faster if you can search all nodes for a certain phrase or keyword. Yet some hypertext designers have had a tendency to shun string searches as outmoded and inefficient. Other hypertext designers have incorporated the traditional string search in their programs to satisfy customer demands. BlackMagic, for example, was first offered without a string search. However, when a major customer indicated a need for a string search, NTERGAID, the maker of BlackMagic, responded by adding this feature to the program and to HyperWriter.

So it is also possible to combine the traditional string search with hypertext. A string search program can be designed to build a control node and put the name of each node that it finds in the control node. Then from the control node the user can jump into any of the nodes that contain the keyword. For example, suppose you have contacted Kristina Black-wood about several projects and recorded notes about your discussions. You would like to see a list of all of the nodes that contain references to her so you can be sure what projects you have discussed with her. A hypertext search program might create a control node like the one shown in Fig. 2-13.

The following nodes contain Kristina Blackwood:
`CBT.kb`
CONTACT: Kristina Blackwood   PROJECT: CBT development
Kristina will be doing the graphic art for the new CBT

`ACC.kb`
CONTACT: Kristina Blackwood   PROJECT: Accounting
Kristina, I need to see your expense report for the month of

`SALES.kb`
CONTACT: Kristina Blackwood   PROJECT: CBT Sales
Kristina is preparing a graph showing our sales growth in

Fig. 2-13 Hypertext control node.

Notice in Fig. 2-13 that after the introductory explanatory sentence, a node name is listed on a line by itself, followed by a line that lists the actual search text. In this case the search text was Kristina Blackwood. In addition, the first line of actual text in the node (other than the header line) is listed. To jump into any one of the nodes, all you need to do is to move the cursor to the node name and press an appropriate "hypertext" key. So you have the best of both worlds. You can get a quick overview of all nodes and if you want, jump into any single node when you want more details.

The illustration in Fig. 2-13 is hypothetical. But since I created that example, a handy memory-resident program called PC-Browse was released by QuickSoft, the company that publishes the popular PC-Write word processor. PC-Browse supports hypertext functionality along with string searches across multiple files. Because PC-Browse is memory resident, you can pop it up and do a search while you are using some other application program, as long as you are not in a graphic mode. Here are the steps you would take to do such a search:

1. Press Shift-Ctrl-F1 to pop up PC-Browse.
2. Press F9 and enter the text you want to search for.
3. Press F8 and tell PC-Browse where to search. That is, type the subdirectory name and file search pattern. For example to search all files in a subdirectory called HCA on Drive D, you would type d:\hca*.*. After typing in such a specification, press the gray + key (to the right of the numeric keypad). This will begin the search.

When the search is complete, a Location List will appear. You can move a selection bar to the file you want to see and press Enter. Then you can jump to the next node on the list by pressing F5. By pressing F5 repeatedly you can cycle through all of the nodes that have been collected on the Location List. When PC-Browse is active, you can get the Location List back by pressing Shift-F4.

To try out PC-Browse, I used it to scan all chapter files in this book to see where I had referred to Guide. Figure 2-14 shows the Location List that PC-Browse prepared.

Although PC-Browse is great for quick look-ups, it doesn't create a control node that you can use for later hypertext browsing. In chapter 4, I show another example of how string searches can be combined with hypertext. In chapter 7, I show how you can use a C library called POWER SEARCH to build your own text search utility for use with a hypertext system.

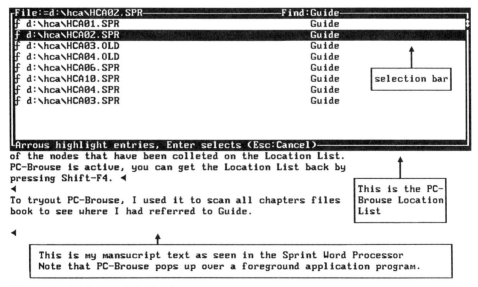

Fig. 2-14 PC-Browse Selection list.

Trails

A *trail* is a record of the nodes that a user has accessed in viewing a hypertext network. Ideally the trail would include "note nodes" created by the user in the process. Some hypothesize that users will blaze exciting, useful or enjoyable trails for others. It might be enjoyable for example, to follow a trail made by others (famous or otherwise) and read their comments on various stories, illustrations, news items and so on.

Chapter 8 shows the source code for The Hypertext Editor (HE), which can record trails. If you have Turbo Prolog, you can compile HE yourself. You can also order an executable version of the program. Trail recording can be a useful tool for refining hypertext networks. If you can study the trails that users take in searching for information or in studying an instructional network, you can spot problems and refine the network. You'll see a specific example of this in chapter 7: you'll see how HE can be used to develop and refine computer-based training materials.

Tours

A *tour* is a trail through a network that a reader may take simply by selecting a button or menu option. HyperWriter has a flexible system for creating tours. One way to create a tour with HyperWriter is to open a document and access the various nodes that you want to be in the tour. HyperWriter will record your trail, or history, as you proceed. You can then turn this trail into a tour by pressing a hotkey, Shift-F9, or by selecting a menu option. HyperWriter then asks how you want to create the tour and you respond by selecting Current History.

You can also create a tour in another way. After selecting the Create Tour option you can begin browsing in a hypertext network and then press Shift-Enter whenever you are in a node that you want to turn into a *tour point* (the node you want to display when the tour is run). When you press Shift-Enter, a dialog box appears as you can see in Fig. 2-15.

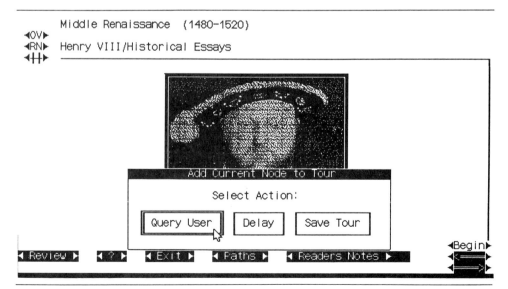

Fig. 2-15 Adding a node to a tour in HyperWriter.

If you choose the Delay option, you can specify exactly how many seconds you want the system to pause on that node. If you choose Query User in the dialog box, you are specifying that you want to let the user click on a Continue button when they are ready to continue or click on a Browse button and then go off exploring virtually any nodes on the system. Figure 2-16 shows the Tour Point dialog box that appears when the user actually runs the tour.

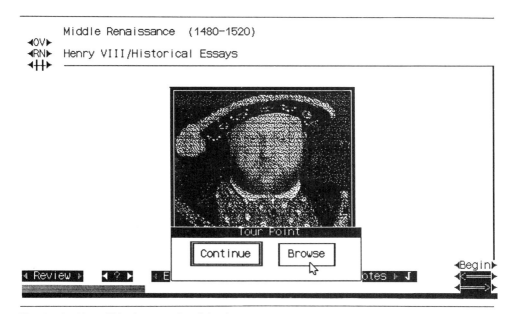

Fig. 2-16 HyperWriter's tour point dialog box.

Incidentally, after breaking out of a tour to browse, you can restart the tour by pressing Shift-F8. Shift-F8 is the shortcut key you can use to activate any of the available tours in the current directory. (Menu options are also available. For example, the user could press F10 and select Utilities, then Navigate, then Tour Function.) As a developer, you can also create a hypertext button and link it to a tour. You can also create *autotours*—tours which will start automatically whenever a user loads a specific hypertext network.

Bookmarks

More and more hypertext systems are adding bookmarks to the bag of navigational tools they offer. Sprint, the system that HyperSprint is based on, comes with a set of 10 bookmarks, numbered 0 to 9. To set a bookmark, you press Alt-M (short for "mark") and then type in a number between 0 and 9. Later during the same session, to return to the exact spot where you placed the mark, you press a hotkey and enter the bookmark number. Once you close a file or exit to DOS, however, the bookmark is removed.

Sprint, however, always inserts a bookmark in a file whenever you exit to DOS even if you exit by pulling the plug to the CPU or pressing that red reset button! One of Sprint's most remarkable qualities is that it is unruffled even if a sudden power failure occurs.

That's because Sprint does a background save whenever you stop typing more than about three seconds—this save includes the bookmarks.

Whenever you restart Sprint it automatically activates any files that you did not explicitly "close." Whenever you return to such a file, Sprint jumps to the bookmark that it placed in that file when you left it. You can select any of the open files by pressing Ctrl-F9 and selecting a node from the menu that appears. I usually leave a control node (a top-level node) open so that I can use it for a jumping off point. Sprint is unusual in that you can have up to 26 files open—you can leave the files open even when you exit to DOS.

NOTE: Technically, as far as DOS is concerned, all files are closed when you exit, but Sprint maintains its own set of pointers into the files and automatically reopens the files when you restart Sprint.

To test Sprint's power to recover from a power failure, I pulled the plug immediately after typing this sentence. (Actually, I just pressed reset.) Figure 2-17 shows Sprint in action after I restarted Sprint and pressed Ctrl-F9 to bring up the open files menu. Notice that Sprint saved the entire file as it existed up to that point—except for the last few words of the sentence. And when I restarted Sprint, it positioned the cursor back to the sentence I was typing when I pushed reset.

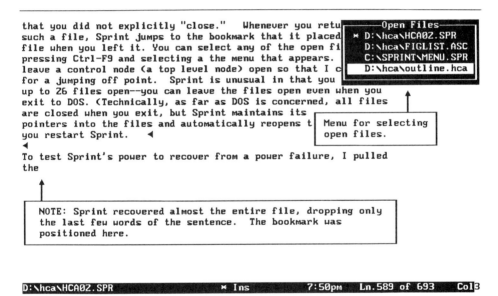

Fig. 2-17 Sprint after recovering from power failure.

Those are the major navigation tools. Closely related to navigation is the concept of a hypertext web. Let's discuss that next.

Webs

The term *web* is sometimes used to refer to any group of nodes linked together. However, more precisely, a node is a subnetwork—a part of a larger hypertext network. In this approach every link can belong to one or more webs. Webs can be active or inactive. When a web is *active*, you can see the buttons that point to the nodes in the web. If the web is *inactive*, buttons that belong to it will be invisible. A user can open a web and then open and look into one or more of its nodes.

The concept of a web is useful because sometimes a large hypertext network can become unmanageable. The concept of a web is relatively new and is still under development. Brown University's Institute for Information and Scholarship first proposed the term web and is working on implementing it in its Intermedia project.

A web is really a subcollection of a complete hypertext network. Ted Nelson refers to the problem of identifying subcollections in a hypertext network as the "framing problem." See Fig. 2-18, an illustration taken from Ted Nelson's book *Literary Machines*.

If a hypertext program has a text search function, you can identify a web or subnetwork of a larger network. A control node that results from a text search shows all of the nodes in a web. However, ideally, a control node should show all of the interconnections between nodes. To date, none of the hypertext programs for personal computers that I have

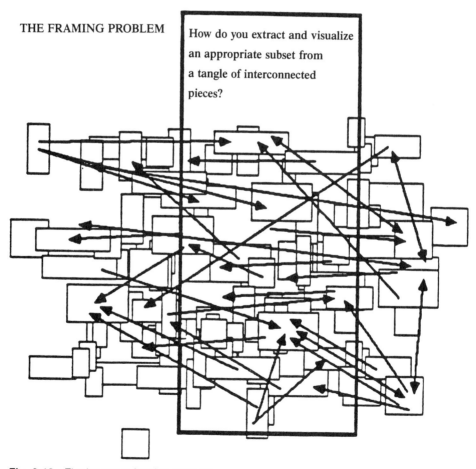

THE FRAMING PROBLEM

How do you extract and visualize an appropriate subset from a tangle of interconnected pieces?

Fig. 2-18 The hypertext framing problem.

looked at have this capability. That's an area that's worth further exploration, research and development.

Built-in programming languages

Some hypertext systems have built-in programming languages so you can customize the system to fit your specific needs. I'll go into some detail on this in chapter 8 and just give you an overview here.

A good example of a program that has a built-in programming language is KnowledgePro. KnowledgePro enables you to build *expert systems*, systems that can emulate the behavior of human experts within a limited subject area. KnowledgePro allows you to store a number of rules in a file called a *knowledge base* using special Knowledge-Pro commands. You can program KnowledgePro to present information and ask questions to help users solve complex problems. KnowledgePro differs from many expert systems in that any word in question or response can serve as a hypertext button. You can program KnowledgePro so that when the user selects a hypertext button, a built-in subprogram is activated. The subprogram may go off on its own tangent—ask questions, branch to other subprograms and so on. Eventually, though, when the user finishes the subprogram, control will return to the node that contained the hypertext button. You'll see a specific example of KnowledgePro in action in chapter 8, Programming Hypertext.

Several other hypertext systems have built-in programming languages. HyperCard on the Macintosh is a language called HyperTalk, which is also examined in chapter 8.

IBM LinkWay also has its own script language, as does HyperPAD. With such a language you can do more than just create a network of nodes: you can create special visual effects, prompt the user for specific input, and process the input—for example, perform mathematical calculations.

Languages like HyperTalk and PADtalk, which works with HyperPAD, are not computer languages in a traditional sense; they are scripts that the hypertext application program reads, interprets and then executes. Still, they qualify as programming languages because they enable you to store a series of instructions that can be activated at the touch of a button.

You don't need detailed technical knowledge about programming to use these built-in languages because the hypertext program provides the interface to the operating system. However, this is still programming and it is not for everyone. In chapter 8 you'll get a taste of three kinds of programming: script programming, memory-resident hypertext programming, and programming that results in stand-alone executable programs.

Summary

Those are the basic elements of hypertext: nodes, links, buttons, editors/browsers, navigational tools, and built-in programming languages. In the following chapters I will explore them in more depth. In the next chapter let's take a closer look at nodes.

3
Hypertext nodes

In this chapter I will take a closer look at nodes and discuss the different kinds of nodes used in hypertext systems. As I said earlier, a node is usually a collection of data related to a specific topic. More broadly, a node is some sort of stimulus material that can be activated and presented to a user. Ideally, it should be possible to embed a button in a node so that it can be linked to another node in the network. In the early hypertext systems nodes were always text nodes. But, there are other possibilities. When you think about it, a node can be anything that can be presented to a user. A node might be:

- text display
- graphic display
- videotape or a videodisc segment
- animated graphics
- recorded speech
- digitized speech
- music
- another person

This view of nodes focuses on the display attributes of the nodes. There are other ways of looking at nodes, too. For example, you might say that nodes can be:

- structured
- semi-structured
- unstructured
- typed
- context-sensitive
- composite

Let's begin our discussion by considering text nodes.

Text nodes

Text nodes can be scrollable or fixed. A *fixed node* is usually limited to just one screen or window of information. In a *scrollable node* you can use cursor control keys or a mouse to travel through the node and expose those parts of it not immediately visible in the window. Systems that allow the user to scroll through a long article in this way are sometimes referred to as *article-based systems*. Systems that offer only fixed screens are termed *card-based systems*.

Hypertext programs like Guide, BlackMagic, HyperWriter and EMPOWERment offer scrollable text nodes so they are said to be article-based. In these programs the hypertext editors have fairly good editing functions. For example, with EMPOWERment, you can use any of the standard WordStar-like cursor control keys to move through a text node. If you don't recall how to scroll, you can press F1 for a help menu as shown in Fig. 3-1. When the help menu appears, you can select a topic of interest.

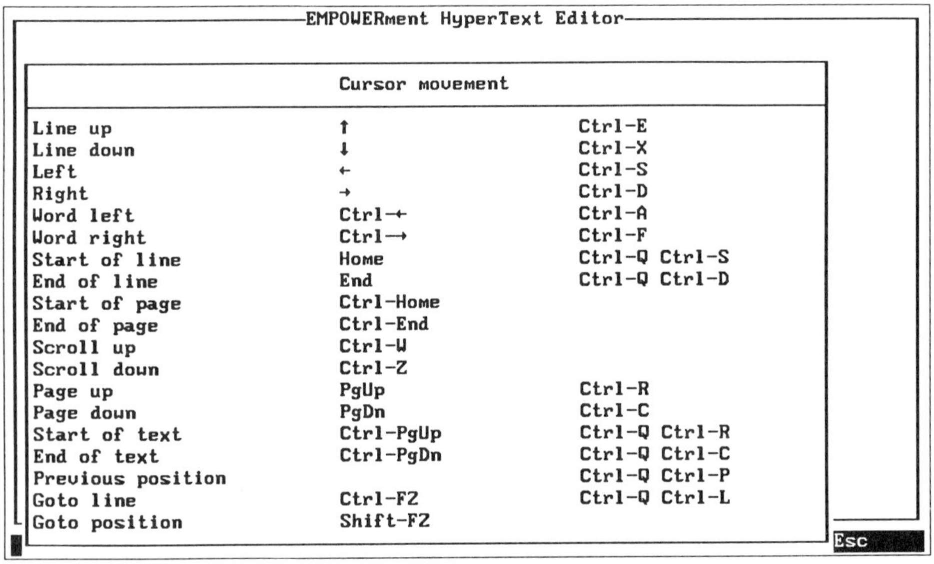

```
┌─────────────EMPOWERment HyperText Editor─────────────┐
│                                                       │
│  ┌─────────────────────────────────────────────────┐ │
│  │                 Cursor movement                  │ │
│  │                                                   │ │
│  │ Line up           ↑              Ctrl-E           │ │
│  │ Line down         ↓              Ctrl-X           │ │
│  │ Left              ←              Ctrl-S           │ │
│  │ Right             →              Ctrl-D           │ │
│  │ Word left         Ctrl-←         Ctrl-A           │ │
│  │ Word right        Ctrl-→         Ctrl-F           │ │
│  │ Start of line     Home           Ctrl-Q Ctrl-S    │ │
│  │ End of line       End            Ctrl-Q Ctrl-D    │ │
│  │ Start of page     Ctrl-Home                       │ │
│  │ End of page       Ctrl-End                        │ │
│  │ Scroll up         Ctrl-W                          │ │
│  │ Scroll down       Ctrl-Z                          │ │
│  │ Page up           PgUp           Ctrl-R           │ │
│  │ Page down         PgDn           Ctrl-C           │ │
│  │ Start of text     Ctrl-PgUp      Ctrl-Q Ctrl-R    │ │
│  │ End of text       Ctrl-PgDn      Ctrl-Q Ctrl-C    │ │
│  │ Previous position                Ctrl-Q Ctrl-P    │ │
│  │ Goto line         Ctrl-F2        Ctrl-Q Ctrl-L    │ │
│  │ Goto position     Shift-F2                        │ │
│  └───────────────────────────────────────────── Esc ─┘
└───────────────────────────────────────────────────────┘
```

Fig. 3-1   Cursor movement Help screen in EMPOWERment.

When accessing an EMPOWERment text node, you have a full range of editing tools. For example, you can delete words, lines, or blocks of text and then undelete them if you wish. Within a node, you can search for specific words or phrases as in a word processor: pressing Ctrl-Q, F brings up a prompt that asks for the word you want to search for as you can see in Fig. 3-2.

A calendar that highlights appointments and deadlines is always active, although it may be covered by the current editing window. You can reveal the calendar by resizing the edit window. To do this you press Shift-F10 and then use the arrow keys. (The calendar has certain hypertext like attributes, which we'll look at later.)

Card-based systems   HyperCard, HyperPAD and LinkWay are examples of card-based systems. The user cannot scroll through a node, but is limited to the text on screen. Although the node (card) itself is not scrollable in these systems, there are ways to work around it that allow you to scroll through long text documents without having to jump from card to card. Sounds like a contradiction doesn't it? Let me explain. In LinkWay you can

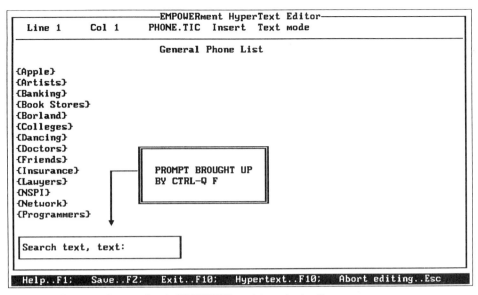

```
┌─────────────────EMPOWERment HyperText Editor─────────────────┐
│ Line 1      Col 1       PHONE.TIC  Insert  Text mode          │
├───────────────────────────────────────────────────────────────┤
│                   General Phone List                          │
│                                                               │
│ {Apple}                                                       │
│ {Artists}                                                     │
│ {Banking}                                                     │
│ {Book Stores}                                                 │
│ {Borland}                                                     │
│ {Colleges}                                                    │
│ {Dancing}                                                     │
│ {Doctors}                         ┌─────────────────────┐     │
│ {Friends}                         │ ┌─────────────────┐ │     │
│ {Insurance}              ┌────────┤ │ PROMPT BROUGHT UP│ │     │
│ {Lawyers}                         │ │ BY CTRL-Q F      │ │     │
│ {NSPI}                   │        │ └─────────────────┘ │     │
│ {Network}                │        └─────────────────────┘     │
│ {Programmers}            │                                    │
│                          ▼                                    │
│  ┌──────────────────────────────┐                            │
│  │ Search text, text:           │                            │
│  └──────────────────────────────┘                            │
├───────────────────────────────────────────────────────────────┤
│ Help..F1;   Save..F2;   Exit..F10;   Hypertext..F10;  Abort editing..Esc │
└───────────────────────────────────────────────────────────────┘
```

Fig. 3-2 Text search operation in EMPOWERment hypertext editor.

create a document button. When you select this button, you are taken to a scrollable text document. The limitation, though, is that you cannot embed links in the scrollable document. In HyperCard, you can create scrollable fields. If you move the mouse pointer into such a field, you can scroll through this field to read the text. Again, the limitation is that you cannot create buttons inside of a scrollable field.

Graphics nodes

Graphics nodes are images that appear when you choose graphics buttons. Graphics on IBM PCs can be bit-mapped graphics or character graphics. You can get the most detail with bit-mapped graphics because the program can control the color of each dot (or pixel) on the screen with a "bit." Some people call this the *APA mode* (All Points Addressable). Using APA you can make complex geometric images, and fill any desired area of the screen with solid colors or blends of colors.

Bit-mapped graphics   In Fig. 3-3 you see BlackMagic displaying a bit-mapped graphics node showing the United States. Embedded in the node (in each state) are buttons that point to text nodes. To bring up this display, I selected a button embedded in California and pressed F1. That popped up the text node you see in the upper right corner of the screen.

There are several ways to prepare bit-mapped graphics for hypertext systems. You can:

- Scan art that exists on paper.
- Buy clip art already in the proper file format.
- Capture graphics generated by other programs with special programs like

HyperWriter's GRABIT, IBM LinkWay's LWCAPTUR, or HotShot's GRAB.
- Use a video camera as an image source and convert the image to a graphics file with a product like the VIMAGER available from P.B. Smith and Associates.

Once an image has been converted to a graphic file format you can usually load it into a node if your hypertext system supports graphics. In some cases you might need to convert a file from one format to another. In PC work I have had good success with a program called HotShot Graphics, which also lets you do extensive editing of graphic images. HotShot Graphics can also capture and print just about any PC screen. Sometimes problems can develop when you try to work with bit-mapped graphics. For example, a .TIFF file is not just a .TIFF file; there are variations that are not completely compatible with all software programs. Sometimes a graphic file might have too many levels of gray to be edited or merged into a hypertext program or a file might just be too large. Sometimes patience is required to get things working smoothly.

Although the all points addressable (APA) mode is great for detailed graphics, there is a price to pay. For example, consider this: in APA mode an EGA screen might be 350 pixels wide and 640 pixels tall. That's 224,000 pixels in all. In 16-color mode, you need 4 bits for each pixel. (You can count to 16 with 4 bits.) So we need 224,000 times 4 or 896,000 bits (or 112,000 bytes) just to display one full screen. A program that has to work with this much data in displaying a screen must be a lot more complex and usually slower than one that displays character graphics. In contrast 4,000 bytes are needed to display 25 rows and 80 columns of characters in 16 colors. IBM and compatibles have a special set of characters that can be used to generate graphics images.

Character graphics Interesting images can also be created just by using the special

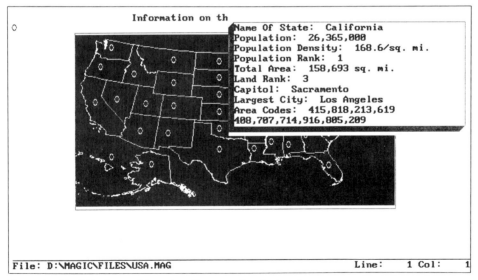

Fig. 3-3 BlackMagic graphic node with popped-up text node.

graphics characters. Although the images are not very detailed, character graphics have advantages:

- Less data is required for storing them.
- The user need not have a graphics card or monitor.
- The images appear more quickly on the screen.

An easy, inexpensive way to create colorful character graphics is to use a shareware program called ANSIANIM. Using ANSIANIM you can select a character paintbrush using function control keys and then draw using the cursor control keys. While using ANSIANIM, you can get a help screen by pressing F1. Figure 3-4 shows ANSIANIM's help screen.

```
                        ANSI-ANIMATOR Help Menu


ALT A ASCII: Switches ASCII character set without clearing screen (no chart).
ALT B Blink: Switches characters from blinking to not blinking and vice versa.
ALT C Color: Changes current drawing color.
ALT D Displays: ASCII character chart and allows change of current symbols.
ALT H Help! This menu.
ALT P Pen: Picks Pen up or puts Pen down.
ALT R Redisplay: Redisplays current screens.
ALT S Save: Saves current screen(s) to disk.  Allows subdirectory paths.
ALT T Text center: Centers a line of text on current row.
ALT W Whirling star: Displays whirling star at current cursor position.


[ESC] Ends ANSI-ANIMATOR and returns to DOS.
[HOME] Clears screen, retaining all previously entered information.
[CTRL][HOME] Clears screen, deletes all previously entered information.
[END] Non-destructively move cursor back 2 spaces(for drawing frame backwards).
[PGUP] Non-destructively moves cursor Up 1 line and back 1 line(for frames).
[PGDN] Non-destructively moves cursor Down 1 line and back 1 line(for frames).




                     Press any key to continue....
```

Fig. 3-4   ANSIANIM's Help screen.

Once you have created a screen with ANSIANIM, you can display it simply by using the DOS TYPE command. For example, if the file created by ANSIANIM is "WARNING," you can display the warning screen with the DOS command:

TYPE WARNING

Figure 3-5 shows a screen created with ANSIANIM and displayed by EMPOWER-ment. Any hypertext program that enables users to create command buttons can display an ANSIANIM screen. For example, if the ANSIANIM screen file name is "WARNING" you could create a WARNING.BAT file containing:

ECHO OFF
CLS
TYPE WARNING
PAUSE

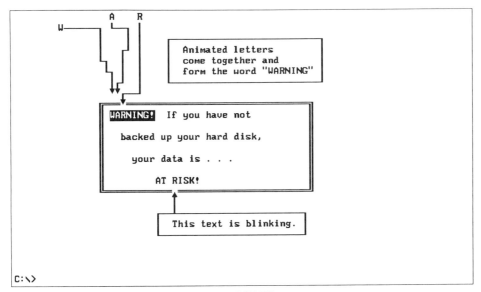

Fig. 3-5 ANSIANIM screen displayed with EMPOWERment.

and then set up a command button that executes the "WARNING.BAT" file.

To be able to use the DOS TYPE command to display an ANSIANIM work, though, the DOS screen driver called ANSI.SYS must be active. To activate ANSI.SYS, just put the line DEVICE = ANSI.SYS in your CONFIG.SYS. You probably already have a file called CONFIG.SYS in your root directory since several programs require that it be present including specific directives. If you don't have a CONFIG.SYS file in your directory, you might want to create it and include these lines:

```
DEVICE = ANSI.SYS
FILES = 20
BUFFERS = 20
```

The FILES = 20 statement helps to ensure that you can have 20 files open at once. The BUFFERS = 20 statement says that you want 20 disk buffers to be set up in internal memory. A *disk buffer* is an area of memory for holding data read from (or to be written to) disk. It is used to increase the speed of data access. When you read data from disk, the system first searches the internal buffers for the data. If the system finds the data, it simply pulls it from the buffer instead of from disk. For example, on a PC, try entering the DIR command twice in succession. Notice how much faster the second one goes. That's because the data has been buffered.

You might be able to download ANSIANIM from a local bulletin board. If not, you can get a copy by sending a formatted disk in a stamped, self-addressed disk mailer to Seyer Associates, 1079 Mohr Lane, D14, Concord, CA 94518.

A key question It's important to realize that most hypertext programs can throw up a graphic image in one way or another and link it to a text node. But a key factor, here, is whether you can embed a button in the graphic image. When evaluating the graphics capability of a hypertext program, always ask: "Can the user move the mouse pointer or the cursor to a hot spot on the screen and then access another node?" This isn't possible using an external program like ANSIANIM.

Although bit-mapped graphics are costly, several PC hypertext systems include this capacity. Examples include: Hyperdoc, HyperWriter, Guide, Plus, and LinkWay. Using these programs you can create or import graphic images and then overlay hot spots (hypertext button). Some of these programs provide built-in paint programs for creating graphic nodes; others require that you create the graphic using an external paint program. Usually, you can also scan a paper-based graphic. In the next chapter I'll go into specifics on how this is done and what to watch out for in scanning graphics.

Graphic nodes in HyperCard HyperCard is specially suited for developing hypertext applications that require graphics and animation. HyperCard has a built-in paint program that you can use to "paint" your own graphic nodes. Because most of you are probably already familiar with paint programs, I won't go into detail. See Fig. 3-6, which shows some of the paint tools available on the HyperCard Tools menu.

- *Import a picture* you have created with MacPaint or a MacPaint-compatible program.

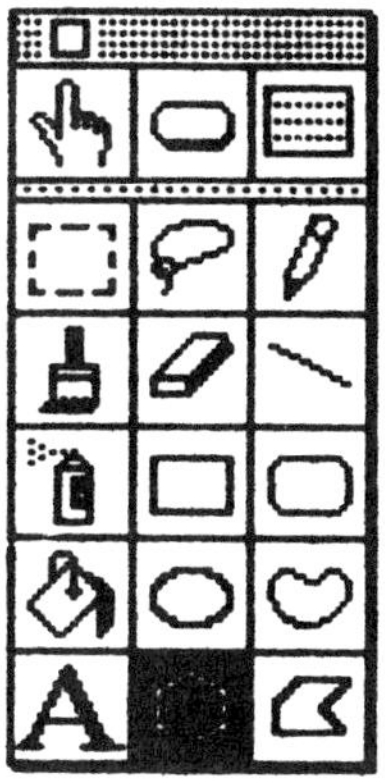

Fig. 3-6 HyperCard Tools menu.

There are several ways to make graphics in HyperCard. You can:

- *Make basic picture elements* (shapes, patterns, contours) using a built-in Tools menu.
- *Borrow pictures* from nodes that already have graphics. (You do this using Hyper-Card's paste and copy commands.)
- *Import a picture* you have created with MacPaint or a MacPaint-compatible program.
- *Import a graphic* that you have created with a digitizing camera, scanner or other device.
- *Touch-up a graphic* using an option called FatBits.

Besides static images, HyperCard is specially good for creating animated sequences. Let's consider it is possible to do this with HyperCard as well as other hypertext programs.

Computer-animated nodes

An animated node can be useful for catching a user's attention and stressing important ideas. HyperCard has built-in routines for copying and dragging objects around the screen.

Animation with HyperCard Usually, in the course of designing a HyperCard screen, you use various "paint" tools manually. However, you can also insert commands into a program to use the various paint tools. For example, you can select and drag objects within a script. In this way you can do a kind of simple animation. Figure 3-7 shows a screen from a HyperCard vocabulary improvement program I am developing.

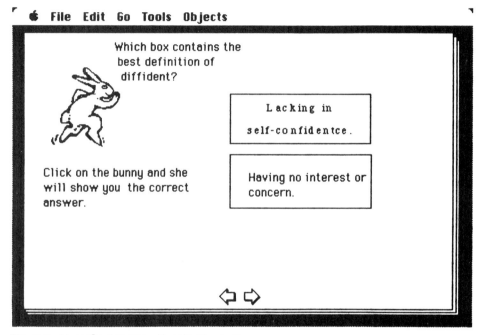

Fig. 3-7 HyperCard screen with animation button.

The bunny at the top left in Fig. 3-7 is one of the many art ideas that comes with the HyperCard program. Using the Edit menu in HyperCard I was able to copy the bunny from the Art Ideas stack and paste it into the card as shown. (In HyperCard, a *stack* is simply a network of nodes.) After pasting in the bunny, I installed an invisible button directly on top of it; this way when you click on the bunny, you activate the button. The button, in turn, activates a short program that moves the bunny across the screen. The bunny "hops" across the screen and touches the top box showing that it contains the correct answer to the question. (Actually, the bunny doesn't hop, she glides. However, with more programming effort, she could be made to hop.)

The animation program, technically, is a *script*. HyperCard, like many other current hypertext programs has a built-in English-like language you can use to customize your hypertext network. (Amanda Goodenough, one of the first people to use HyperCard's scripting language, has made a series of interactive stories about her cat Inigo.)

Figure 3-8 shows a script that moves the bunny across the screen when you click on her. I'll discuss HyperCard scripting in more detail in chapter 8, but you can get the gist of scripting by studying Fig. 3-8 along with the explanation that follows.

The on mouseUp in Fig. 3-8 tells HyperCard to execute the following commands only when the user clicks and then releases the mouse button. The choose select tool command activates a special HyperCard tool that lets you select objects on screen. The next command, drag from 40,40 to 150,150 actually creates a selection box whose left corner is at column 40, row 40 and whose lower right corner is at column 150, row 150. The next command, set dragspeed to 100 sets the animation speed.

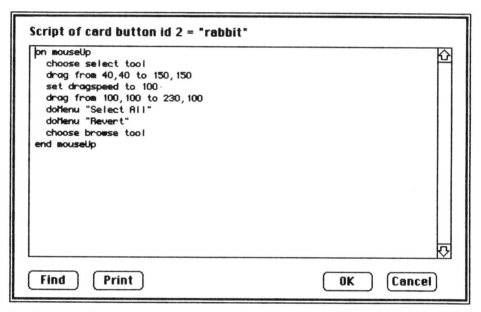

Fig. 3-8 HyperCard animation script.

The command drag from 100,100 to 230,100 moves the bunny from left to right across the screen—from column 100 to column 230. Because the row coordinate stays the same, the bunny moves horizontally. You could make the bunny move diagonally with a statement like, say:

drag from 100,100 to 230,300

The doMenu command in *HyperTalk*, the name for HyperCard's scripting language, is a powerful one. It allows you to script most of the menu commands that a user would normally access manually. The Select All and Revert commands are needed, here, to return the bunny to her initial screen position—otherwise the bunny will be left standing next to the correct answer. Now, previously HyperCard was in a *selection mode*. While in this mode, objects can be dragged around the screen, but buttons are not active. Buttons are only active in HyperCard when the system is in a *browse mode*. The choose browse tool command serves to return HyperCard to the browse mode, so that the user can continue to click on buttons and browse through the network of nodes.

Note that this script does not specifically animate a bunny. It will move any object that happens to be in the boxed area selected by the command drag from 40,40 to 150,150.

Although animation is relatively easy with HyperCard, you can create similar effects with other hypertext programs as well. For example, the IBM LinkWay ToolKit (which enhances IBM LinkWay) has an animate command, which allows you to animate objects with the MCGA 256 color mode. (MCGA is the system used with PS/2, model 25 and 30 computers). By the time you read this, the new version of IBM LinkWay will have a bit command and a move command that will make it easier to do animation on other systems. In Guide3 you can animate an object by loading it into a small window and then moving the window repeatedly. You can set the attributes of the window so that it does not have a border. This way when you move the window, it appears that only the object is moving. To allow you to move a window, Guide provides a special command aptly named MoveWindow.

PC-KEY-DRAW, a comprehensive shareware drawing program with hypertext capability, offers a special animation function. You can use this function with a Key Macro command to jazz up slide shows that you create with the program. Another possibility is that PC-KEY-DRAW could be called and fed keystrokes by other hypertext programs that have "command button capability."

Another way to create a simple animation with most any PC hypertext system is to create an animation file with the ANIANIMAT public domain program. As you create the file, you can draw an image, erase it, and then redraw it in a slightly different position. If you repeat this draw, erase, redraw cycle several times, the image on the screen will be animated when you use the TYPE command to display the image. Sometimes you can create an eye-catching display by animating letters that move around the screen and finally come together to form words.

FANTAVISION, from Broderbund, is an inexpensive program by Scott Anderson that you can use to create impressive animation nodes. Scott calls these nodes "movies." FANTAVISION automatically takes care of creating all of the in-between drawings needed for the animation effect. You can work with graphic shapes or text. You can make text as well as images spin, rotate, grow, enlarge, shrink or just move across the screen. When you save your animation, it is saved in the form of a file that ends in an .MVE extension (short for "movie"). Any hypertext program that can launch an external program can start up PLAYER.EXE which comes with FANTAVISION. Currently, when you start PLAYER.EXE, it will immediately start displaying all of the .MVE files in the current subdirectory. You could create multiple animation nodes, though, by creating a command node that first copies the appropriate .MVE files into the subdirectory that contains the PLAYER.EXE program and then executes PLAYER.EXE.

Figure 3-9 shows a "still shot" from a FANTAVISION "movie" that I used to help illustrate a talk on hypertext at the 1989 NSPI Conference. NSPI (National Society for Performance and Instruction) has headquarters in Washington, D.C.

Figure 3-10 shows another "still shot" with a different perspective and position. I created these two still shots and FANTAVISION did the rest, creating the in-between frames needed to animate the image.

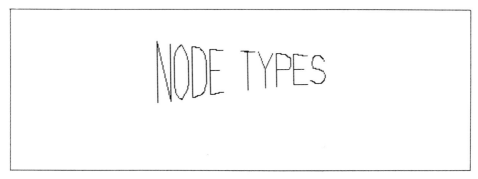

Fig. 3-9 Still frame from FANTAVISION movie.

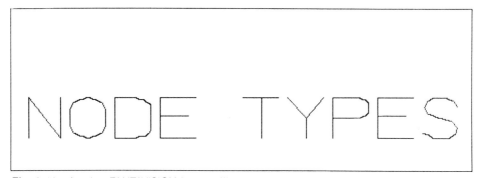

Fig. 3-10 Another FANTAVISION frame, different perspective.

FANTAVISION is great for making impressive animations of simple geometric shapes. Also, you make rather detailed backdrops for animation sequences using PC paint programs like PC Paintbrush. If you need a more realistic visual display—for example to show a surgical procedure to medical students—you could create a link that starts up a videodisc player.

Video nodes

Any hypertext program that has command buttons can have video nodes. The command button need only run the program that launches the video tape or videodisc segment. What good is the advantage of this? The advantage is that a user can first work with text, which is much cheaper than video, and can access videodisc segments only when they are needed. Using a hypertext system, you can easily embed references to videodisc segments in instructional materials, or adventure games, or promotional materials. You can ask users what they would like to see next or what they would like to do next. When the user selects a certain option the appropriate video segment can spring into action. Several programs are available that allow you to control videodisc players. One such program is Video Lesson Writer 42 produced by Whitney Educational Services. (See chapter 10 for details.)

Hyperdoc, an "industrial strength" hypertext program, can work with video nodes in a powerful way through a special Hyperdoc Action Language. With the use of a Video logic MIC controller and Hyperdoc you can display a video sequence on your EGA or VGA monitor along with computer-generated hypertext buttons. The buttons can serve as a menu leading to the selection of various videodisc sequences. See Fig. 3-11, which shows a screen with computer-generated text combined with a motion video being displayed in a small window at upper left. Hyperdoc is controlling the screen in this figure. By clicking on Citizen Kane the user could activate that video.

Fig. 3-11 Combining computer graphics with video.

HyperWriter is another program that has built-in support for controlling a videodisc player. Using HyperWriter, you can attach a special video command to button. For example, a button can activate the command:

@PLAY [REV] from to"

where from is the starting videodisc location and to is the stopping location of the video segment. Here, REV is an optional argument you can include if, for some strange reason, you want to play the segment in reverse.

Buttons on video displays

Although I haven't seen it demonstrated, the Hyperdoc folks say that with their system (along with a video overlay board) you can suddenly freeze a video segment and then superimpose computer-generated buttons over the frozen video image. This capability could be quite useful in computer-based training programs where the learner needs to make important visual discriminations.

Musical nodes

MIDI is an acronym for *Musical Instrument Digital Interface*, which is a system that allows you to capture musical performance in digital form in computer data files. MIDI data shows which keys were pressed on a musical instrument—how fast they were pressed, when they were pressed, and when they were released. MIDI data is analogous to a player piano roll.

Although I am not aware of any music software that makes systematic use of hypertext, some music software has hypertext-like features. A good example is WinSong for IBM PCs and compatibles, which runs under Microsoft Windows. This program will record the performance of a musical instrument that is connected to the PC through MIDI interface. Besides recording a musical performance in digital form, WinSong can translate the data to conventional musical notation. The user can then edit the musical notation, correcting errors or elaborating on the musical performance. (Think of what Beethoven could have done with this!)

When working with musical notation in WinSong, the various musical symbols that appear are actually hypertext buttons. When you point to a musical symbol and click the mouse button, additional information or options will appear. For example, Fig. 3-12 shows the pointer pointing to the treble-clef symbol, at the upper left.

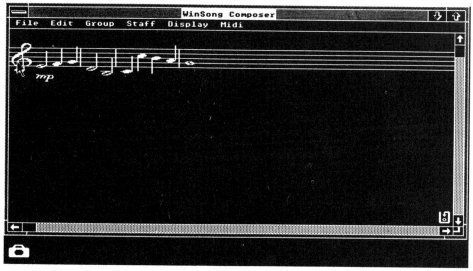

Fig. 3-12 Pointing to treble-clef.

After you click the mouse button, the node shown in Fig. 3-13 appears. This node shows that the selected object is a treble-clef. Notice that the button to the left of the word Treble has a dark circle in it showing that it has been selected. The user could select a different clef by pointing to the appropriate button and clicking the mouse. If the user did that and then clicked on the "OK" button, the treble-clef symbol would automatically change to the new clef.

In the same figure, in the box to the right, notice that the button to the left of "C" has a dark circle in it. This shows that the piece of music is in the key of C. By selecting a different button, the user could transpose the musical notation to a different key center. (Don't worry if you don't understand this musical jargon—just focus on the hypertext concepts.)

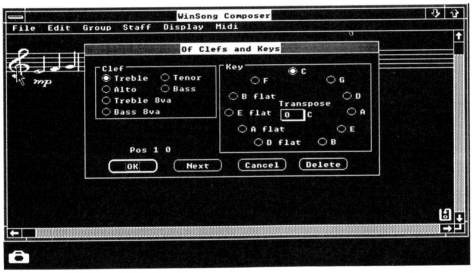

Fig. 3-13 "Of Clefs and Keys" node.

Let's look at another example from the same program. In Fig. 3-14 the user is pointing at a particular note in the musical score. Figure 3-15 shows the node that pops up when the user clicks the mouse button. This node shows a lot of information about the note: its length, pitch, volume, position in the song and so on. The user is free to edit this information if desired. For example, if the user puts a larger number in the box to the left of volume, the note will sound louder when the piece of music is later "performed" by WinSong.

An important hypertext idea to note, here, is that a node can do more than just display information. For example, after clicking on a note, a user gets information: the name of the note, its note number, its pitch and so on. But, in addition, the user can do different things to the note, such as delete it or modify its characteristics.

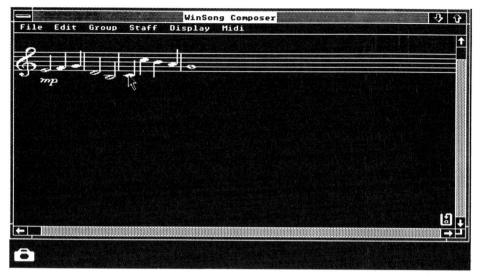

Fig. 3-14 Pointing at a note.

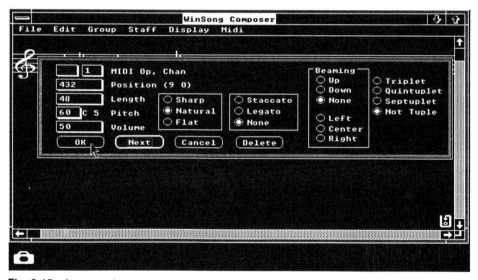

Fig. 3-15 A note node.

Using macro scripts to refine commands

Even if a MIDI program does not have hypertext, if you have a general hypertext program
like Guide, HyperWriter, EMPOWERment and a MIDI instrument and MIDI software,
with a little imagination, you can create a musical hypertext jukebox. Here's how.

Using Borland's SuperKey (or any other suitable macro program), create a self-starting macro that will start up your MIDI software and begin playing a specific song. You can store this self-starting macro in a file named, say, PFPEACE.MAC. See Fig. 3-16, which shows a sample of a self-starting macro. This macro is designed to work with Sequencer Plus mk III from Voyetra Technologies.

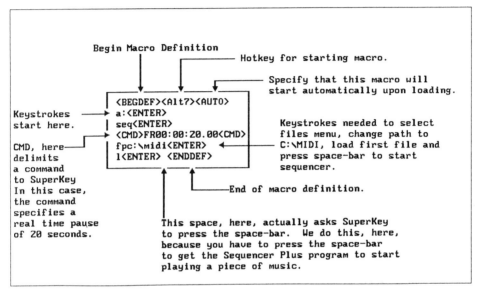

Fig. 3-16 Self-starting SuperKey macro.

To activate the sample SuperKey self-starting macro, you would just give this DOS command:

KEY /ml PFPEACE

KEY is the executable program that you fire up when you start SuperKey—the complete name is KEY.COM. The following characters /ml PFPEACE are commands to SuperKey: The slash (/) means "bring up the main SuperKey menu." The l means "load a macro." PFPEACE is the name of the macro to load.

In Fig. 3-16 notice how the macro contains <AUTO> at the end of the first line. This instructs SuperKey to begin immediately executing the keystrokes that are specified. I also included a hotkey for starting the macro, since Superkey requires that some hotkey be specified.

In this macro I included a delay of 20 seconds, because Sequencer Plus takes about that long to load into memory and start executing. I found that if I did not include this delay, Sequencer Plus would not pick up the keystrokes made previous to its loading. Some programs do that—they throw away keystrokes that have been stored in the keyboard buffer.

Anyway, once this works, the rest is easy. You just include a Command Button in your hypertext program that changes to the proper subdirectory and executes a KEY /ml pfpeace-.mac command.

In a text node, which contains the music command button, you could have detailed notes about the music—the composer, performer, and so on. You could create your own "jacket notes." If you're not yet familiar with MIDI, you might want to investigate it. Some predict that the time is coming soon when every television will also have MIDI capabilities.

Even if you are not interested in MIDI or computer music, this last example is still important. Why? Because it shows how you can use a macro script to specify exactly how a command node will be executed. Notice that you can do more than just start up other programs from within a hypertext node—you specify exactly which keystrokes will be fed to the external application program.

Digitized voice nodes

Sometimes it can be more effective or convenient to hear information than read it on the screen. Voice nodes might be especially appropriate for proofreaders, writers, small children or those engaged in language study. Writers can benefit from hearing the computer speak aloud what they have written. It's hard to explain why, but it's easier to detect errors and badly written sentences when the computer reads them aloud.

IBM PC hypertext programs that have command buttons, can easily link to voice nodes by making use of the SPEECH THING and SmoothTalker, both relatively inexpensive products. The SPEECH THING is a sound converter that attaches in-line with the parallel printer port. (It doesn't interfere with the printer.) SmoothTalker is a software program that works with the SPEECH THING; it accepts text input from the keyboard or from any ASCII text file. To create a voice node, all you need to do is create an ASCII file that contains the words that you want the computer to speak. Then—provided that the SmoothTalker driver is properly installed—you can simply create a command button that invokes a DOS command to process the ASCII file. The DOS command would just be:

```
SPEAK MESSAGE.TXT
```

where MESSAGE.TXT is any ASCII file with English text. The ASCII file will be displayed on the screen and will be read aloud simultaneously by SmoothTalker. SmoothTalker's speech is clear and understandable, but the synthesized speech does have a Swedish accent. If you have an application, such as language training, where you want to use digitally recorded speech, rather than synthesized speech, you can do that using the Voice Mastery Key System. Both the SmoothTalker and Voice Mastery Key System are available from COVOX. (See chapter 10 for details.)

Using HyperCard you can also create voice nodes. No additional hardware need be purchased. There is an interesting program that uses this capability to help you learn the writing and pronunciation of Japanese characters. (See chapter 10 for details.)

People as nodes

You can think of a person as a kind of dynamic node, that you might be able to access with a hypertext button. How? Well, for many years now, we've used the telephone as a means of linking directly to people in remote locations. Some hypertext systems provide direct support for making phone calls. By selecting an "autodial" button, you can have the system start a phone call. Even more than that, by linking to an external voice messaging system, such as WATSON, you can even have the computer repeatedly call an individual until contact is made and then carry on a conversation with an individual who knows the proper access code. You can program WATSON to deliver different messages to an individual depending on how the individual responds. The individual can respond by pressing different keys on a touch tone phone. In the future, when voice recognition software matures, individuals will be able to respond directly with their voice. The main point here though, is that you can activate an external program like WATSON and feed it specific keystrokes simply by selecting a hypertext button.

Faxable nodes

Services such as MCI Mail and CompuServe now offer Fax dispatch. You can upload an ASCII file to these services and type in instructions to fax the file to a fax machine attached to a specific phone number. The cost is minimal—about a dollar or two for a full page. Using the capabilities in most hypertext programs combined with a telecommunications program like, say, ProComm, you could create a "fax" button which would upload the current node to MCI mail with special instructions to fax it for you. The program could also throw up a selection node, from which you could select the phone number to use for faxing. EMPOWERment, a special purpose hypertext program designed to increase business productivity has a built-in menu option that does just that.

In this chapter we've explored different ways of looking at nodes. In the next chapter, we will explore buttons and links which enable us to interconnect nodes to form a network.

4
Buttons and links

As I mentioned in earlier chapters, a *button* in hypertext is an object that shows that more information is available. A button, also called a *point*, "points out" that there is a link between the current node and another node. A button might look like the kind of button you press—a doorbell button, for example. Or a button might be a word, special character or other symbol. A button might be text that is highlighted in some way. In other cases, a button might be invisible or it might be a reference to another file or topic, like this:

    see projects.tic

Here it would be clear to the experienced user of EMPOWERment that projects.tic is the name of a file. The period between projects and tic is a giveaway to an IBM PC user that this is a DOS file name. By putting the cursor on the first letter of the file name and pressing F10, the hypertext key, the user can immediately jump into that file. So in EMPOWERment, words that are valid DOS file names are potential hypertext buttons. This is probably the simplest implementation of a hypertext button.

Several hypertext systems have a similar, simple design for hypertext buttons. A good example is the Thinker, which runs on an Amiga. The Thinker is a hierarchical text processor with hypertext. As in EMPOWERment, any word in a Thinker document is a potential hypertext button. A text string, however, can also be marked as buttons by putting them between angle brackets (< >). In this way a hypertext button can contain a space. For example, <target income> would be a button showing a link to another node in a Thinker document. Whereas an EMPOWERment hypertext button links to an external file, a Thinker button links to a node that is contained within the current document. The Thinker term for such a node is a *statement*. Thinker buttons may also point to nodes in external files. To make this work, you just separate the external file name from the node name with a comma. The Amiga disks have string names and you can use these disk names along with a file name to give the complete path name. You separate the disk name from the file name with a colon. So to specify a node called "target income" in a file called "goals" on a disk called "Thinker," you would use a button like this:

    <Thinker:goals,target   income>

Here, Thinker is the disk name, goals is the file name and target income is the node name.

A useful feature of the Thinker is the ability to display only the first line of each node. This lets you see a large part of the document all at once. If you move blocks of text while the document is in "outline form" all of the text associated with a single line of text gets moved too.

The Thinker has an interesting and quite useful "see-thru button" (referred to as a *see-thru link* in the Thinker documentation). If a button consists of a string surrounded by angle brackets, you can select a menu option so that the Thinker displays the contents of the node pointed to. Notice, here, that you are not going to the remote link. Rather you are "peeking," as it were, through a window. You can enable and disable a see-thru function. When you disable see-thru, only the button is visible. If you move the button to a new location in the document and then enable see-thru the text will again become visible, but in its new location. If the external document is modified, then the display of that document in the secondary document is automatically updated. This is a valuable feature because all documents that quote from a source document with a see-thru button will automatically be updated when the source document is updated.

The Thinker can link to several different kinds of nodes:

- Thinker documents
- An Amiga picture file (known as IFF)
- An external application
- A communications port (known as an ARexx port)

The Thinker has many features but I only have space to describe a few of them here. If you are an Amiga user, I highly recommend the Thinker; it will let you tap into the power of hypertext. (For information about the publisher see chapter 10.)

Guide buttons

As you have seen, different hypertext systems have different kinds of hypertext buttons. Now, let's look at the buttons used in Guide, a relatively high-end hypertext system, which runs on both the Macintosh and IBM PCs and compatibles. Guide uses four different kinds of buttons:

- Expansion buttons
- Reference buttons
- Note buttons
- Command buttons

Expansion buttons

When you select an expansion button (by clicking on it with a mouse), it expands and instantly reveals text that is hidden from view. This "expansion" text is not stored in a different file—it is embedded in the current file. Control characters in the file signal the editor not to display the hidden text until the user clicks on an appropriate expansion button.

When you see text that is boldfaced, you know it is some kind of button. When you move the mouse pointer over the boldfaced text, the pointer changes so you know what kind of button you are dealing with. Figure 4-1 shows a screen from Guide. Notice that the mouse pointer is just below the expansion button—boldfaced text that says Why does WordPerfect ask you this? This screen shows part of a quiz I developed to help employees learn WordPerfect. Trainees can type an answer to the question and check their work. They check their work by clicking the mouse button to reveal the replacement text, which contains the correct answer.

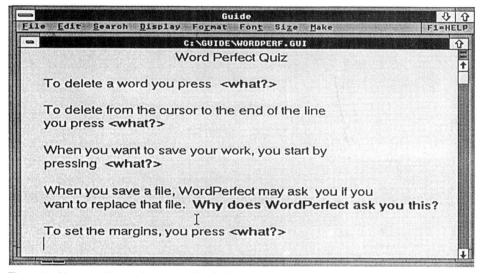

Fig. 4-1 Mouse pointer below expansion button.

Now look at Fig. 4-2. In this figure you see how the mouse pointer changes to a cross hair when you move it over the button. The cross hair tells the user that this is an expansion button.

Figure 4-3 shows how Guide reveals the replacement text after the trainee clicks on the expansion button.

After accessing the "expansion text" you can fold it away by moving the mouse pointer until it turns into a square and then clicking the mouse button. Figure 4-4 shows how the mouse button turns into a square showing that it is possible to fold away the expansion text by clicking the mouse button.

In Guide, replacement text can also contain buttons. This lets you provide another level of detail if the reader needs it. For example, I could rewrite the expansion text shown in Fig. 4-4 so that it contains another expansion button. For example the words "already saved some work" might be in boldface. If the user clicked on this boldfaced phrase, Guide would, in turn, reveal a more detailed explanation.

Note buttons

When you choose a note button, (by clicking the mouse button or pressing an appropriate hotkey), a note will pop up in a small window. This note is a *terminal node*. That is, it

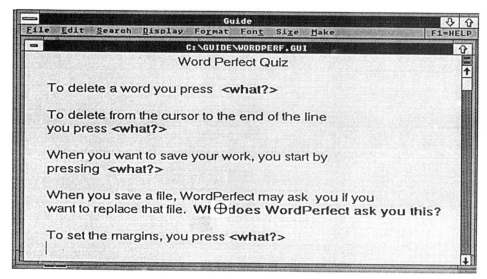

Fig. 4-2   Mouse pointer on expansion button.

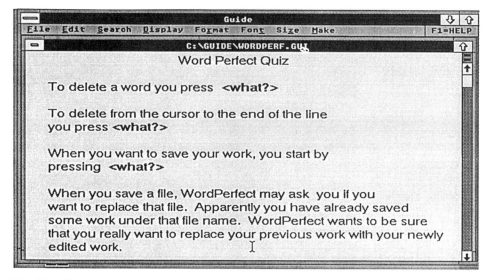

Fig. 4-3   Expansion text.

cannot point to other nodes. Note nodes are useful for annotating text or drawings when you want the reader to be able to pop up a short comment or explanation of existing text. Usually the reader can see the note and the main text at the same time. Note nodes are designed to allow the reader to quickly return to the main text. In Guide, the reader presses and holds the mouse button to read the note node. When the reader releases the mouse button, the note immediately disappears.

Earlier, I showed how, using BlackMagic, you can display a map of the United States.

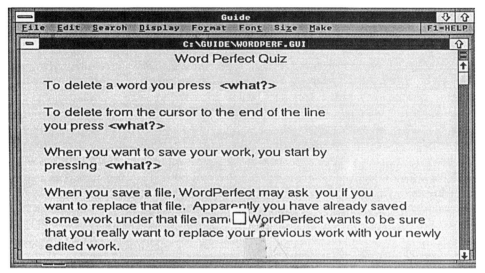

Fig. 4-4 Folding away expansion text.

By pointing to a state of interest and pressing a designated hypertext key, the user can pop up a note containing information about that state. See Fig. 4-5, which repeats the figure shown earlier for your convenience.

If this were hypertext, instead of a book, I could just refer you to this figure with a reference button instead of having to repeat it. Let's discuss reference buttons and consider how they differ from expansion buttons.

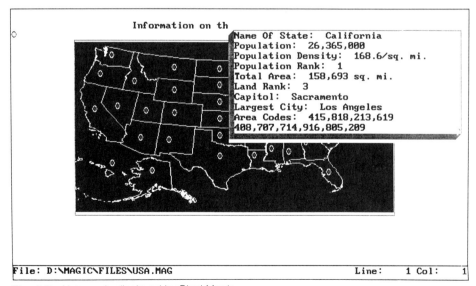

Fig. 4-5 Note node displayed by BlackMagic.

Reference buttons

A reference button differs from an expansion button in that it points to a particular point in a file. The file may be the current file or an external file. (An expansion button, on the other hand, points to concealed text—when a reader selects an expansion button, the concealed text becomes visible and replaces the expansion button without really changing the apparent position in the file.)

A reference button refers readers (and transports them) to a new point in a file. The point to which a reference button points is called the *reference point.* (This is similar to what is called a *statement label* in Thinker.)

You have seen how, in Guide, that the crosshair symbol marks a Replacement button. You've also seen how the box symbol shows that the current text is replacement text. In the same way, the mouse pointer turns into an arrow when it is over a reference button. It turns into a bent arrow when it is over a reference point as you can see in Fig. 4-6.

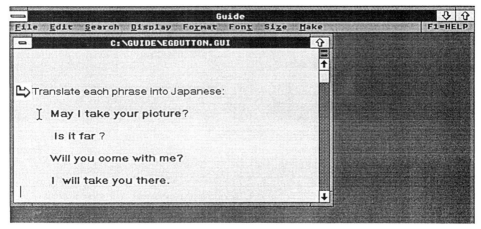

Fig. 4-6 Guide reference point shown by bent arrow.

The value of a reference button is that you can refer the reader to a specific point in a document that already exists. In this way you can make use of existing documents without having to edit or modify the existing document.

Making a reference button/reference point pair These are fairly easy to make in Guide but it takes some know-how. It might help you to understand reference buttons and points if you see exactly how they are created in Guide. The best way to create a reference button and its corresponding reference point pair is to define the reference point first. Here are the steps:

1. Open the file that you are going to reference. Use the mouse to move through the file until you find the point you want the reader to reference. Then highlight a heading or keyword. (In Microsoft windows this is called "selecting.")
2. Pull down the Make menu and choose the Reference Point command.

3. Go to the place where you want the reference button to appear and highlight (select) some keyword. To do this you might need to open another file—or if that file is already open, just move the mouse pointer to its window and click on it.

4. Once you have selected the word to be the reference button, pull down the Make menu and pick the Reference command. The word you last highlighted is now linked to the reference point you created in steps 1 and 2.

Quiz time Most readers, I've found, appreciate quizzes in computer texts because they help them stay alert. Feel free to skip this if you want. Now, earlier, when I introduced the hypertext buttons in the Thinker (on the Amiga) I said that, by default, these buttons point to nodes within the current document.

Q. Would you say the default Thinker buttons are reference buttons?

A. Yes, the default Thinker buttons are reference buttons because they refer the reader to nodes that are located in the current document. Now let's look at another system that enables reference buttons.

HyperSprint reference buttons

HyperSprint is a hypertext interface that Seyer Associates developed for use with Sprint, a customizable word processor. Unlike almost all other word processors, Sprint is fully customizable because it comes with a full-fledged language complete with IF statements, DO loops, and programmable calls to DOS, memory variables, and so on. Programs written in Sprint's macro programming language can be compiled to a binary overlay file for fast execution. The binary overlay file is linked to Sprint at run-time.

Creating a reference button

Using the compiled HyperSprint interface you can create a reference button by marking it as "underlined text." This is easy to do using Sprint's menu-driven system. You just highlight the text you want underlined: move the cursor to the start of the text to be underlined, press F3 and move the cursor to the end of the highlighted text. Then you press Alt-T to bring up the Typestyle menu and choose Underline. (You can choose an option here by moving the selection bar or by pressing the first letter of the menu option.) See Fig. 4-7, which shows me in the process of marking text as "underlined text" using the Typestyle menu.

Creating a reference point

To create the corresponding reference point (in the same file), you just move the cursor to the desired location and insert the same text that appears in the reference button—only this time you italicize the text. To activate a reference button, you just move the cursor to underlined text and press an appropriate hypertext hotkey. Sprint then "automatically" searches for the reference point: an italicized version of the underlined text. To return to the reference button, you just press an appropriate hotkey such as Alt-B (B here being

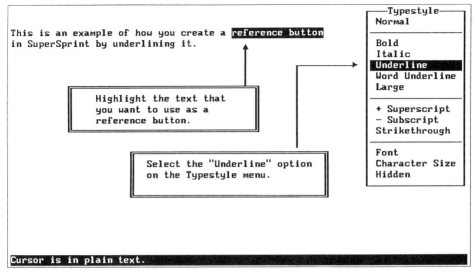

This is an example of how you create a `reference button` in SuperSprint by underlining it.

Highlight the text that you want to use as a reference button.

Select the "Underline" option on the Typestyle menu.

┌─Typestyle─┐
Normal

Bold
Italic
Underline
Word Underline
Large

+ Superscript
- Subscript
Strikethrough

Font
Character Size
Hidden

Cursor is in plain text.

Fig. 4-7   Creating a reference button with HyperSprint.

short for go Back to the reference button). Using HyperSprint you can easily create many reference buttons in a file, all of which will refer the reader to the same reference point. This way, whenever readers need an amplification of a keyword, they can get it simply by pointing to the word and pressing the hypertext hotkey. When they press Alt-B they will go back to whichever reference button they came from last.

Reference buttons in EMPOWERment

EMPOWERment, an IBM PC hypertext program designed to help individuals manage appointments, projects, and programs, enables reference buttons in a different way.

To create a reference button using EMPOWERment, you enclose the reference button text in braces. To specify the reference point (or destination button), you surround text with periods. To activate a reference button in EMPOWERment, you put the cursor on an opening brace and press F10. EMPOWERment then moves immediately to the matching text which is enclosed with periods. If you press F10 with the cursor on the period, or on any other period, EMPOWERment returns immediately to the previous reference button.

Figure 4-8 shows how I use reference buttons with EMPOWERment to index a project management file. The index at the top of the file tells readers what the file contains and makes it easy for them to jump to a topic of interest, read or edit as needed and then jump back to the index. I'll discuss the usefulness of this approach later. For now, let's take a look at the buttons available in IBM LinkWay.

LinkWay buttons and objects

LinkWay, a program from IBM that resembles HyperCard on the Macintosh has several different kinds of buttons. LinkWay takes a different approach to button categorization.

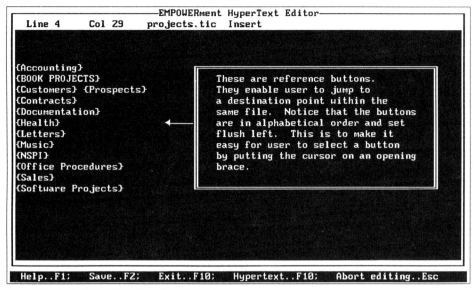

```
┌─────────────────EMPOWERment HyperText Editor─────────────────┐
│   Line 4      Col 29      projects.tic  Insert                │
│                                                               │
│ {Accounting}                                                  │
│ {BOOK PROJECTS}           ┌────────────────────────────────┐ │
│ {Customers} {Prospects}   │ These are reference buttons.   │ │
│ {Contracts}               │ They enable user to jump to    │ │
│ {Documentation}           │ a destination point within the │ │
│ {Health}              ◄───│ same file.  Notice that the buttons │
│ {Letters}                 │ are in alphabetical order and set │ │
│ {Music}                   │ flush left.  This is to make it  │ │
│ {NSPI}                    │ easy for user to select a button │ │
│ {Office Procedures}       │ by putting the cursor on an opening │
│ {Sales}                   │ brace.                         │ │
│ {Software Projects}       └────────────────────────────────┘ │
│                                                               │
│ Help..F1;   Save..F2;   Exit..F10;   Hypertext..F10;   Abort editing..Esc │
└───────────────────────────────────────────────────────────────┘
```

Fig. 4-8   Indexing a file with reference buttons.

There are no reference buttons or expansion buttons, but there are these six other kinds of buttons:

- Go
- Link
- Text pop-up
- Picture pop-up
- Script
- Document

To understand these buttons it helps to know a little bit about how LinkWay is structured. In LinkWay *nodes* are single, non-scrollable screens called *Pages*. A network of Pages are stored in a document called a *folder.*" Pages can contain three kinds of *objects*:

- Buttons
- Pictures
- Fields

Buttons you already know about. *Pictures* are graphic images that you create with a special LinkWay paint program called LWPaint. You can also capture graphics that you have created with the other programs. Almost any picture you can display on your monitor you can move into LinkWay as a picture object. (I might add, here, that Guide, BlackMagic, HyperWriter, Hyperdoc and other hypertext programs also offer a similar capability.)

Fields are definable input/output areas on a page that allow you, the hypertext developer, to output text. Fields also allow users to input text. Note that you cannot just create a new Page in a folder and immediately start entering text unless a field has previously been defined for this purpose. This adds a certain "cognitive overhead." It can slow you down. You have to "work at it" to develop a network of nodes. You can't just pop open a node and start writing unless you or someone else has previously designed a folder of nodes with a Base Page, which is similar to a template for all other pages, that has input fields.

Each LinkWay folder has a *base page*. Any buttons, fields, or pictures that you put on the base page are automatically displayed on the regular pages in a folder.

Go buttons   A Go button in LinkWay allows you to link a button to the base, first, last, next or previous page in a folder.

Link buttons   A Link button lets you link the current card with some other specific card, which may be in another folder. You must know the ID code of the card you want to link. (This is similar to a reference button in Guide, BlackMagic, or EMPOWERment.)

Find buttons   When a user clicks on a Find button, LinkWay searches through a specific field (or all fields) in a folder for the string you specify. When LinkWay finds the first occurrence of the string, it stops on that card.

Text Pop-up buttons   When a user clicks on a Text Pop-up button, a window the same size as the button will appear. The user will be able to scroll the text in this window. One drawback, here, is that you can't define a small button area and then pop up a window that is larger than the button. You have to make sure the button area, itself, is large enough to hold the text comfortably.

Picture Pop-up buttons   A click on a picture pop-up button will result in the display of a Picture that you have previously captured or created with LWPaint.

Script buttons   When a user clicks on a Script button, the commands embedded in the script will be executed. I'll go into more detail on scripts in chapter 10.

Document button   This button, when selected, will pop up a scrollable text document in the LinkWay editor. One drawback, here, is that this scrollable text node is a terminal one; that is, you cannot have buttons embedded in the document that point to other nodes. This limitation does not exist in systems such as xText, EMPOWERment, HyperTIES, Guide, TransText, Hyperdoc, KnowledgePro, which are primarily designed for hypertext rather than hypermedia. Again, I'd like to stress that it is important to know whether the node that a button creates can be linked to other nodes. Keep this in mind when evaluating various hypertext systems. A program that has a lot of capability in this area is HyperWriter, a commercial product that was an outgrowth of the BlackMagic shareware program. Let's look at the buttons and links in HyperWriter next.

HyperWriter buttons and links

Before getting into a discussion of what HyperWriter links, I'd like to mention that in the HyperWriter documentation, buttons are referred to as links. As you might recall in this book, I use the term button to refer to a visual cue, on screen, that tells a user that there is a hypertext link to another node. I think of the link as the actual data that the hypertext program uses to bring about the hypertext jump. The link is usually hidden behind the button. If the button is moved, then the link moves with the button. However, to stay consistent with the HyperWriter documentation, I will use the term link interchangeably with button in this discussion.

HyperWriter has three basic kinds of links:

- Text links
- Graphics links
- Action links

Furthermore, some of these basic kinds of links have variations. For example, a text link can be a:

- Jump
- Comment
- Swap
- ASCII file

The options don't stop here. A Jump link, in turn, can jump to a new window, an existing window, or to an external document. See Fig. 4-9, which summarizes the possible link types available, what colors they appear in, and how you get started creating them.

TEXT LINKS (in green, created with F3)

    JUMP LINKS
        To new window
        To existing window
        To external document
    COMMENT (popup) Links
    SWAP (replacement) Links
    ASCII FILE Links.

Fig. 4-9 Link types in HyperWriter.

GRAPHICS LINKS (in blue, created with Shift-F3)
    To full screen (.PCX images)
    To popup window (.MGR images)

ACTION LINKS (in red, created with Alt-F3)
    Script execution
    HyperWriter menu operations
    DOS programs

Let's take a closer look at these HyperWriter links and how you create them. Let's start with Text links.

Text links In HyperWriter, a link (hypertext button) appears as text that is delimited with triangular-shaped symbols. To create a text jump link:

1. Mark a block of text that you want to turn into a link. (Hold down the Shift key and press the Right arrow key. As you press the Right arrow key, the text will start to be highlighted.)

2. Press F3. When a dialog box appears, choose the type of text link that you want to create. You can choose from jump links, comment links, swap links or ASCII file links. See Fig. 4-10, which shows the dialog box popping up over a HyperWriter

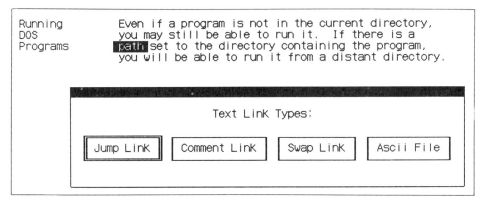

```
Running         Even if a program is not in the current directory,
DOS             you may still be able to run it.  If there is a
Programs        ▊path▊ set to the directory containing the program,
                you will be able to run it from a distant directory.


                              Text Link Types:

        ┌─────────────┐  ┌──────────────┐  ┌────────────┐  ┌──────────────┐
        │  Jump Link  │  │ Comment Link │  │  Swap Link │  │  Ascii File  │
        └─────────────┘  └──────────────┘  └────────────┘  └──────────────┘
```

Fig. 4-10   HyperWriter text link dialog box.

screen. In Fig. 4-10 I am in the process of turning the word "path" into a hyper-text button.

Text jump links   If you say that you want to create a Jump link, HyperWriter will ask whether you want to link to a new window, an existing window, or another document. Figure 4-11 shows the dialog box that appears.

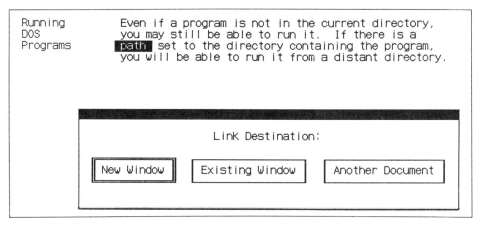

```
Running         Even if a program is not in the current directory,
DOS             you may still be able to run it.  If there is a
Programs        ▊path▊ set to the directory containing the program,
                you will be able to run it from a distant directory.


                              Link Destination:

        ┌─────────────┐  ┌─────────────────┐  ┌──────────────────┐
        │  New Window │  │ Existing Window │  │ Another Document │
        └─────────────┘  └─────────────────┘  └──────────────────┘
```

Fig. 4-11   HyperWriter jump link dialog box.

Text jump to new window   If you say you want to link to a new window, HyperWriter will display a blank screen and you can type in the next text for the new node. After typing in the new text, just press Esc to return to the parent node and complete the link.

Text jump to previously defined window (node)   If you choose to create a link to a previously defined window, HyperWriter will go into Point Mode and wait for you to navi-gate to the destination point and mark a block (by holding down Shift and pressing the Right arrow key). After marking the destination point, you press Esc to complete the link. A handy feature, here, is that all of HyperWriter's navigation tools are active. You don't have to remember some cryptic node ID. If you want, you do a text search through a network of nodes to find the one you want to use as the destination of the link. Note that the destination point is not just a node, but it is a specific point within a node. This is quite useful because HyperWriter supports scrolling nodes.

Text jump to external document If you choose to link to an external document, HyperWriter will ask you for the name of that document. You can enter the name or select it from a menu of files. After HyperWriter loads the file, navigate to the node you want to link to (using any of the navigation methods available). Then mark the destination as described earlier and press Esc. HyperWriter will then take you back to the parent node. The cursor will be on the button you just created, which the NTERGAID folks refer to as a *link anchor*.

Text comment link A comment link displays a pop-up node (which appears in a separate window). To create a comment link, press F3 and choose C for Comment link. Enter the text that you want to appear in the pop-up window and press Esc to finish the linking process.

Swap (replacement) link A swap link is like a "replacement button" in Guide. That is, the swap link is replaced with new text. This is done in the same window. The text seems to "expand." To create a swap link, mark a block of text, press F3 and choose S for Swap. A window will appear for you to enter the replacement text. Press Esc to finish up.

ASCII file link An ASCII file link, as its name implies, displays an ASCII file which you can browse through. The procedure for creating this link starts out the same: you mark a block and press F3. Then you choose Ascii File from the dialog box. You can then type in the name of the ASCII file you want to link to or choose it from the dialog box. After you specify the name of the file you want to link to, that file will appear on screen. You can now link to a specific line in this file. Just scroll to the desired line and press Esc. An important limitation, here, is that you cannot embed links in the ASCII node itself. That is, after the users access the ASCII file, they cannot branch to other nodes by selecting links.

Graphics link A graphic link appears as text delimited with blue triangular symbols. When you select such a link, HyperWriter displays a graphics image. Before you can link to a graphic image, you must have that image stored in an external file. You can create the image with any graphics "paint" program that can generate files in .PCX format. Alternatively, you can capture a screen generated with any graphics program using HyperWriter's screen grabber, a separate program named GRABIT.COM. The graphic can appear in a full window or a pop-up window. If a graphic appears in a full window it must be stored in a .PCX file format. Pop-up images are stored in the .MGR format, which is a format created by GRABIT.COM.

NOTE: Although GRABIT is a handy program for capturing most screen images, it won't work with Microsoft Windows or GEM. There is a workaround, though, using a program called HotShot Graphics.

Linking to a graphic To create a link to a graphic, start by marking some text as a block. Then, as usual, press Shift-F3. A dialog box will pop up and you can press F to choose Full Screen or P for a Pop-up graphic. Another dialog box appears in which it lists the names of the appropriate graphic files in the current default subdirectory. You can enter a file name or choose it from the list. After you select the graphics file, HyperWriter loads it into the current window. To complete the link, you press Esc. Figure 4-12 shows a sample pop-up graphic. When the user clicks on Philip C. Seyer the graphic pops up as shown. The graphic is a cartoon drawing of me sitting at my favorite PC. The cartoon was first drawn on paper, then scanned using a ScanMan Plus hand-held scanner. This created a .TIFF file. Next the file was edited using HotShot Graphics and then the image was captured using HyperWriter's GRABIT program.

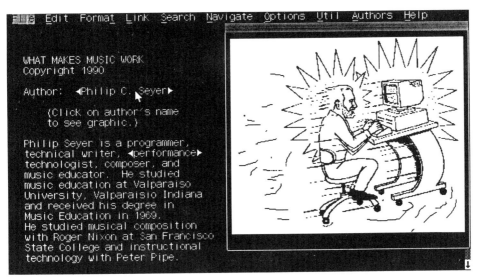

Fig. 4-12 Linking to a pop-up graphic.

Importing graphics It is also possible to import a graphic stored in .MGR format into a HyperWriter network. A good way to do this is to first create a text jump link to a new window. Be sure to complete the link first. Then go back to the destination node and position the cursor. Press Alt-F9 and select the .MGR file image that you want to import. In this way you can create a link that displays a full-screen .MGR image. Or if you like, you can add text to the screen if the graphic doesn't fill up the entire screen.

Creating links from graphics

Many programs can create jumps to graphic images. What distinguishes a well-developed hypertext program, however, is the ability to embed links in the graphic images themselves. With HyperWriter, you can embed links in either pop-up graphics or full screen graphics. To put a link into a graphic image, you follow these steps:

1. Display the graphic.
2. Press Alt-F4.
3. Position the link anchor (the button) where you want it on the graphic, using the arrow key. Then press the Spacebar.
4. Adjust the size of the button by pressing the arrow keys. When you have the button

the size that you want it to be, press the link key, Shift-F3, and choose the type of link you want to create.

5. When the destination window opens, enter the contents of the link and press Esc to finish the linking process.

Action links Action links appear as text delimited with red triangular shaped symbols. You can use action links for: Script execution, HyperWriter menu operations, or DOS programs.

To create an action link:

1. Highlight a block.
2. Press Alt-F3. A dialog box will present a menu. You can choose the type of action link you want to create—script, menu operation, or DOS execution.

If you are linking to a menu operation, HyperWriter will give you a selection of menu operations to which you can link. Otherwise, HyperWriter will give you a blank window in which you can enter your action commands.

DOS link If you are creating a DOS link, you can just enter a series of DOS commands as if you were writing a DOS batch file. One difference, though, is that you must put @RESTART itself after executing the DOS commands.

Creating graphic nodes As I mentioned earlier, if you have a graphic image in .PCX format you can use it as a full screen node in HyperWriter. But what if your graphic is in a different file format? Then, it is probably best to use HyperWriter's GRABIT.COM utility program to capture the image in .MGR format. In most cases, you don't want a graphic to fill the entire screen anyway, you want to add in a few introductory words or a caption for the illustration. To use GRABIT:

1. Exit to DOS and make sure you are in your HyperWriter subdirectory.
2. Enter the command GRABIT filename.mgr where filename.mgr is the actual name you want to use for your captured image.
3. Run the program that will display the screen you want to capture.
4. When the proper screen comes up, press Alt-G. GRABIT will now display a sizing box that you manipulate to specify exactly what you would like to "grab." Use the Spacebar to choose the corner of the box that you want to move. Use the arrow keys (or Shift-arrow keys) to actually size the box.
5. Once you have sized the box, press Return to capture the screen image.
6. After you have captured an image with GRABIT, the next step is to merge it into a HyperWriter screen. This is easy.
7. Put the cursor where you want the image to appear.
8. Press Alt-F9.
9. Select the proper .MGR file from the list of files in the dialog box that appears. (If the file name doesn't appear in the directory, you can click on the OK button to select a different subdirectory.)

Limitations of GRABIT In general GRABIT works well, but there are a few limitations. GRABIT can't grab an entire screen image, although it comes close. This is done by design to ensure that all screen images captured can be distributed on all computers.

Another limitation is that GRABIT works only on graphics screens. GRABIT also cannot capture graphics screens displayed by Microsoft Windows or GEM products.

Using HotShot Graphics   You can get around these problems with an excellent screen capture and graphics editor called HotShot Graphics. Using HotShot Graphics, you can capture almost any graphics screen and edit it at the pixel level. Once you have captured a graphics screen with HotShot Graphics, you can recapture it with GRABIT or export the captured file to .PCX format. The .PCX format generated by HotShot Graphics is compatible with HyperWriter so, if you like, you can create a full screen graphic node. HotShot Graphics will come in handy if you want to scan images and create full screen nodes. That's because your scanner software might not be able to create .PCX files that are HyperWriter-compatible.

For example, one of the projects I am working on is the creation of an extensive hypertext tutorial on music theory. Because I earlier authored a book on this subject that contained hundreds of illustrations, I decided to use a scanner to capture the images. Although I could easily scan the images, my scanner (ScanMan Plus) produced files in .TIF format. Because ScanMan Plus comes with a conversion utility, I converted the .TIF file to .PCX format. However, this file was not HyperWriter-compatible. Next I tried reading the .TIF file into PC Paintbrush and then saving the file in .PCX format. Again, the .PCX file produced by PC Paintbrush could not be read. HotShot Graphics came to the rescue. Its conversion worked without a hitch.

Command buttons

A *command button* is a button that can give a command or series of commands to the computer just as if they had been typed at the DOS prompt. You've already seen a kind of command button in the HyperWriter action links. Now let's examine the way some of the other hypertext systems enable command buttons.

EMPOWERment command buttons

Using EMPOWERment you can create command buttons in three different ways:

1. Put one or more DOS commands in brackets (with each command on a separate line).
2. Put one or more DOS commands in a standard text file and just put the file name in brackets.
3. Put a single DOS command in parentheses.

For example suppose you want to change to a subdirectory called LOTUS and then run the 123.EXE program. You could write the command button like this:

```
[CD \ 123;123]
```

Notice that multiple DOS commands can be enclosed in brackets if a semicolon is used to separate each command.

Another approach might be to create a file called, say, GOLOTUS. In the LOTUS file you would put the CD \ and 123 commands. Then in the EMPOWERment file, the command button would look like this:

[GOLOTUS]

Notice that with this method, the GOLOTUS file does not need an extension. You could use any convenient extension, however. You might want to use an extension to categorize various kinds of command buttons.

In enabling both of these command buttons, EMPOWERment exits and frees up all memory to the external program. But after the external program finishes, EMPOWERment returns. How is this possible? It's done with a simple DOS batch file trick. In this example, EMPOWERment reads the LOTUS file into memory, writes a temporary batch file, and then terminates. Because EMPOWERment is always started by a batch file, after EMPOWERment exits, this batch file continues on with the next command, which is to run a temporary batch file. This temporary batch file is the one EMPOWERment created just before it terminated itself! So the temporary batch file runs the external program and then restarts EMPOWERment—the last line of the temporary EMPOWERment file is always EMP, which is the batch file that launches EMPOWERment. See Fig. 4-13, which shows a diagram that illustrates this DOS chicanery.

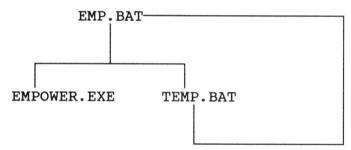

NOTE: EMPOWER.EXE writes TEMP.BAT on the fly just before it exits to DOS.

Fig. 4-13   How EMPOWERment frees up all memory.

The third way to create a command button in EMPOWERment is to put a single DOS command in parentheses. This is called a *Quickie Command button* because EMPOWERment executes the command directly and stays resident in memory so that it can pop back into action with the cursor exactly in the same place in the parent node.

If you need to execute two or more commands with this method, for example, change to the LOTUS subdirectory and run 123. You could put these commands in a DOS batch file called, say, LOTUS.BAT. The Quickie Command button would then look like this:

(LOTUS)

This works well as long as the external program does not require too much memory. It is possible to run Lotus 1-2-3 with a quickie command in this way. But if you need to load a huge spreadsheet memory problems could result. In that case, it is better to use an external command button, which is always delimited with square brackets. An external command button carries out these actions:

1. Terminates the hypertext program (EMPOWERment, for example). This frees up all memory previously occupied by the hypertext program.
2. Loads and executes the external program.
3. After the external program finishes, the hypertext program restarts.

Because external command buttons free up memory, they are effective when you need to launch a big external program. The disadvantage, though, is that the process is slower because time is required to reload the main hypertext program. Also, when a hypertext program exits to the operating system, it is more difficult for it to maintain the user's place in the hypertext network.

Command buttons in Guide

To create a command button in Guide, you start by entering a special script. You must create the script in a Definitions window. To do this, you pull down the Display menu and choose Show Definitions. The Definitions window appears and you can enter the script. The script for running Lotus 1-2-3 would be:

```
#LAUNCH
CD \LOTUS
123
```

Notice that the script must begin with the key word #LAUNCH on the first line. After typing in the script, you highlight it, pull down the Make menu and pick Definition.

After writing the script and storing it as a definition, the next step is to create the command button. To do this you go to a file, which Guide calls a Guideline, and enter some text. Then you highlight the text, pull down the Make menu and pick the Command option. Now the command button text will normally be italicized. When you move the mouse pointer over that italicized text, it will turn into a distinctive black arrow showing that it is a command button.

This works well for Windows applications. If the external program is a non-windows application, however, you need to create a *program information file* (PIF) file. You do this using the PIFEDIT.EXE program that comes with Microsoft Windows.

Command buttons in Guide can also control devices connected to the serial port. There are a number of simple commands you can use to select a COM port for input or output, set the baud rate, parity, data bits and so on. In making a script for a serial device, you make the first line #SERIAL. Of course, a serial device could also be controlled by calling a DOS .EXE program designed to control the serial device.

LinkWay external command buttons

I've discussed the types of buttons that LinkWay is capable of creating, but I didn't go into too much detail about how you make a button and link it to a specific kind of action. Let's do that now with the "command button." Actually, LinkWay does not support a command button directly, but you can create a command button indirectly using a script. To create any kind of LinkWay button, you go through several steps using a system of menus.

It's rather difficult to describe the steps for creating a button. It's really visual and kines-thetic requiring a mouse. Once you do it a few times, it is relatively easy. Here are the steps:

1. Select the Object menu (from the pull-down menu at the top of the screen).
2. Select the New option from the Object menu. A menu box appears; click on Button and then click on the dot in the upper right corner of the menu box. (Clicking on this dot always closes a box or window.)
3. After you carry out the previous step, a dotted outline cursor appears. Drag this outline to the spot where you want the button to be. Then click the mouse to anchor one corner of the button area.
4. Move the mouse and notice how the size of the button changes. When the size of the button area is the way you want it to be, click the mouse again.
5. Next, LinkWay will pop up a menu box as shown in Fig. 4-14:

Fig. 4-14 IBM LinkWay Button Type menu.

```
BUTTON Type
    Go
    Link
    Text Pop-Up
    Picture Pop-Up
    Script
    Document
```

As you can see, this is where you tell LinkWay which kind of button you want to create. Since LinkWay does not directly support command buttons, you need to select the Script option here. To do that you click on Script and then click on the dot in upper left corner of the box. After you click on the dot, a box appears in which you may name the button. If you want to name the button, you click on a spot between parentheses and type in the button name. Then you again click on the dot in the upper left corner of the box to close the box.

6. Next, a box appears where you can pick out the symbol that you want to use to represent the button.
7. Then a window will open for you to enter a script, which is one or more commands that will later be interpreted as a computer program and executed when you later select the button. The script command for executing an external program is:

DOS "command-line-expression";

Suppose you want to fire up dBASE by clicking on a LinkWay button. A simple script command to do that would be:

DOS "dbase";

Sometimes LinkWay will be in graphics mode when you launch an external program. If you want to reset DOS to character mode before calling the external program and ensure that you return again to graphics mode, you can do that by including two pound signs (#) in the script command, like this:

```
DOS # "dbase"#;
```

You can do a lot more with LinkWay scripts than just creating command buttons. For more details on scripting, see chapter 8, Programming Hypertext.

Controlling external programs

Although command buttons launch external programs, they usually relinquish control to the external program. But what if you want a command button to do more than that? One solution is to make use of the command tail. The *command tail* is the string of characters that you can enter after the program name on the command line. This string is stored in memory and any DOS program can access it, although some DOS programs don't.

For example, when you start up WordPerfect, you can immediately tell it which file to edit on the command line if that file already exists:

```
WP filename
```

Using the Norton Editor, you can even specify which line you want to jump to on the command line. After the command NE (short for Norton Editor), you put a plus sign (+) and the line number where you want to go. Then you put the name of the file you want to edit. For example, to load a file called "secrets" and jump to line 387, you would give this command:

```
NE +387 secrets
```

Ize, an information manager with some hypertext features, allows you to feed a few keystrokes to a program even after it has launched the program. These keystrokes instruct the external program how to load a file in the case where the program cannot get this information from the command line. Multimate, for example, doesn't accept a file name on the command line. So Ize allows you to define some keystrokes that will be passed on to Multimate so it can load a file.

If a hypertext program lacks the ability to feed keystrokes to an external program, you can still do that by using a memory-resident program like SuperKey. For example, in the previous chapter I showed how to launch a musical node with a DOS command like:

```
KEY /ml PFPEACE
```

where KEY loads SuperKey if it is not already resident in memory. The /ml PFPEACE means load the PFPEACE macro. For this to work, PFPEACE should be designated as an autostart macro. SuperKey will immediately start executing this macro because AUTO appears at the end of the first line. (See Fig. 3-16 in chapter 3.) You might also use a program called KEY-FAKE to enable *hotlink*—links that feed keystrokes to external programs and thereby allow you to control the external program. KEY-FAKE is available from *PC Magazine* through a service called PC MagNet. You can access PC MagNet directly or through CompuServe.

To download a program from PC MagNet with your modem, set your modem to 7 data bits, even parity, 1 stop bit and full duplex. Then call the nearest PC MagNet number (you can find out the nearest number by calling (800) 346-3247). When your modem connects to this number, press Enter. At the HOST NAME prompt, enter PHONES. Then just follow the prompts and make a note of the number that is nearest you.

After you find the closest PC MagNet number, hang up and dial again using that number. After you connect with PC MagNet, carry out these steps.

1. Press Ctrl-C.
2. At the HOST NAME prompt, enter CIS.
3. At the USER ID prompt, enter 177000,5000.
4. At the PASSWORD prompt, enter PC*MAGNET.
5. At the ENTER AGREEMENT NUMBER prompt, enter Z10D005.
6. Once you are on PC MagNet, choose PC Magazine Utilities from the menu.
7. Next choose Direct Utility Download.
8. At the next menu enter KEY-FAKE.
9. Several KEY-FAKE files will be displayed. Pick the file you want to download. I suggest you first download KEY-FAKE.COM and then KEY-FAKE.DOC which documents the program.
10. Answer yes by pressing Y at the DO YOU WISH TO DOWNLOAD prompt and press Enter to see the transfer protocols. Choose a protocol that matches the protocol you have available on your modem program.
11. As soon as you see the "downloading" message appear, press the appropriate key to activate the downloading function in your modem program to start downloading the file. (For example, using a modem program called ProComm you would press the PgDn key.)

Using KEY-FAKE within a command button

To use KEY-FAKE you normally set up a batch file. On the line preceding the one that invokes an application program, you give a KEY-FAKE command. This pumps some key codes into the keyboard buffer so that when the application program starts (via the next line in the batch file) the application program is tricked into thinking that someone actually made those key presses. The application program is "faked out," hence the name "FAKE-KEY." To give the FAKE-KEY command you type KEY-FAKE, leave a space and then specify the keys you want to be faked by your "phantom" typist. On the next line in the batch file you give the name of the program you want to launch.

In specifying the keys that you want pressed, if the keys can be expressed with simple ASCII codes you can just put the characters in quotes or use the decimal ASCII code. For example, 13 is the ASCII code for the Return key and 27 is the code for the Esc key. Ctrl-A is represented by 1, Ctrl-B is 2, Ctrl-C is 3 and so on so that Ctrl-Z is 26. To specify an extended ASCII code (a scan code), you precede the number with @. For example, @61 is the scan code for F3. See Table 4-1, which is a table of the IBM PC scan codes for keys that do not have ASCII codes.

Let's apply this to a practical example. Suppose you want to create a command button that launches WordPerfect and instructs it to load a certain file and immediately jump to a specific reference point in that file marked by a unique string. If the file is called PCON-

Table 4-1. PC Scan Codes.

Key	Scan code	Key	Scan code
Shift-Tab	15	Ctrl-F1	94
		Ctrl-F2	95
Alt-A through Alt-Z		Ctrl-F3	96
		Ctrl-F4	97
Alt-A	30	Ctrl-F5	98
Alt-B	48	Ctrl-F6	99
Alt-C	46	Ctrl-F7	100
Alt-D	32	Ctrl-F8	101
Alt-E	18	Ctrl-F9	102
Alt-F	33	Ctrl-F10	103
Alt-G	34		
Alt-H	35	Shift-F1	84
Alt-I	23	Shift-F2	85
Alt-J	36	Shift-F3	86
Alt-K	37	Shift-F4	87
Alt-L	38	Shift-F5	88
Alt-M	50	Shift-F6	89
Alt-N	49	Shift-F7	90
Alt-O	24	Shift-F8	91
Alt-P	25	Shift-F9	92
Alt-Q	16	Shift-F10	93
Alt-R	19		
Alt-S	31	Alt-F1	104
Alt-T	20	Alt-F2	105
Alt-U	22	Alt-F3	106
Alt-V	47	Alt-F4	107
Alt-W	17	Alt-F5	108
Alt-X	45	Alt-F6	109
Alt-Y	21	Alt-F7	110
Alt-Z	44	Alt-F8	111
		Alt-F9	112
		Alt-F10	113
Function keys			
		Ctrl-Alt combinations	
F1	59		
F2	60	Ctrl-Alt-=	131
F3	61	Ctrl-Alt-0	129
F4	62	Ctrl-Alt-1	120
F5	63	Ctrl-Alt-2	121
F6	64	Ctrl-Alt-3	122
F7	65	Ctrl-Alt-4	123
F8	66	Ctrl-Alt-5	124
F9	67		
F10	68		

Key	Scan code	Key	Scan code
Ctrl-Alt-6	125	Ctrl-PrtSc	114
Ctrl-Alt-7	126	Ctrl-Right Cursor	116
Ctrl-Alt-8	127	Cursor Down	80
Ctrl-Alt-9	128	Cursor Left	75
Ctrl-Alt-minus	130	Cursor Right	77
		Cursor Up	72
Cursor control keys		Del	83
		End	79
Ctrl-End	117	Home	71
Ctrl-Home	119	Ins	82
Ctrl-Left Cursor	115	PgDn	81
Ctrl-PgDn	118	PgUp	73
Ctrl-PgUp	132		

TACT.DOC and the string you want to go to in the file is "E. BLACKWOOD", the batch file might look like this:

```
KEY-FAKE @85 "E. BLACKWOOD" @85
WP PCONTACT.DOC
```

In EMPOWERment you could write this directly into a text node on one line like this:

```
[KEY-FAKE @85 "E. BLACKWOOD" @85;WP PCONTACT.DOC]
```

The first argument to KEY-FAKE here is @85, which you can see from Table 4-1 (in the function keys section) is the code for F2. Why do we want WordPerfect to think we pressed F2? Because in WordPerfect, F2 is the function key you press when you want to start a search operation. The next argument is the string "E. BLACKWOOD", which is the search string. Next comes another @85 to repeat the F2 because this is what you do in WordPerfect to activate the search function. Notice that after the @85 there is a semicolon. A semicolon, remember, is used in EMPOWERment to separate multiple DOS commands from each other in a command button. Next comes WP PCONTACT.DOC. The WP invokes WordPerfect. PCONTACT.DOC is the name of the file we want WordPerfect to load in this example.

Script files and command buttons

Some DOS programs read script files. A *script file* is an ASCII file that contains instructions for an application program. If a program can read a script file, you can create a command button that will make the program do just about anything you want. Some programs can take their input from a file if the redirection symbol, <, appears on the command line after the program name. For example, if you want to run the DOS DEBUG.EXE program and instruct it to carry out certain actions, you can put the keystrokes in a file called, say, SCRIPT.DBG. DEBUG is quite powerful. It can read virtually any file, search for specific strings of characters and change them to anything you want. Of course, this makes

DEBUG dangerous as well as powerful. To run DEBUG and tell it to take its keystrokes from a script file, you might give a command like this:

```
debug < script.dbg
```

PC Magazine often publishes useful script files for DEBUG in its "User-to-User" column. A good example was a script created by Sigurd P. Crossland of Centerville, Virginia. The script appeared in the June 13th, 1989 issue (Volume 8, Number 3). This script instructs DEBUG to read the contents of a 360K floppy disk and move its entire contents to a single file. The advantage is that all files on the diskette (including hidden files and system files) are retrieved and saved in a single file. If you want, you can then send the file via telecommunications and it's just like sending an entire disk. The command to read a floppy disk and put it into a file could be:

```
debug < getdisk.dbg
```

If you use Crossland's script, a file called DISKFILE will be created. DISKFILE will contain all the files that were on the diskette. To restore to diskette format, you insert a diskette in Drive A and give the command:

```
debug < resdisk.dbg
```

Now, if these commands will work from DOS, they will work from hypertext programs that support command buttons. For example, in EMPOWERment you would have a node that contains DOS utilities. This node could have buttons that look like this:

[debug < getdisk.dbg] Copy diskette in Drive A to DISKFILE
[debug < resdisk.dbg] Restore diskette from hard disk file

If you are interested in creating hypertext command buttons that do some interesting things with DEBUG and other DOS programs, I suggest you browse through the "User-to-User" column in *PC Magazine* regularly. In the meantime, here is a simple example you can try with EDLIN, another DOS program. EDLIN comes with DOS. Every PC user has EDLIN. Although EDLIN is often criticized as being a clunky line editor, it can be fast and convenient if you know how to use it. With EDLIN you can often make a change in an ASCII file and get on with your next program even before you could load your favorite word processor into memory.

To use EDLIN with a script file you might give a command like this:

```
EDLIN Phone.tic < Script
```

Here, Phone.tic is the name of an ASCII file containing phone numbers. Script is the name of a file containing the commands that you might type manually. For example, Script might contain these lines:

```
sKumiko Seyer<Return>
e<Return>
```

In this example, <Return> refers to a carriage return press. That is, you would just press the Return key. You would not literally type <Return>.

The lowercase s instructs EDLIN to search. The rest of the line, Kumiko Seyer, is what EDLIN will search for in the PHONE.TIC file. Notice that Kumiko comes immediately after the s. If you were to enter s Kumiko, EDLIN would search for <space> Kumiko. The letter e instructs EDLIN to save the file and exit to DOS.

CAUTION: If you try this be careful. You must be sure to include the e and a carriage return; otherwise, EDLIN might just sit there forever—or until you reboot the system.

Anyway, if the Script file contains the proper commands, to look up Kumiko's phone number in the PHONE.TIC file, I could give the command EDLIN Phone.tic < Script as mentioned earlier. A command button in EMPOWERment to look up her number, might look like this:

```
(EDLIN Phone.tic < Script)
```

If I activate such a button, the screen will clear, Kumiko's phone number will appear on the screen for about five seconds, and then the original text screen will return. Keep in mind that although this is a simple example, more complex operations are possible with EDLIN or DEBUG.

By the way, Sprint, Borland's word processor, can take its input in this way, that is from a file instead from the keyboard. For example, you can start Sprint like this:

```
SP < control
```

where control is the name of a file that contains the keystrokes you want to feed to Sprint. In setting up the control file, you could use the key code table in Appendix E of the *Sprint Advanced User's Guide*. This means that a hypertext program could contain a button that would call Sprint and jump to some predefined location or carry out some other action—print the file, sort it, do a spelling check and so on. Most application programs these days don't take redirection in this way, but SPRINT is an exception.

Linking with other computers

Telecommunications programs can usually read script files. Do you see the implications? Using a hypertext program that can create command buttons you could create a button for logging onto a mainframe computer or service, such as CompuServe, and check for electronic mail. Another button might automatically log on to CompuServe and send a file to a subscriber. Such a button would enable novice input clerks to carry out telecommunications faster than experienced users—this could amount to quite a savings at the current hourly rates for such services. Another related idea involves sending fax messages via hypertext buttons. MCI Mail provides a fax dispatch service. So it is possible to create a command button that will invoke a telecommunications program and upload a file to MCI Mail along with instructions to send that file to a specific fax telephone number. I've used this approach quite successfully and I invite you to give it a try. Of course, if you have your own fax machine or a fax board, this idea might not be for you.

Advantage of command buttons

I've spent quite a lot of time discussing command buttons and showing how they can be installed in different hypertext programs. What's so great about all this? One advantage in creating these command buttons is that your utility programs don't become forgotten orphans. Do you have a utility folder or subdirectory on your hard disk? If so, take a look at what's inside. Do you see any little utilities there whose purpose you can't remember? If so, why don't you remember or why don't you have notes on what the programs are for? Because it's just not convenient to do so given the normal way that most operating systems work. But hypertext command buttons solve that. If you were to create a hypertext control node from which you launched all your utilities, inside of that control node you could easily make notes about the purpose of those various little gems.

Date buttons

Another value of hypertext is that it can stimulate you to think in new ways. Perhaps now that you have been mulling over the concept of buttons and links, you will think of a new kind of link—one that will be especially useful to you in your work.

A good example of this is the date button. For quality control purposes, a customer had asked us to develop a tickler program—one that would remind him of important tasks. The first version of the program automatically put the user into a project file when that project was due. Later, after we had worked with hypertext for a while, the idea occurred to use date buttons; that is, buttons that would appear in a "to do file" only after a certain date. By using date buttons we were able to give the user a quick picture of all of the projects that were coming due within X number of days. Then, if desired, the user could immediately get more detail by accessing the hypertext node pointed to by the date button. Figure 4-15 shows a sample planning node with date buttons.

Notice in Fig. 4-15 how each button appears at the left edge of the screen and to the right, on the same line, there is a brief description of the task to be performed. By putting the cursor on the first character of the date and pressing F10, the user can zoom into the date node.

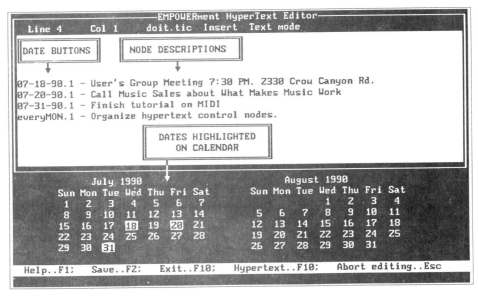

Fig. 4-15 EMPOWERment date buttons.

Automatic linking

Automatic linking is a powerful concept, but one which is still emerging. It would be useful to be able to ask a system to automatically link to the current node all other nodes which deal with a similar topic.

Several PC programs are available that can search text files for keywords, but not many integrate hypertext linking. For example, Norton's TS.EXE utility (short for text search) will search a group of files for a string and report the line number at which it found the keyword. The report is displayed on the screen or it can be redirected to a file. A hypertext extension of this would put the results of the search in a control node from which you could jump into any of the files containing the keyword. In fact, something like this is already available in EMPOWERment. Also, a personal information management program called Ize can do dynamic linking of nodes that have been previously indexed. Let's look more closely at how EMPOWERment and Ize do this automatic linking.

Automatic linking with EMPOWERment

Figure 4-16 shows the Automatic Linking menu in EMPOWERment. In using this feature, you enter this information:

1. File specification, which tells which files should be searched.
2. Keyword to search for
3. Name to use for the resulting output file.
4. Subdirectory name

The subdirectory name tells which subdirectory you want to search. If you want, you can also ask EMPOWERment to search several subdirectories. If you press just the Return

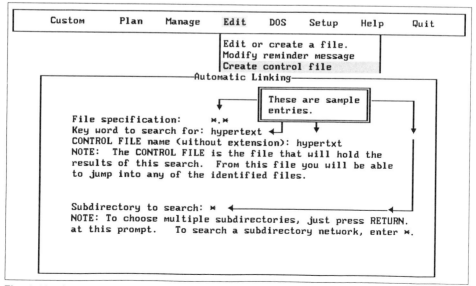

Fig. 4-16 Automatic Linking screen from EMPOWERment.

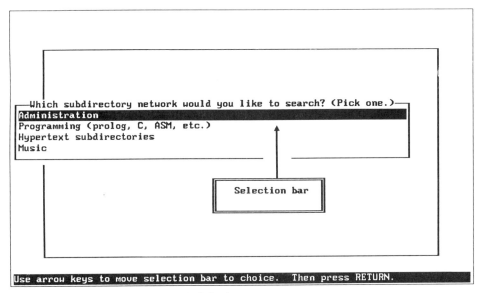

Fig. 4-17 EMPOWERment's Network Selection menu.

key at the subdirectory prompt, the program will give you a menu of all of the subdirectories on the current drive. You can then mark the subdirectories you want searched.

EMPOWERment also lets you search a predefined network of subdirectories. If you enter an asterisk, *, at the subdirectory prompt, EMPOWERment asks you which subdirectory network you want to search. A network of subdirectories is simply a group of subdirectories you have previously lumped together and identified with a descriptive name. See Fig. 4-17, which shows EMPOWERment's Network Selection menu.

So far, this is not too different from a traditional search program. The difference, however, is that the program automatically links the files that are identified in the search to the control node that you specify. After the AUTOLINK program finishes the search, you find that you are in a hypertext control node that lists all of the identified files—files that contain the keyword. From inside this control node you can immediately access any of the files and also add your own documentation of them if you wish. Once you have this control node, you can use it later as the starting point for a search related to the keyword you specified. You can also edit this control node as you work and create new files.

So that the control node does not get lost, EMPOWERment automatically links it to a master control node, CONTROL.CTR. The master control node never gets lost because you can access it from the EMPOWERment Edit menu. See Fig. 4-18.

Building your own automatic linking system

If you are interested in building your own automatic linking system and you program in C, you might want to consider using POWER SEARCH from Blaise Computing, Inc. POWER SEARCH is a library of C functions for searching for character strings in DOS. POWER SEARCH routines can be simple and extremely fast, or based on a pattern and highly flexible. See chapter 10 for more information about POWER SEARCH.

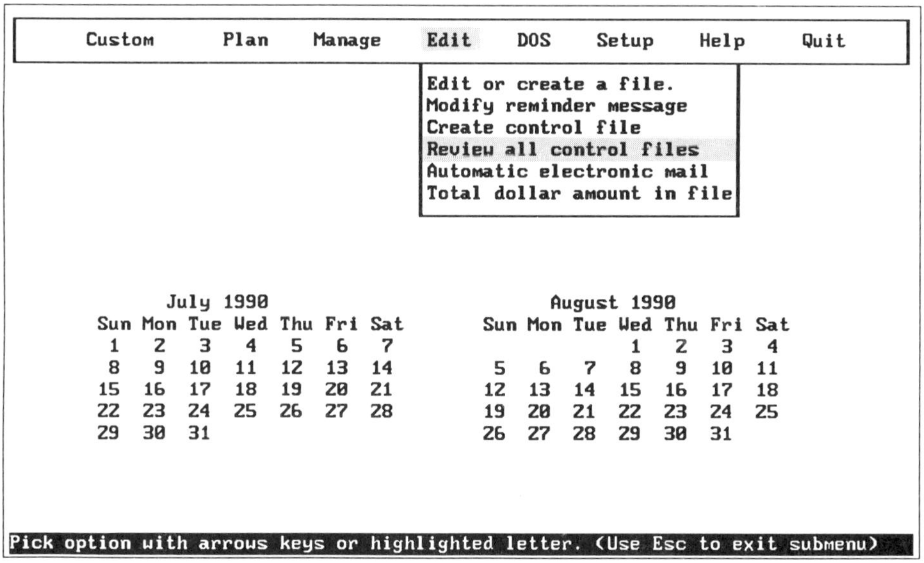

Fig. 4-18 EMPOWERment Edit menu.

Automatic linking with Ize

Ize is an information manager that has its own unique style of hypertext. With Ize you store all information in nodes called *texts*. A text can be just one word or it can be up to 30K in size. You can store many texts (up 32,000!) in a network, which Ize calls a *text-base*. You retrieve texts by their keywords. When you save a node (a text) in Ize you must assign at least one keyword. Texts in Ize are stored in a special Ize format. You can't just link standard ASCII files like you can in EMPOWERment. If you have ASCII files or files in special word processing formats, you need to import them into Ize. A powerful feature of Ize is its ability to "automatically" create keywords for each text that you import into it. Ize then uses the keywords as the basis for a hypertext-like access system. Before Ize can automatically generate keywords, you need to give Ize some guidance.

One way to do this is to define several words that you want Ize to associate with a text if those words exist in the text. Another way is to define a certain area of text that you want Ize to use as the basis for generating keywords. You do this by specifying a starting string and an ending string. Ize will use all the text in between the starting and ending string as the basis for the keywords. But it will also delete those words that you specify. When importing a large ASCII file—like the chapter of a book, you can have Ize automatically split it up into nodes (or texts as Ize calls them).

To give Ize a test run, I tried this with the first new chapters of this book. I first converted three of the chapter files to ASCII and then merged them into one large ASCII file. Next I imported the ASCII file into an Ize textbase. In the process of importing the file I instructed Ize to split the file automatically whenever Ize encountered the string "HEADINGB." ("HEADINGB" always marks a second level heading in my chapters.) I asked Ize to use the heading as the basis for creating keywords for each node. Also, I gave Ize a list of words to use if Ize would find them in any given node.

Figure 4-19 shows an Ize screen on which I specified some of these parameters.

After you have created or imported several texts into Ize you can search the textbase by keyword—so far this is not hypertext. But when you give a search request, Ize automatically builds an outline that acts somewhat like a hypertext control node. Figure 4-20 shows an outline that Ize automatically constructed when I searched the test textbase with the keyword "hypertext."

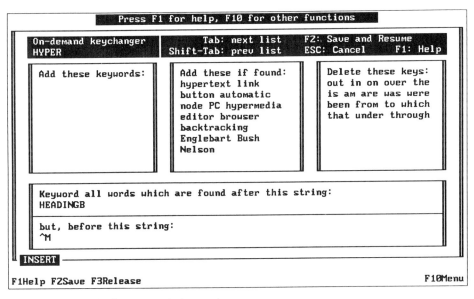

Fig. 4-19 Telling Ize how to create keywords.

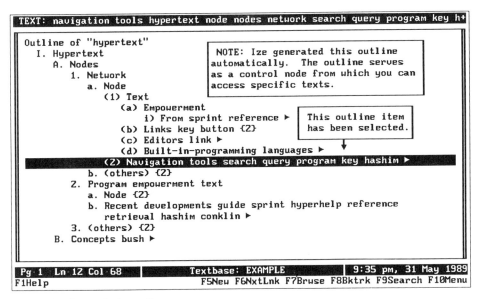

Fig. 4-20 Automatic Ize outline.

In Fig. 4-20 you can see that I have highlighted an item that begins Navigation tools. This line points to a specific node that discusses hypertext navigation tools. The other words on this line are the additional keywords associated with this node. In Ize you browse by pressing F7. Figure 4-21 shows the node that appeared when I pressed F7 with the selection bar on Navigation tools.... As I mentioned earlier, Ize also allows you to create command buttons (hot links) that can launch external programs.

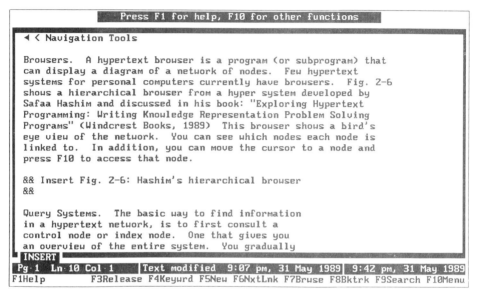

Fig. 4-21   Ize text displayed when outline item is selected.

Typed links

Some hypertext systems allow users to describe the relationship that exists between two nodes. In so doing, the user might be said to be declaring that the link is of a certain type. For example, if node B gives an example of a rule or principle presented in node A, the link that connects A to B might be called an "illustrated" link. But suppose there exists another node, C, which is a more detailed explanation of node B (the example node). You might say that the link between B and C is an "amplification" link. See Fig. 4-22.

```
NODE A <------------> NODE B <------------> NODE C
          illustrates                amplifies
```

Fig. 4-22   Typed links.

With this type of network, there must be a separate data entity that describes each link. The link entity must exist separately from the node because any given node could be linked in different ways to other nodes. (See the chapter on programming considerations for an example of how this might be implemented.)

Value of typed links

What good does it do to type links? For one thing, before transversing a link, you can have some advance information about the nature of the destination node. Also, theoretically, with an advanced query system, you could query the system in a structured way. For example, you might be able to ask:

- Which nodes support a position refuted by a majority of the design engineers?
- Which position nodes have no supporting examples?
- Which examples are refuted by at least one node?

Hypertext system knowledge

Notice here that the system has knowledge about the relationships between nodes. With typed links we have the potential of developing intelligent hypertext. That's because an important aspect of knowledge involves information about how two things relate to each other. Facts, ideas, even rules and principles are of little value until we can see how they relate to each other and to other information.

If a network has knowledge about the relationship of various nodes to each other we might be able to query the system about its knowledge. For example, we might ask:

- Show me all the nodes that discuss X or something similar to X.
- Show me all the nodes containing information that is contrary to or the opposite of X.

Few of the commercial PC hypertext systems that I have examined support typed links, but the PC IBIS system developed by Safaa Hashim does. It appears that further research and development is needed before typed links will be put to practical use in microcomputer hypertext systems. (See chapter 10 for more information about Hashim's program.)

Summary

This chapter presented a variety of buttons:

- Expansion
- Note
- Reference
- Command
- Date
- Text
- Go
- Link
- Picture
- Text pop-up

You've seen how you can use these different kinds of buttons and links to organize information for easy retrieval. You've also seen how some hypertext programs can scan existing data files and automatically create "control nodes." In addition you've learned about typed links and how you might use them for more intelligent processing of hypertext networks. I've got more to tell you about nodes and links as you will see in the coming chapters, especially chapter 8, which discusses how buttons and links can be embedded in PC memory-resident programs. By now you have a good understanding of the fundamentals of hypertext, so in the next chapter you will learn why hypertext is valuable.

5

Why use hypertext?

Now that you have a fairly good idea of what hypertext is and the features found in hypertext programs, let's consider why hypertext is valuable. Why would you want to switch from a traditional word processor or database system to one that has hypertext capability? There are a variety of reasons. Hypertext has the potential to help you:

- Maintain continuity in your work.
- Capture brainstorms.
- Produce better organized, more creative paper documents.
- Manage projects.
- Create help systems for fast information retrieval.
- Learn new material more effectively.
- Design more flexible learning systems for others.

Let's consider each of these benefits of hypertext in detail.

Maintain continuity

A hypertext program can help you maintain continuity while enabling diversity. For example, while working on this chapter, an associate called me and asked if he could send me a copy of a document he was working on via telecommunications. With ordinary software, I would need to exit from my word processor; start up ProComm, my telecommunications program; carry out the file transfer operation; then reload my file and try to find where I was when I left off. But because I was using HyperSprint, I just typed a command button directly into the text I was writing and then executed it. Figure 5-1 shows a screen from HyperSprint. I have annotated the screen so you can easily see the ProComm command button.

When I activated the command button, it launched ProComm and I carried out the file transfer. Later when I exited from the telecommunications program, HyperSprint restarted itself and returned me to the exact spot in the file where I was working. To continue, all I needed to do was to delete the command button. Creating the command button

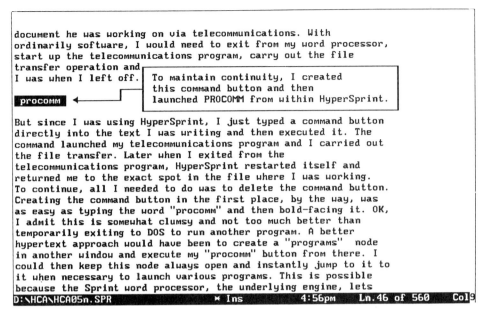

```
document he was working on via telecommunications. With
ordinarily software, I would need to exit from my word processor,
start up the telecommunications program, carry out the file
transfer operation and┌──────────────────────────────────────┐
I was when I left off. │ To maintain continuity, I created     │
                       │ this command button and then          │
 ■ procomm  ◄──────────┘ launched PROCOMM from within HyperSprint.│
                       └──────────────────────────────────────┘
But since I was using HyperSprint, I just typed a command button
directly into the text I was writing and then executed it. The
command launched my telecommunications program and I carried out
the file transfer. Later when I exited from the
telecommunications program, HyperSprint restarted itself and
returned me to the exact spot in the file where I was working.
To continue, all I needed to do was to delete the command button.
Creating the command button in the first place, by the way, was
as easy as typing the word "procomm" and then bold-facing it. OK,
I admit this is somewhat clumsy and not too much better than
temporarily exiting to DOS to run another program. A better
hypertext approach would have been to create a "programs" node
in another window and execute my "procomm" button from there. I
could then keep this node always open and instantly jump to it to
it when necessary to launch various programs. This is possible
because the Sprint word processor, the underlying engine, lets
```
`D:\HCA\HCA05n.SPR          × Ins        4:56pm   Ln.46 of 560    Col9`

Fig. 5-1 Maintaining continuity with hypertext.

in the first place was as easy as typing the word procomm and then boldfacing it.

OK, I admit this is somewhat clumsy and not too much better than temporarily exiting to DOS to run another program. A better hypertext approach, however, is to create a "programs" node in another window and execute my ProComm button from there. I could then keep this node always open and instantly jump to it when necessary to launch various programs. This is possible because the Sprint word processor, the underlying engine, lets you keep 24 files open at once.

The main point here, though, stands: hypertext can help you maintain continuity in your work because you are able to tie many programs, files, or nodes together into a whole.

Capture inspirational thoughts

Hypertext can help you capture inspirations that come to you when you are working on various projects. You can still keep your place in the current project while you move into a new node and jot down your ideas.

Traditional word processing tools tend to lock writers into a fixed linear sequence in writing. With a traditional word processor you usually need to know where an idea fits into a larger document before you start developing it. In other words, you need to have an outline. But this need for a structure before starting can easily lead to writer's block!

Hypertext gives us the freedom to think and develop ideas before we have worked out a full-blown outline; as a result it increases our productivity. We can create a node that focuses on a topic without knowing (or worrying about) where the topic will fit. We can then link this "dangling" node to a control node under a heading such as "Where does this go?" Doing this will help to ensure that we don't lose this node in our vast sea of hard disk files on our system. The maximum "out of sight—out of mind" does have a ring of truth, especially when it comes to files on a hard disk. With a traditional system, I would be reluctant to jump in and work on an idea in its own file because I would be afraid that I would lose track of the file or forget about it. Some word processors give you a lot of flexibility—they allow you to have many windows and many files open at once. But the crucial missing element in plain word processors is that you can't link one idea to another; yet that's the way our mind works.

So hypertext can give you a decided advantage over an old-fashioned word processor. But for this to work well, the hypertext system needs to be easy to use and not require the user to do a lot of thinking about how to set up a mode, link it, "type the link" and so on. Although link typing (discussed in chapter 4) certainly has advantages, it can cause "cognitive overhead." That is, it can be mentally tiring to use a sophisticated hypertext system that requires you to answer a lot of questions every time you create a new node.

Hypertext as a writing tool

I made extensive use of hypertext in developing this book. I used HyperSprint (the hypertext interface my company developed from Borland's Sprint). One of the main uses I made of this program was to keep the outline of the book in view and then quickly move to any one of the chapters by moving the cursor to the appropriate file name and pressing return. I created a command that automatically inserted the headings at the top of each chapter. Then by treating each of these headings as a reference button, I was able to quickly jump to any of the major sections of the chapter.

Write now, organize later   Hypertext allows a writer to work more naturally. Although when writing textbooks you usually develop an outline before writing, many writers just don't work this way. After all, how can you develop the outline before you've had a chance to thoroughly research and think through your topic. In the days before word processors, writers would often work with note cards—small cards on which they would write ideas related to a single topic. In this way, when taking notes, or working out a discussion of a topic, they didn't have to be concerned with the overall structure of the work, continuity, transitional paragraphs and so on. They were free to just focus on the topic at hand. Then, because each card focused on one idea, it was easy to rearrange the cards and unfold the structure of the writing piece.

When word processors became popular using note cards became less fashionable. It was just too much trouble to write out everything by hand and then retype it into the computer. (Also many users of word processors have discovered that their handwriting has deteriorated!)

At first it would seem that a word processor obviates the need for note cards. After all, can't a writer just create a separate file for each card and then later merge the files as desired to produce the final document? The problem with this approach is the "out of sight out of mind problem." Note cards are tangible. It is easy to pick them up on a desk top and move them around. Files are stored on disk and once saved are often forgotten.

Now with hypertext, you have the ability to reference the various files in a control node, so they don't get lost. When I first began writing this section of the book, for example, I didn't know exactly where it would fit into the outline. I did know that the topic was "the value of hypertext" so I created a node called valuehyp.hca (actually just a DOS file in Sprint format). Then I linked valuehyp.hca to a control node called menu.spr. Menu.spr is a control node that helps me organize all of my word processing activities.

Another technique I have found useful is to create a "follow-through" node. When an idea occurs to me I jump into this node and make a quick note of it. Then when I have "dealt with" the idea, either integrated it into the book or perhaps discarded it, I mark the idea with an asterisk. To help ensure that I don't forget about my follow-through node, I put a follow-through button in another node that I routinely access called outline.hca. This node contains a button for each chapter in the book along with other related items like personal contacts, figures, research and so on. Figure 5-2 shows part of the outline.hca node.

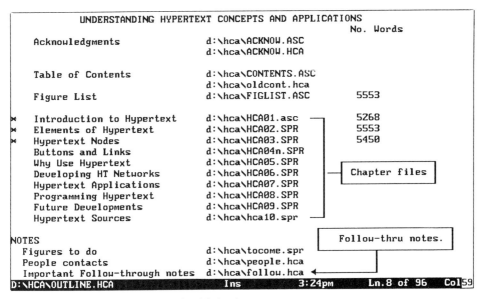

Fig. 5-2 Node used to help organize this book.

Unfortunately, hypertext isn't a panacea; in spite of all the advantages it offers, you still have to do your research, organize, write, rewrite, and reorganize.

Better organized, more creative documents

Another benefit of hypertext is that it inspires us to think in new ways. For example, hypertext may stimulate us to create new kinds of paper documents.

Hypertext, by our definition, is non-sequential text. Usually this is best done on computer screens. But it is possible to take the concept of hypertext and use it to structure a paper-based document. A good example of this is the MIX Publication entitled *HyperMedia* (Summer, 1988). The Table of Contents reflects a hypertext design. The title of each article is in boldface. Immediately beneath the title is a byline and a brief description of the article's contents in smaller print. Then to the right of each description is a small photograph or color illustration relating to the article. These illustrations almost look like hypertext buttons that you might press to bring up the article. The article also shows the influence of hypertext thinking.

Key terms are highlighted in the text and a line connects these words to a note of explanation or a reference to another article. A light yellow color is used for the highlighting and connecting lines so that the hypertext references are quite subtle. Icons (small graphic images) consistently appear in the upper right corner of the page. These icons let the reader see at a glance what the major topics covered in the publication. (These same icons also appear on the cover.)

Another good example of hypertext design elements in a paper document is the book *Hypertext Hypermedia* by David H. Jonassen. In this book terms are sometimes enclosed in boxes with page references next to them. (This is like a reference button.) The first page, after the table of contents, is a wheel-type diagram, which is similar to the cover of the HyperMedia publication mentioned earlier. Jonassen refers to this as a *hypermap*. The hub of the wheel contains the title of the book, Hypertext. The spokes of the wheel connect to shapes that look like buttons or perhaps miniature computer screens. Inside these buttons are the subtopics—which correspond, perhaps, to what would be the chapters of a book. The reader is invited to select a topic and turn to the appropriate page.

If I were to use this approach in writing this book, I might have created a "hypermap" like the one in Fig. 5-3.

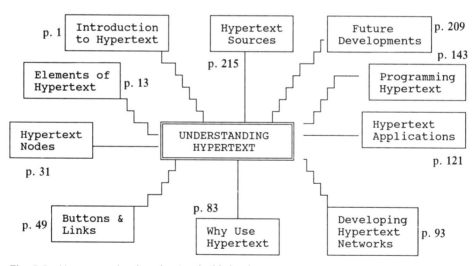

Fig. 5-3 Hypermap showing chapters in this book.

When you turn to the first page of a subtopic, the book presents another wheel-type diagram with sub-subtopics and more page references, which is like having a table of contents at the beginning of each chapter in a book—not a bad idea. When you choose a sub-subtopic and turn to the corresponding page, you are presented with a page of text. The author has broken the page into several blocks and each block of information is labeled as to its type in a style of writing called "Information Mapping" developed by Leonard

Horn. (See chapter 10 for more details on Information Mapping and Hypertext/Hyperme-dia.) Typically such pages contain these kinds of information blocks:

- Description
- Example
- Links to other text block
- Links to other documents

The links to other text are shown in a graphic form. The main topic on the page is inside of a box and miniature computer screens enclose related topics. Lines connect these nodes and symbolize links. Each "link" is labeled as to its type. Jonassen uses links such as:

- example of
- required by
- supports
- organized by
- enabled by
- implementation of
- described by
- influences
- provides structure for
- produces
- represents
- provides components

and so on.

The multiple cross-references and diagrams in this book make it easy to use and easy to find information. After experimenting with using it as a hypertext network, though, I began to feel quite uncomfortable—I wondered if I was missing something by creating my own path through the network. I decided to back up and read the book sequentially and use the various links to other parts of the book only when I needed them for clarification or when I was specially interested in a topic. This approach worked better for me and I didn't get that "lost in a network feeling." Still, when reading Jonassen's book sequentially I greatly appreciated the convenience of having references to external documents always placed in a convenient block on the page. Jonassen links almost every subtopic to an external document.

Another book that has a hypertext feel is *Mapping Hypertext* by Robert E. Horn. Information mapping works well with hypertext and helps to give it structure. (I'll have more to say about Information Mapping in chapter 6.) Horn's book is very graphic. On almost every page there are graphics, buttons, and (as it were) pop-up nodes. Horn's book might be the closest you can get to hypertext with paper.

Project management

Hypertext can help you manage projects. Typically, in managing a project you need to keep track of many diverse things: people, proposals, companies, equipment, budgets, ideas, meetings, schedules, artwork, models, and promotion. Often information about these elements are stored in a computer in many different files, in different programs. With hypertext you can tie all this information together in one control node. Then from the control node, you can easily access any part of the project by "pointing and shooting."

As you know, I used hypertext to help me write this book. Earlier I needed to make a reference to another point in the book where I had discussed Information Mapping in some detail. I couldn't remember in which chapter I had done this. So I used a search program I developed with POWER SEARCH (discussed in chapter 8) to build a control file that showed all references to Information Mapping. Figure 5-4 shows this control file. Notice that the file names are on the left. Opposite each file name is the line that contains the word "mapping." From this control file I could easily pop into various files—I just had to point to a file name (with the cursor) and press a hotkey. This made it easy to find out which chapter had the detailed discussion of Information Mapping.

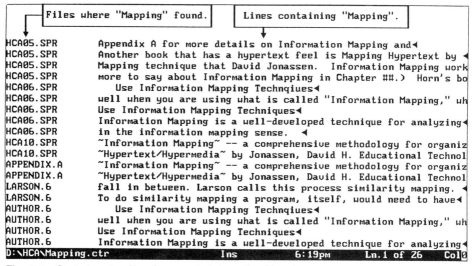

Fig. 5-4 Control node with references to Information Mapping.

Hypertext help systems

Using hypertext you can design help systems that are easier to use and more effective than conventional help files, databases, or hard copy documentation. In the traditional approach you have to know the jargon of a field before you can effectively carry out a database search. Also if the system uses a query language, you have to understand how to construct queries, which often must follow a rather rigid grammar. Using hypertext you can browse through a network and explore various topics—you don't need to enter a direct query first. Browsing can be fun and an excellent way to learn. (Ted Nelson, himself, claims that he got most of his education from browsing in book stores—not in school.)

Run-time hypertext help systems

Several hypertext systems are becoming available that are dedicated to specific subject areas. You can use these to quickly find information that you need or to explore new ideas.

I'll discuss these in detail in chapter 7, Hypertext Applications. You'll also find information about how to order these programs in chapter 10.

In addition to these reference tools, more and more hypertext tutorials, and simulations are being developed. Keep your eyes out for these products. I predict that this is how we computer types will do most of our learning in the 1990s. The main advantage to these systems is that they give you much more flexibility. If you want to review a key term, you can do it instantly by pointing and clicking. Some of these tutorials are really fun to use. Some have animation, sound or video nodes that might surprise you. Again, stay tuned for further details on these programs in chapters 7 and 10.

Custom help systems

Improved Learning Researchers have found that hypertext is especially useful to those who design original hypertext networks. Hypertext helps designers because it makes their task easier and it also helps them learn the subject matter they are putting into the system. In the process of designing a hypertext help system, the designer must face important issues like:

- What are the key actions that people need to carry out?
- What steps are needed to carry out these actions?
- What prerequisite skills must a person have to carry out each task?
- What are the major topics of interest? Subtopics?
- What are the relationships among the various tasks, topics, subtopics?

In the process of learning Sprint macro programming, I needed to refer to an encyclopedia of macros quite often. The entries were arranged alphabetically, but it was still difficult to look up information because at first I did not know what to find. For example, when I wanted to do I/O operations I didn't know what macros to find. My first thought was "INPUT" as in BASIC, but no such macro was available. How about GETLN or GETLINE? No luck there either. I finally stumbled upon the macro I was looking for, no thanks to the alphabetical listing of macros.

Gradually I began developing a help system that would enable me and other users to find information quickly. Using HyperSprint, a hypertext interface for Sprint, I prepared a hierarchical control node that would allow me and others to find information quickly. This hierarchy helps me, but perhaps more importantly, the process of preparing this hierarchy gave me a cognitive structure and made it easier for me to learn the Sprint macro language. (See the next chapter for some specific examples of HyperSprint control nodes.)

Hypertext helps you learn because it encourages you to focus on the relationship of facts and ideas and because it encourages you to develop hierarchical structures. These structures can become cognitive structures (structures that you store in your memory). Cognitive structures help you organize and remember new information; they give you a place in memory where you can insert cognitive links.

More flexible learning systems

Hypertext is not limited to text. As you have seen in earlier chapters, various kinds of nodes can be created. Instructors and training specialists are finding that hypertext is useful because it can integrate a wide variety of media. Sometimes music, voice, video, graphics, or animation can convey information more effectively than text. Hypertext, sometimes called hypermedia, can make it easy for users to choose various kinds of nodes, depending on their needs, interests, or special abilities. Chapter 10 contains more information about products and companies that enable you to create a hypermedia network.

Other advantages

Updating information   Hypertext, if it is structured properly, can simplify problems associated with updating information. Imagine that document B references document A with a hypertext button. If the information in document A is updated, then B is almost automatically updated.

This can work especially well if a "see-thru" button is used. As mentioned earlier, a "see-thru" button allows you to peek through it and see the node to which it is pointing. It appears as if you are reading the current node, but you are actually reading the text from the external node. With a "see-thru" button, the text has not been imported into the current node. That's why if the external document is changed, then all other documents that quote from it with "see-thru" buttons will be instantly updated.

Less typing   Hypertext can save you work because less redundancy is required. You don't have to keep repeating yourself to be sure that the reader knows what you are talking about. Some research shows that up to one-third fewer words are needed to convey the same information with hypertext than with traditional linear documents. Another related benefit is that you can be free to reuse drawings, explanations, and other nodes in many places without worrying about repeating yourself too much or about using up too much memory.

Annotations are encouraged   With hypertext, readers are often encouraged to mark up or annotate nodes. These annotations can benefit future readers of the document. Wouldn't it be enjoyable and instructive to read a document and explore the comments made by one of your favorite luminaries or gurus?

Networks can adapt to readers   Different pathways through a document can be provided for different kinds of readers. Unlike a paper document, which usually has only one path, a hypertext network can provide many trails.

Group decision making   As I've discussed earlier, some hypertext systems can provide a map of a group discussion. As the group continues to discuss a problem electronically, the hypermap grows and helps to pinpoint the main issues, positions on those issues, objections to positions and so on. As the map grows the group's understanding of the problem also increases.

Faster access to ideas   Although research currently doesn't yet support this claim, it seems evident that hypertext will allow us to access information faster—especially when the search is a complex one. (Research shows that for simple look-up tasks, a paper document with a good index is faster than a hypertext look up.)

Easier to create new forms Hypertext allows the average person, who has little formal training in computer programming, to develop interesting and useful applications. New forms are emerging like electronic hypertext magazines, travel guides, hyper resumes, hyper cookbooks. In chapter 7 you'll learn about a successful magazine published electronically in hypertext format, called *ComputorEdge*.

Hypertext has other advantages, too, like the ones associated with other electronic documents:

- Duplication can be done more quickly and at less cost.
- As memory storage improves, larger and larger documents can be stored in a small space.
- Documents can be transmitted electronically.
- You can do a brute force search for key ideas.
- Editing is easy.

I hope now you are convinced that hypertext is a productivity booster. But I caution you. There are good and bad hypertext networks. In the next chapter, you'll find some guidelines that will enable you to create a useful and well-structured hypertext system.

If I don't want to switch

At the beginning of this chapter, I suggested that you might want to switch from your current non-hypertext program to one that includes hypertext capability. But you might not want to switch or you might not be able to (because of corporate policy that dictates what software you must use). Even if you don't switch to a hypertext word processor, you can still use hypertext to organize your work and your data files.

When necessary, you can activate a command button that will activate your word processor, database system or spreadsheet. You can usually design the button so that the external program will immediately spring into action and start carrying out a predefined function.

For example, I am currently in charge of a job referral service for members of a local professional society. I like to keep the information about hiring companies, contact people, and so on in a traditional database so I can easily sort the information and prepare various kinds of reports. But I like to link the database to a hypertext system. The hypertext system helps me keep track of the relationship of this project to the other tasks that I am doing. When I am ready to access the information, I can easily do so by selecting a hypertext button that launches the database system and also loads the appropriate database file.

6

Issues in developing
hypertext networks

Niel Larson of MaxThink in Kensington, CA has done a lot of research on hypertext and has developed several hypertext systems. (See chapter 10 for more information.) Niel stresses that it doesn't take much to build a hypertext system. He says: "Everyone will be doing it. But what is more important than programming of links, nodes, and buttons is the theory behind how you go about building a hypertext network." However, perhaps to the chagrin of computer scientists and professors, in this chapter I won't delve that deeply into the theory of hypertext. Instead I'll stay practical and present some useful approaches and rules of thumb I think will help you create effective hypertext networks. I'll start by discussing various approaches and then move on to a discussion of some rules of thumb. The approaches include:

- Table of contents approach
- Hierarchical
- Hypermaps
- Summary
- Guided Tour
- Decision Table
- Empirical
- Index

Let's look at each of these approaches in detail.

Table of contents approach

In the table of contents approach you create a control node that has a table of contents, much like that at the front of a book. By moving the cursor to a topic and pressing a hot-key you can move directly to the appropriate node. In this approach, the table of contents may be a scrollable node that itself contains a lot of detail with several levels of headings. You can see an example of this approach in a hyperdocument entitled "Doing Business in

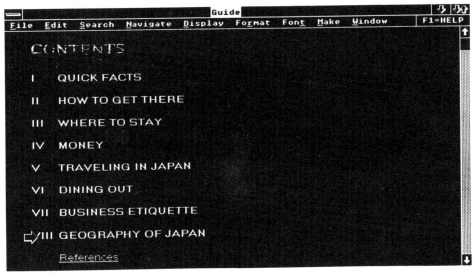

Fig. 6-1 Table of contents for "Doing Business in Japan."

Japan" with the Guide hypertext authoring system. After an attractive title page appears, the program presents you with a table of contents as shown in Fig. 6-1.

Notice that I have moved the mouse pointer to Geography of Japan. When you click on this button, a map of Japan appears, which itself has several buttons on it. See Fig. 6-2.

When you move the mouse pointer to Naha at the bottom left of the screen the pointer turns into a pointing finger, indicating that a pop-up node can be activated. Figure 6-3 shows the Naha node that appears when you click on the Naha button.

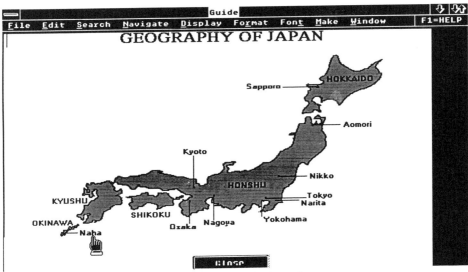

Fig. 6-2 Graphic node in Guide's "Doing Business in Japan."

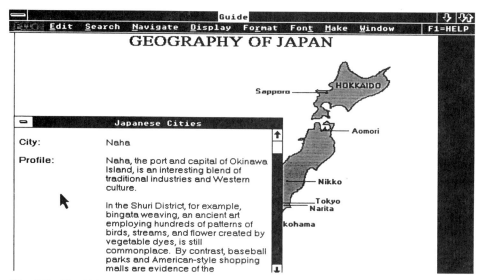

Fig. 6-3 The Naha pop-up node.

Hierarchical approach

In a hierarchical approach, you identify the major subtopics or skill areas and display them on the opening screen. As a user, when you pick a subtopic, the system takes you to another screen which lists sub-subtopics. You keep exploring in this way until you arrive at the node that contains actual contents rather than just a list of nodes.

In developing a hierarchical network, you might find it useful to carry out a hierarchical skill analysis. This involves asking the questions "What does this node enable users to do? What skills do users need before they can master this node?" These questions may generate, say, two new nodes. Then take each of those nodes in turn and ask the same questions. Keep going in this way until you reach the point that you are describing skills that you assume your "target population" of users has already acquired. It might help to include some assumed skills in your hierarchical analysis, too. It might turn out that some of these assumed skills do not actually exist in your target population.

This is one case where the best tools for your first initial analysis are a large sheet of paper and a pencil. You can sketch the hierarchy diagram quickly and immediately see the relationships in front of you. Besides, it's good to get away from the keyboard for a while—it helps you to see things from a different perspective. Alternatively, you might want to use a program like Org Plus, which was specifically designed to help users create company organizational charts.

Figure 6-4 shows an introductory screen for a WordPerfect hypertext help system. If you wanted help on, say, how to import an ASCII file, you would start by selecting Files.

Next the File Operations node appears, as shown in Fig. 6-5. From here, you would pick import ASCII file.

Next, the node shown in Fig. 6-6 appears, which gives the three steps needed for importing an ASCII file. Notice that the words proper import option are highlighted. This

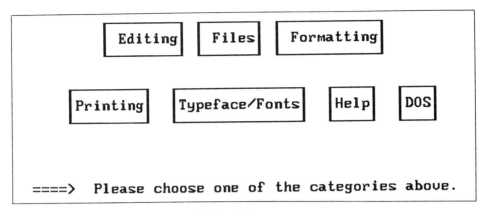

Fig. 6-4   Introductory screen for WordPerfect Help.

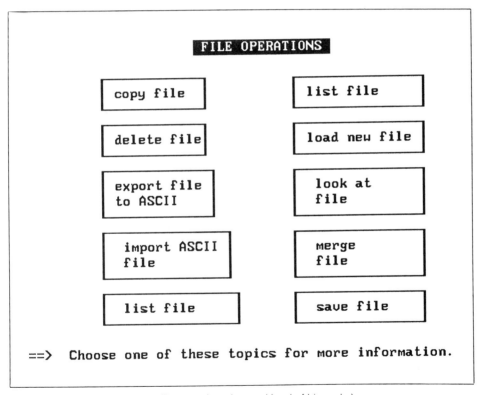

Fig. 6-5   Help on WordPerfect file operations (second level of hierarchy).

shows that further detail is available if you need help on selecting the correct import option.

This approach works well for certain kinds of subject matter, but not others. It can be

```
To import an ASCII file:


    1. Tap Ctrl-F5

    2. Choose  proper import option  from menu.

    3. Enter name of the ASCII file you want to import.
```

Fig. 6-6 Hypertext help on WordPerfect import options.

frustrating to use an exclusively hierarchical hypertext if you don't know which subtopic to choose first on the opening menu.

Hypermaps

A *hypermap* is a graphical depiction of a part of a hypertext network. The idea behind hypermaps is that knowledge has structure. By showing a map that depicts this structure, you might help the user to see relationships. Also the hypermap might give the user a cognitive structure that promotes learning. A hypermap, then, can act as an illustration as well as a navigational tool. As a user repeatedly encounters a hypermap in navigating through a network, the user has an opportunity each time to see a picture of network's structure. Figure 6-7 shows a hypermap I made for HyperSprint using the line drawing capabilities of Sprint.

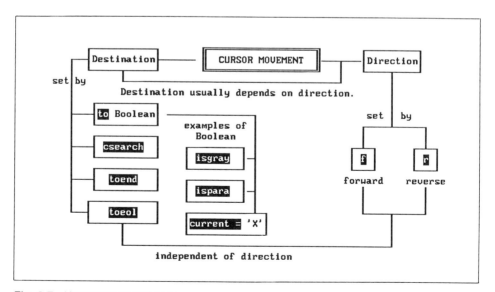

Fig. 6-7 Hypermap control node.

The main topic in this hypermap appears at the top in a double-lined box. The map shows that there are two main concerns in controlling cursor movement, the direction of the movement and the final destination of the cursor. The line connecting destination and direction helps to strengthen the idea that there is a relationship between the two. The text below the line helps to clarify the relationship. The areas in reverse video are hypertext buttons.

Summary approach

In the summary approach to designing a hypertext network, you begin with a narrative summary rather than a map or list of key topics. In this summary, you make certain keywords or phrases into buttons. An experienced user can use this summary for a quick review. A novice can explore the hypertext as needed. Figure 6-8 shows an example of the summary approach applied to the topic of cursor control in Sprint macro programming.

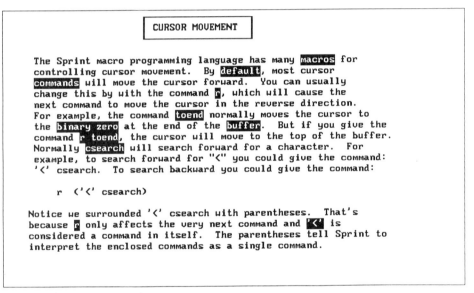

Fig. 6-8   Summary approach.

Guided tour

In the guided tour approach, a network of nodes might already exist. But the timid novice user might not know how to access the information. A control node that leads the novice through the network can help to overcome this problem. Figure 6-9 shows how the guided tour approach might be applied to the subject of cursor control.

Notice in Fig. 6-9 how the user "walks" through the network. I explain which nodes to go to and in which order to go into them. Then I ask the user to answer a multiple-choice question. The question is designed to verify that the user has understood the material presented in the nodes. This type of presentation takes on the characteristics of a

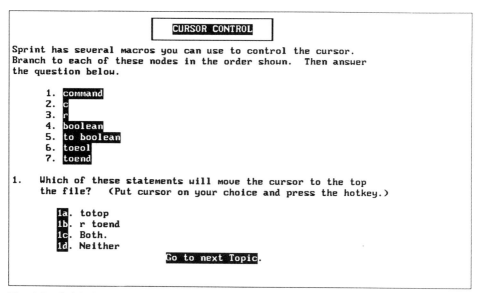

Fig. 6-9 Guided tour approach.

conventional linear instruction. However, each node in the hypertext network is still available for review on a direct access basis.

Decision table approach

A decision table (sometimes called a logic table) is a table that shows what outcomes, decisions, diagnoses, etc., are appropriate when certain rules or conditions are met. Figure 6-10 shows the start of a simple decision table for an eating style recommended by Anthony Robbins, a success guru and author of the book *Personal Power*. (Never say "diet.") The decision table is not complete and does not show all of Tony's recommendations—it does not handle all conditions and outcomes—but it shows how a decision table works.

Traditionally, you put conditions on the top of the table and outcomes or decisions at the bottom of the table. An X indicates that an outcome is appropriate if the conditions listed above are met. To read the table, you scan the columns vertically and look for a yes or no answer about current conditions. Each column, in effect, is a rule.

For example, according to the table if it is still morning, you may eat only fruit. Notice that if condition 1 is yes, then conditions 2 and 3 are irrelevant. Rule 2 says that you can still eat fruit in the afternoon if it has been three hours since you've eaten fats or carbohydrates. Rule 3 says that you can eat fats, carbohydrates or vegetables in the afternoon if it has been 10 minutes since you've had fruit.

You can use a decision table as a control node from which a user can branch to get detailed advice. Often with some analysis, an expert system can be reduced to a simple decision table with supporting hypertext nodes. For example, outcome cells in the decision table can be buttons that lead the user to a detailed step-by-step procedure to be followed when certain conditions are true.

		RULES		
		1	2	3
CONDITIONS	1. Still morning?	Y	N	N
	2. Three hours since you've eaten fats/carbohydrates?	–	Y	–
	3. 10 minutes since you've eaten fruit?	–	–	Y
OUTCOMES	OK to eat: Fruit	X	X	
	Vegetables			X
	Fats/carbohydrates			X

```
N = No
Y = Yes
- = Condition is not important.
X = Take this action.
```

Fig. 6-10 *Start of decision table for eating style.*

Figure 6-11 shows part of an expert system in the form of a decision table. This expert system gives advice about a medical condition involving "feeling faint." (This figure is based on a table taken from the documentation that comes with a program called the Logic Gem, which I'll discuss shortly.) I've chosen to use HyperWriter to display the decision table, but you could also use any of the hypertext systems I've discussed.

Figure 6-12 shows how HyperWriter can pop up a comment node that gives advice when the user clicks on one of the advice buttons at the bottom of the screen.

Decision tables sometimes work well in communicating information, but another important use for a decision table is that it can help you analyze a problem. Decision table analysis has been around for a long time but it hasn't been too popular even among "left-brained" programmers and hackers. That's probably because it can be tedious to organize and to sort columns and rows. Fortunately, though, at least two PC programs are now available to help generate and simplify decision tables: Sterling Castle's Logic Gem and Peter Pipe's Decision Table Algorithm System. Using either of these programs, you can analyze your table and check for conditions for which no outcomes have been specified. Another benefit is that in the process of analyzing the table, you can simplify it and make it easier to read. Decision table analysis can help you identify rules that are not required and it can help you simplify rules by eliminating conditions that don't contribute toward making a rule unique. This can also have the effect of making any computer program based on the table run faster. If the decision table ends up being the front-end for a hypertext system, the table will be easier to use.

CONDITIONS	1	2	3	4	5	6	7	8
Did you feel you were spinning?	Y	N	N	N	N	N	N	N
Did you stand up suddenly after sitting, lying down or stooping?	–	Y	N	N	N	N	N	N
Were you exercising more than usual or were you out of breath?	–	–	Y	N	N	N	N	N
Taking blood pressure for drugs?	–	–	–	Y	N	N	N	N
Are you diabetic or was it a long time since you last ate?	–	–	–	–	Y	N	N	N
Had you spent several hours in strong sunshine or in very hot or stuffy conditions?	–	–	–	–	–	Y	N	N
A D V I C E	DI	LO	RB	BR	DP	LB	HE	CO

Fig. 6-11   Expert system in a decision table.

CONDITIONS

Low blood sugar is probably causing your feeling of faintness. You might want to eat somethng sugary or starchy if you are still feeling faint. NOTE: if you are diabetic, consult your physician.

CONDITIONS	1	2	3	4	5	6	7	8
Did you feel you were spi...		Y	N	N	N	N	N	N
Did you stand up suddenly after sitting, lying down or stooping?	–	Y	N	N	N	N	N	N
Were you exercising more than usual or were you out of breath?	–	–	Y	N	N	N	N	N
Taking blood pressure for drugs?	–	–	–	Y	N	N	N	N
Are you diabetic or was it a long time since you last ate?	–	–	–	–	Y	N	N	N
Had you spent several hours in strong sunshine or in very hot or stuffy conditions?	–	–	–	–	–	Y	N	N
A D V I C E	DI	LO	RB	BR	DP	LB	HE	CO

Fig. 6-12   Comment node used with decision table.

Figure 6-13 shows a sample decision table before simplification. Notice that there are 10 columns. Each column in a decision table, remember, is a *rule*.

Figure 6-14 shows how the table came out after I ran it through Pipe's program. Notice that after simplification, the rows and columns of the table are sorted: rows with the most N responses are moved to the top of the table and rules with the most Y responses are moved to the left. By following its built-in logic, Pipe's program determined that two rules were redundant; note that the simplified table has only eight rules.

Also notice that the rules are simpler. For example, rule 1 now only asks two questions whereas before, this rule involved five questions. The program has determined that

			0	0	0	0	0	0	0	0	0	1
			1	2	3	4	5	6	7	8	9	0
A	?	Older than 65?	Y	N	N	Y	N	N	Y	N	N	N
B	?	15 or younger?	N	N	Y	N	N	Y	N	N	N	N
C	?	Previous record?	Y	N	N	N	Y	Y	N	Y	Y	N
D	?	Still employed?	Y	Y	-	N	N	-	Y	Y	Y	N
E	?	Dependents?	N	Y	-	N	N	-	N	N	N	Y
X	:	Program A	x		x				x			
Y	:	Program B		x			x	x		x		
Z	:	Not eligible	x			x						x

Fig. 6-13 Decision table before simplification.

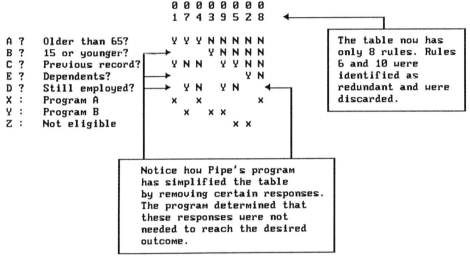

Fig. 6-14 Decision table after simplification.

the extra conditions in rule 1 do not contribute to making the rule unique so therefore they are logically not needed in the rule. In other words, as long as you answer Y to questions A and C, the outcome must be X because no other rule in the table has a Y answer to questions A and C. Pipe's program seems to really excel when it comes to rule simplification.

The Logic Gem, though, has some features that are not contained in Pipe's program. For example, based on a decision table, the Logic Gem can automatically generate code in several different computer languages including, dBASE, C, BASIC, Fortran and even English!

Have I convinced you that decision tables will brighten your life? Probably not. Even so I recommend you look at both Pipe's Decision Table Algorithm System and the Logic Gem. You can find details about how to order them in chapter 10. For now, though, let's move on to the empirical approach, which is a technique you can use in any endeavor that involves observable outcomes.

Empirical approach

Strictly speaking the empirical approach relies only on direct experience or observation, without benefit of theory or science. Today, many writers use the term "empirical approach" more loosely to refer to a process that stresses direct observation rather than "armchairing" (sitting around in comfortable armchairs and speculating without getting out into the real world and doing direct testing and observation).

Using the empirical approach, you develop a hypertext network, try it out, and carefully observe the behavior of users. When observing users you look for: (1) Paths that users typically follow in searching for information. (2) Information that users have difficulty in finding, find difficult to use, need to look up frequently, or don't need. In addition, Niel Larson suggests that you ask these questions:

- Can a user go through the network and find all the ideas—or are some of them hidden or nested in some obscure node?
- Is the vocabulary controlled? Can a novice who doesn't have the knowledge to begin learn from the network by exploring definitions of keywords?
- Are there "transitive nodes" that help a user move through the network and find what they are looking for? A *transitive node*, which I've called a "control node" earlier, is a node that does not contain much information, but helps the user in navigating through the network to find nodes that contain information: facts, rules, examples, definitions.
- Are the ideas in the network appropriately classified? Larson suggests breaking every transitive node in a network down into five categories. He suggests that more than five tends to make the network too complex and that less than five results in a topic that is usually not fully explored or developed. (Others have suggested that seven is perhaps a good number here.)
- Is the system "idiot proof?" Can people find what they are looking for in the network within about 10 keystrokes?

Making revisions   Based on your observations of real users using your hypertext, you can often make significant changes that will greatly improve its effectiveness. If you know that users typically follow path Z when searching the network, you can embed links to important nodes in that path. If you discover that users have difficulty finding node X, you can try linking it in a new way, or embedding more links to it. If users find nodes difficult to apply, you can revise their contents. After revising the network, it is important to continue your observations to see if your changes have worked.

One-on-one testing   It is often effective to do your first testing with just one individual. This initial testing will usually turn up some clear-cut shortcomings in the hypertext network. Revise and test again with another individual, then another, etc. After about 6 to 12 such test and revision cycles, the network will be much improved and you can move to small group testing.

Index approach

Whatever approach you take, you can probably combine it with an alphabetical index. But don't limit the terms in the index to just the key terms used for creating links. Use synonyms and cross-references. Empirical testing of your hypertext can help you uncover the key terms that users use most often when searching for information. For example, suppose you are providing information about how to get the character position in a file—the offset in characters from the beginning of a file. The correct macro in Sprint is "offset." But users might not know to think of this term when searching the index so you might include several entries, like this:

character offset...see **offset**
cursor position.. .see **offset**
offset from top of file

During developmental testing (an important process) you might discover that users frequently look for the term "position." You can then add this entry:

position in file see **offset**

The boldfaced words, here and above, are hypertext buttons that take the user to the text explaining the "offset" macro.

HyperWriter's built-in help system is similar to a hypertext document with an alphabetical index as its "root node." Figure 6-15 shows the index node from this help system. Notice that the approach is to put as many terms as possible on one screen. This simplifies the process of visually scanning the index for the term that you are looking for (although some might argue that it is better to put fewer buttons on one screen to make the screen easier to read). To select a button on this screen you press the Tab key repeatedly until the topic you want has been selected. Then you press F1.

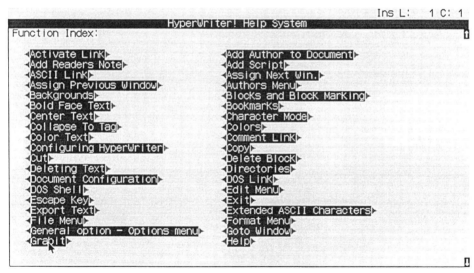

Fig. 6-15 HyperWriter Help index node.

Combine the approaches

If you like, combine several approaches. There is no reason why you need to use any one approach exclusively. The Guide help system illustrates this principle. When you first

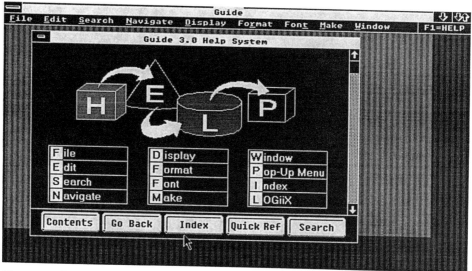

Fig. 6-16 Guide Help table of contents node.

enter the Guide help system you are presented with a table of contents, as shown in Fig. 6-16.

If you want, you can click on any of the major topics and branch off from there. But notice that at the bottom of the screen there are several other buttons that give you different options. You can even do a traditional text search. Or if you prefer to use an Index, you can click on the Index button. To try out the system, I decided to try using the Index to find information about "Command Buttons."

Modified alphabet   The Index button takes you to a screen that shows an enlarged view of a "modified" alphabet—only those letters that have entries for the index are included. See Fig. 6-17.

Notice that there is no J, Q, V, X, Y or Z since there are no entries which start with those letters. In this figure notice that I have the mouse pointer on the C button. When I clicked on this button, Guide took me to the beginning of all of the words starting with C in the index. See Fig. 6-18.

Continuing my search, I moved the mouse pointer to Command Button, as you can see in Fig. 6-18. As you can see, the mouse pointer changed to an arrow showing that further information would be forthcoming via a reference-button jump. Figure 6-19 shows the node I arrived at with information about the Command Button. From here I could also continue and branch to information about how to create a Definition. Notice that the pointer is positioned over the word Definition, another hypertext button.

Authoring guidelines

Now that you've looked at some of the basic approaches to authoring hypertext, let's consider some more specific rules for building a network of nodes. These rules have to do

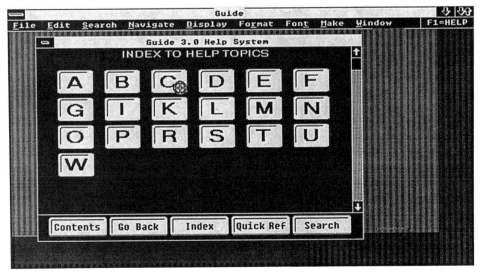

Fig. 6-17 Modified alphabet.

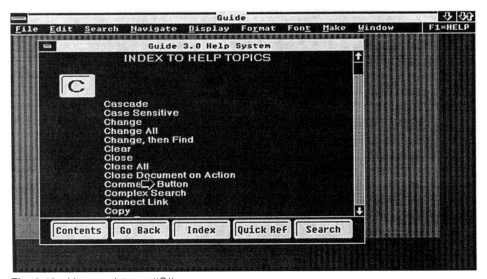

Fig. 6-18 Mouse pointer on "C."

with these topics:

- Using related topics
- Orphan nodes
- Network revision
- Screen design
- Use graphics
- Help users keep their place

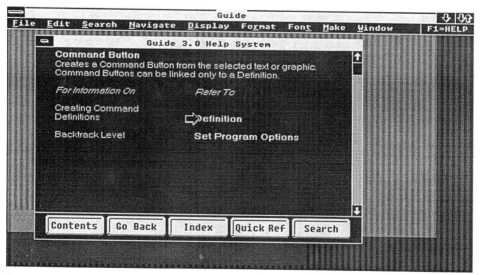

Fig. 6-19 Information about command buttons.

- Use information-mapping techniques
- Writing style

Using related topics

To help users branch to related topics, it's helpful to include a "related nodes" information block in each node that warrants it. I think of an *information block* as a labeled section
of a node that contains a specific kind of information. For example, a *definition block* contains only definitions, an *example block* contains only examples. A *related-nodes block*
would contain only references to related nodes—nothing else.

Figure 6-20 shows an example. This is a resume-control node. It is sometimes useful
to keep different versions of your resume on file—to emphasize different skills and experience when applying for different jobs. But how do you find the proper version of your
resume when you need it? A hypertext control does the job well. While in this node, you
can quickly review the various types of resumes you have and then jump into any one for
editing or printing.

But while in the resume-control node you might want to jump into a related node—
like a node listing all of the cover letters you've written, or a node listing all of the job
prospects. Notice how the related nodes information block helps you tie all of this together
into a network.

Orphan nodes

Some hypertext systems enable you to create nodes without linking them. Or you might
create nodes with software external to your hypertext system, where there is a danger that
you might create a node intending to link it, and then forget to do so. The result is an
orphan node, one that does not have any parents. Orphan nodes are generally undesirable

```
┌────────────────────────────────────────────────────────────────┐
│                 ▐ Resume Control File ▌                          │
│                                                                  │
│   Resumes for Faxing                                             │
│        Programming ...........  c:\empower\program.fax           │
│        Technical support ......  c:\empower\techsup.fax          │
│   No specific job target ....  d:\resumes\short.SPR              │
│   PC Training ..............  d:\resumes\train.SPR               │
│   Tech. Specialist ..........  d:\resumes\ba.spr                 │
│   Technical writer .........  d:\resumes\RANDOLPH.RES            │
│   Summary style resume  .....  d:\resumes\NEWRES.ASC             │
│                                                                  │
│                                                                  │
│   ▐ Related Nodes ▌                                              │
│                                                                  │
│   Wealth Control ...........  c:\empower\wealth.ctr              │
│   Cover Letters  ..........  c:\jobs\letters.ctr                 │
│   New job listings .........  c:\jobs\jobs.new                   │
│   All jobs prospects .......  c:\jobs\jobs.all                   │
│                                                                  │
│                                                                  │
│                                                                  │
│▐D:\resumes\RESUMES.CTR        ┃ Ins      11:44am   Ln.15 of 76   Col 1│
└────────────────────────────────────────────────────────────────┘
```

Fig. 6-20   Referencing related topics.

because it is easy to lose track of them and they might continue to hang around on the system taking up valuable storage space even after you no longer need them. A good way to avoid this problem is to get into the habit of always creating a button for a node before you create the node itself. Put the button in a control node and write a brief statement about the node—what it contains and what its relationship is to other nodes in the system. For example, using EMPOWERment, you can create a button by typing a file name within an existing node. To create the corresponding node, you just put the cursor on the first character of the file name and press F10. The main point, here, is to start by creating the button. Then create the corresponding node.

Network revision

If you find that you have difficulty locating a node because you can't remember its exact name or where it fits into your network, you might want to try creating a wildcard node search if your system allows it. For example, HE (the shareware Hypertext Editor supplied in source code form in chapter 8) lets you create a wildcard button such as:

< hashim *.* >

If HE finds more than one node that matches this specification, HE will display a menu. HE will also automatically create a wildcard specification on its own if it cannot find the file name you specify.

   If a wildcard search for a likely node names doesn't turn up the proper node, you might want to use a traditional text search or automatic linking. If you can remember an important keyword from the node or if you have specifically embedded keywords in the file, retrieval might be relatively easy with the proper software.

   As discussed earlier, EMPOWERment can automatically search multiple subdirectories and create a control node that references nodes that contain a keyword. Another alternative is to use a text search utility such as TS.EXE from the Norton Utilities and redirect the output to a file. The file can then be used as a control node to access the appropriate node. This only works, of course, if your hypertext system uses files that are readable by the text search program.

Revising   Once you locate the node, you might want to insert some additional buttons into appropriate control or "root" nodes. This way you won't have the same problem next time you want to access the node. Also, consider reorganizing your hypertext network, especially the top level nodes in your network. Try using one of the approaches suggested earlier or combining methods as in the Guide help system.

Screen design

Research has clearly demonstrated that people have more difficulty reading traditional computer screens than paper documents. But by using good screen design principles, you can do a lot to improve the readability of your hypertext networks. You can improve screen readability by observing a few simple guidelines:

- Use short lines and captions to label information blocks
- Group related ideas
- Place comments before buttons
- Improve readability with centering
- Use all caps only for short captions
- Use graphics to stress important ideas
- Avoid placing captions above graphics

Use short lines and captions   One simple, yet useful technique is to limit the length of text lines to between 40 and 60 characters. Often, the temptation is to use long lines to try to squeeze as much information in as possible. Although this works in some situations, it is usually a bad idea. In addition to using short lines, I recommend that you use a wide left margin and put brief captions in this margin. This works well when you are using what is called "Information Mapping," which I describe later in this chapter. Compare Fig. 6-21 with Fig. 6-22. They both contain basically the same text. Which one is easier to read?

Group related ideas   To help readers see the structure of information, it helps to group related ideas together. To do this you can use color, inverse video, space, graphics, and varying typefaces. Space, as you saw in the previous figures can help readability. Graphics can be used to group text, too. For example you can draw a box around text that belongs together.

Comments first   When I first started creating control nodes using ASCII-based hypertext systems, I got into the habit of putting the hypertext buttons at the far left margin and the explanatory comments on the right, like this:

```
<fingoals> Financial goals
<friends> Friends' names and addresses
<musicstud> Music students
<prospects> Business prospects
<wealth> Ideas on generating wealth
```

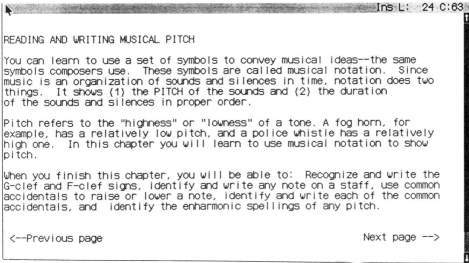

Fig. 6-21 Long text lines with no captions.

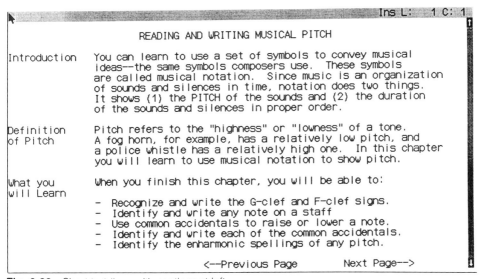

Fig. 6-22 Short text lines with captions at left.

I did it this way to make it easy to move the cursor onto the hypertext button. In fact, you might see such an arrangement in some of the illustrations in this book. The problem with this method, though, is that it makes the screen hard to read, especially when the node contains a large number of hypertext buttons. That's because we are trained from youth to read from left to right. After some experimentation, I found that a better approach was to put the comments on the left, like this:

```
Business prospects . . . . . . . . . . . . . <prospects>
Financial goals . . . . . . . . . . . . . . . . <fingoals>
```

```
Friends' names and addresses  . . . .  <friends>
Ideas on generating wealth  . . . . . . .  <wealth>
Music students . . . . . . . . . . . . . . . .  <musicstud>
```

Easier to read isn't it? In an ASCII-based system with no mouse, it takes a little long to move the cursor to the button this way. But I think the improvement in readability makes this approach well worth it.

Use of capital letters   Avoid using all capital letters for anything but short captions. All caps are sometimes useful for emphasizing important ideas. But stay away from using all caps in the text or in long captions. Compare these two captions. Notice how the second one is easier to read:

REMEMBER: THE PAST DOES NOT EQUAL THE PRESENT.

Remember: The Past Does Not Equal The Present.

Use graphics

Graphics can add "punch" to hypertext networks and help you clarify or stress important points. Often you can scan a hard copy of a graphic and merge the graphic into a node. If you are developing computer-based training with hypertext, it's probably better to avoid the use of purely ornamental graphics. Graphics can be expensive, so it makes sense to save graphics for those learning objectives that involve the user in an active way. It's not enough just to involve the user in some fun clicking activities. Ideally, the hypertext should give the learner an opportunity to practice important visual discrimination skills.

For example, you can define specific parts of the graphic as hot spots or hypertext buttons. Then the user can click on a part of the graphic. Users will learn more if they are encouraged to make some decision or recall something before clicking on a part of a graphic. What happens after the user clicks can serve to confirm the correctness of the user's response or offer corrective instruction.

Figure 6-23 shows a good example of how hypertext combined with a graphic can help students learn to identify key elements of a chest radiograph (X-ray image). In this node, created with HyperWriter, the program is asking the learner to look at part of a radiograph and click on an anatomical part called the "costro-phrenic angle." The user has moved the mouse pointer over an area in the lower right corner of the radiograph and is about to click the left mouse button.

Figure 6-24 shows how the program responds when the user clicks on the correct part of the radiograph. Notice how the pop-up node confirms the user's response. Another approach would be to branch to a new node that shows the part correctly labeled when the user clicks on it.

Caption placement   When you have a strong graphic, avoid putting a line of text above it. Graphics tends to be overpowering and a line above a graphic is likely to get lost. Instead, put the text under the graphic or to the right or left of the graphic. If you want to encourage the reader to read the text before looking at a graphic, put the text to the left of the graphic. If you want the reader to look at the graphic first and then read the text, put the text to the right of the graphic or if you want even more control, put the text in a pop-up window.

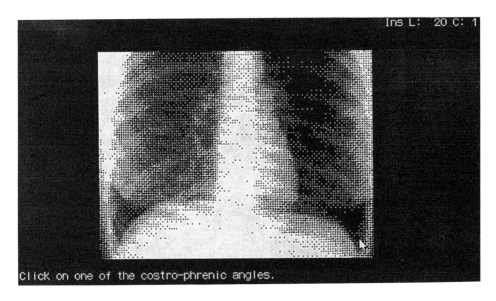

Fig. 6-23 Hypertext used to teach chest radiography.

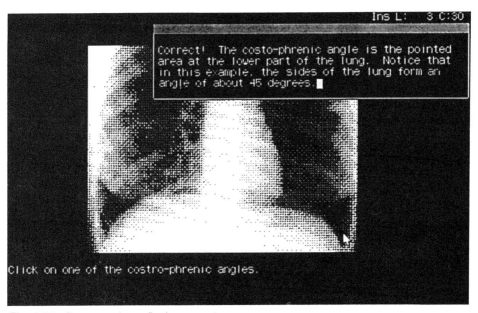

Fig. 6-24 Pop-up node confirming correct answer.

ASCII graphics Even if your hypertext development system does not support bit-mapped graphics, there is still a lot you can do with plain old ASCII characters. For example you can make arrows like this:

————>

or this:

```
       \
        \
=====    \
          \
=====    /
        /
       /
```

You can box important text:

```
= = = = = = = = = = = = = = = = = = = = = =
|                                          |
|          You can box important text.     |
|                                          |
= = = = = = = = = = = = = = = = = = = = = =
```

Help users keep their place

One of the big complaints beginning users of hypertext have is that they have a feeling of being lost. You can do a lot to deal with this problem by designing your hypertext system carefully. Many hypertext systems now have good navigational control tools and clues that help readers keep track of their location. The problem is, though, that it takes some experience with a hypertext system before a user is aware of these tools and clues. One solution might be to develop your own introductory tutorial that explains to the user how to do such things as:

- Review a previous node
- Jump to the first node in a network
- Activate a map of all nodes in the network
- Set and use bookmarks

and so on. Some systems come with a fairly good tutorial built-in. In such a case, you might want to provide a hypertext button in your introductory material that takes the user to this built-in tutorial.

Use Information-Mapping techniques

Information Mapping is a well-developed technique for analyzing and categorizing information. With this technique you break information you are conveying into topics that you can typically handle in a page or two of text. Each topic is called a *map*. Then you break each map down into a series of small sections called *blocks*. You always label each block as to its type. Block types that occur frequently are:

- Definition
- Example
- Non-example
- Rule
- Principle
- Fact
- Procedure

- Algorithm
- Introduction
- Summary
- Contradicting comment
- Supporting comment
- Source document reference

There are strict guidelines for what belongs in an information block. If a block is labeled "example" then only text that illustrates or gives an example of some principle or rule is permitted in that block.

The theory is that if you label each information block, you make the structure of your document explicit and help readers digest and retrieve information. In fact, some carefully controlled research studies support this claim. (See "The Potential Benefits of the Information Mapping Technique" by Eric M. Schaffer in the *NSPI Journal*, February 1982, p. 33−38 and "The Effects of Headings in Text on Recall, Search, and Retrieval," by Harley and Trueman in the *British Journal of Educational Psychology*, 1983, volume 53, pages 205−214. Also see the excellent summary of these studies in the book *Mapping Hypertext* by Robert E. Horn. Horn's summary, of course, is presented in Information-Mapping style.)

You might want to consider combining the Information Mapping methodology with hypertext technology. In doing this, you might treat each map as a named node. You could make the information blocks as lower-level typed nodes. Or if your hypertext system supports fields within nodes, you could put each information block into separate named fields.

Think of the possibilities. Imagine that you have an extended document on some topic and that each example node (or field) is named in such a way that it is identified as an example. Then you could create an "example control node" that would allow you to easily access every example in the network. You could do the same with all of the rules, all of the comments, all of the algorithms, if you were systematic in naming the nodes or fields or in typing the links in the network. In the same way you might create a "guided tour" or trail that would be limited to a certain kind of "information block" in the Information Mapping sense.

To find out more about Information Mapping, you might also consider taking a formal course. (See chapter 10 for details.) In my view, Information Mapping definitely improves the readability of both paper and electronic documents. You can see the influence of Information Mapping in several paper documents including:

Correspondence (Independent Study) courses offered by the University of California Extension, Berkeley, California. Information Mapping was used in developing courses on real estate appraisal, radiologic technology, and credit union management.

The documentation that comes with ToolBook, a hypertext development system for Windows 3.0. A nice feature of this documentation is that chapters are broken down into information maps and each chapter begins with a table of contents, much like a control node in hypertext.

The book *Hypertext/Hypermedia* by David Jonassen, published by Educational Technology Publications.

Writing style

I mentioned earlier the research concerning the difficulty of reading computer screens compared to printed text. I implied that a part of this difficulty can be overcome by following good screen design principles. Another way to deal with this problem is to follow basic principles of clear writing. It is unfortunate that some authors have gotten the idea that elegant, yet hard-to-read prose is somehow superior to simple, clear, down-to-earth writing. In your hypertext writing, unless you are writing the great American novel, I urge you to consider adopting a friendly, concise writing style in which you:

- Talk directly to the reader
- Use the active voice
- Cut out unnecessary words
- Use short sentences
- Prefer short words to long ones
- Use personal words
- Avoid words that convey a parental tone

These aren't principles of hypertext writing so much as they are just principles of good business writing in general. Still these principles make good sense for hypertext writing too and deserve some attention here. So let's consider them in more detail.

Talk directly to the reader   Instead of using the third person and talking about someone else, your writing will be more powerful if you talk directly to the reader. For example, instead of saying:

> The writer of hypertext documents should be careful to avoid creating orphan nodes.

you could be more direct and say:

> Be sure to avoid creating orphan nodes.

Use the active voice   Probably the most common fault in writing style is overuse of the passive voice. Generally, the active voice makes a sentence stronger, more direct, more explicit, easier to read. In my experience, many beginning writers are unable to tell whether a sentence is in the passive or active voice. In the *active voice*, the subject of the sentence is active—it is doing something. In the *passive voice*, the subject of the sentence is passive—it receives the action. Often in this case, the person or thing doing the acting is undefined, which leads to vagueness and uncertainty. Here are some examples that might help to clarify the difference between passive and active.

Passive: Links can be created both to and from graphics by the user.

Active: You can create links both to and from graphics.

Passive: This topic will be covered in chapter 11.

Active: We'll cover this in chapter 11.

Passive: Videodisc commands can be attached to any link.

Active: You can attach videodisc commands to any link.

Active: HyperWriter can attach videodisc commands to any link.

Whenever you can, change to the active voice. But if you know what you are doing and you have a reason for using the passive, go and use it. Sometimes, for example, you might not want to say explicitly who did something:

Passive: A diskette was left out of the package.

Active: I left a diskette out of the package.

Sometimes, you may want to emphasize a certain word by putting it first.

Passive: Our building was hit by a gang of con artists.

Active: A gang of con artists hit our building.

Notice how the passive construction emphasizes "our building" because "our building" comes first in that sentence.

Cut out unnecessary words   Unnecessary words slow down readers and waste space, time, and energy. In school, did your teachers force you to come up with 1000-word essays? If so, they might have rewarded you for packing your writing with fluff. In any case, you can always improve your writing by looking for ways to chop out needless words. Here are some examples:

Wordy: After you have entered the above script and pressed Esc, you are ready to test the link.

More concise: The next step is to test the link. (The information about entering the script and pressing Esc came earlier; there's no need to repeat it.)

Wordy: The first step in the actual construction of this hypertext document was to decide where to break the document into separate nodes.

More concise: As a first step, we decided where to break the document into separate nodes.

Often it is useful to write the stem of a sentence and then list a number of items in a column. Each item then completes the thought started in the stem of the sentence. You can often cut unnecessary words when you list items in a column. A good rule of thumb is to look for words that you find yourself repeating in each item and move these words up into the stem of the sentence. For example, instead of writing:

The responsibility of the copy editor is to:

- Ensure that each author's work is clear.
- Ensure that each diagram is complete in its own right.
- Ensure that spelling and grammar are correct.

you could move "Ensure that" up into the stem like this:

The responsibility of the copy editor is to ensure that:

- Each author's work is clear.
- Each diagram is complete in its own right.
- Spelling and grammar are correct.

Use short sentences   When writing business material, a good rule is to strive for an average sentence length of about 17 words. Avoid long sentences of more than, say, 30 words. If you find yourself writing a long sentence, look for ways to break it up. Divide and conquer. Think small. Another useful technique is to vary the length of sentences. Balance longer sentences now and then with some very short ones. Of course, to make this work, you might have to tangle with pedantic editors and grammarians who still insist that every sentence must have a subject and a verb.

Prefer short words to long ones Bureaucrats are known for using long, pompous words. But longer words slow us down. I suggest that you make every effort to help your hypertext readers by picking the shorter of two words whenever possible. Your writing will be clearer, easier to read and have more punch. For example, prefer "carry out" to "implement," "stop" to "impede," "stupid" to "ill-advised," "stress" to "emphasize." An excellent book that has sharpened my awareness of pompous words is *The ABCs of Style* by Rudolph Flesch (Harper and Row). I have also found automatic style checkers, such as Grammatik and Right Writer useful in this regard.

Use personal words Personal words such as personal pronouns, and proper nouns add interest to your writing. Be bold. Don't be afraid to say "I." For example, instead of saying:

The writer has developed a hypertext help system on music theory.

say:

I've developed a hypertext help system on music theory.

Instead of saying:

The student will benefit from the quiz.

say:

You will benefit from the quiz.

Avoid words that convey a parental tone We were all children once and some psychologists insist that we all still have an inner child. This inner child resents being told it should do this or should do that. One way to avoid a parental tone is to avoid the word "should." The word "should" implies that the listener ought to carry out a certain action out of a sense of obligation just because we said so rather than because it might be useful to do so. Here are some examples of sentences containing "should" along with suggested rewrites:

Parental tone: The document should make the structure explicit.

Revision: You can help readers grasp your organization, by making the structure of your document explicit.

Parental: A user should be able to backtrack immediately if he wishes.

Revision: Well-designed hypertext systems allow users to backtrack immediately. (As an aside, notice how I avoided the use of sexist writing in the revision by using the plural.)

Parental: The most important rule for a writer is that he should understand his audience. He should define their skills, interests, abilities, and characteristics.

Revision: A crucial first step in writing is to think clearly about your audience: what are their skills, interests, abilities, characteristics?

Selecting a hypertext system

There are many hypertext systems available now for IBM PCs and more and more available for other personal computers. There are several issues to consider when choosing a system. Here are some questions to ask yourself.

Is there a "run-time" engine of the program you can use to distribute your hypertext system widely? If so, what royalty, if any, does the publisher charge?

Is the software copy protected? (Yes, some companies still have the archaic policy of copy protecting their software.)

Do you need bit-mapped graphics in your presentation? If so, does the hypertext system support graphic nodes? Can you define hot spots on the graphics and what kinds of links can you create from graphics? What is the required file format for the graphic? Does the program provide a program for capturing screens displayed by other programs? Does the program provide a built-in picture editor or painting program? How easy is it to incorporate graphics?

What kinds of buttons and links are supported? Command buttons? Reference buttons? Jump-to-new-text node buttons? Jump-to-graphics buttons? Can you create invisible buttons and place them over graphics? Can you jump to external files? To specific points in external files? Can you launch other programs? If so, does the hypertext application save its current state? What support does the system provide for linking to a videodisc? Are there specific video commands or do you have to write your own scripts? Are there any specialized kinds of hypertext buttons like date buttons or autodial buttons?

Do you intend to use ASCII files? If so can the hypertext system work directly with ASCII files? If not, can you import ASCII files into the special format required by the system? How difficult is it to import files?

Is end-user scripting supported? Does the script language support variables? Can you check a user's data entry against information stored in a variable? How complete is the script language? How many commands are provided? How powerful are those commands? Are there specific commands for interacting with specific hardware devices, such as videodisc controllers?

What hardware is required? Is a hard disk required? How much disk space do you need? Can run-time versions be distributed on floppy disks? Do you need a graphics monitor? If so, what kinds are supported? Required? Does the software automatically detect the monitor type and display graphics appropriately? What model computer is required? For example, some systems require at least a PC AT computer while others will run on an original PC or a simple barebones laptop like a Toshiba 1000. Is a mouse supported? Is a mouse required? Is a specific graphic user interface required?

How fast is the system? Do you have to compile your hypertext network before you can access it?

Can you create autotours (automatic tours through a hypertext network)? What degree of control do you have when setting up an autotour? Can the user interrupt it?

Can you capture trails taken by users? How easy is it to do this? Does it require scripting?

Can you unfold a document so that different layers of information can be exposed?

Can you develop card-based systems or article-based systems with the system? An *article-based system* lets you create long scrollable documents. A *card-based system* forces you to create cards (single screens) one at a time.

Do you want to be able to pop up a hypertext network while you are using some other program? If so, can the hypertext program reside in memory with other programs? How much memory is required?

Is it possible to search a network for a simple string of characters? Can you specify whether you want the search to be case sensitive? Can you construct more complex queries using "regular expressions?" Can the system automatically create a control node that you can use to later scan all nodes that meet your search criteria?

Can you define fields within nodes? Must you define fields before you can enter text?

How easy is it to use the system? How easy is it for authors to create new documents? For readers to browse? How many nodes per day can a productive hypertext writer create? Does the system require a lot of effort to link nodes? Does it require excessive "cognitive overhead?"

What kind of support does the company provide? Is the company likely to be continuing to improve the system? What is the upgrade policy of the company? Most hypertext programs are still in their infancy and we can usually look forward to significant upgrades. A related question, here, is this: how responsive is the developing company to your suggested improvement? Is the company willing to create a customized version of the program to help you meet your special purposes?

Does the system have word processing features or must you switch to a word processor to prepare a paper document?

Summary

In this chapter I've presented some approaches to hypertext development, principles for constructing useful, well-designed networks, hypertext writing guidelines, and questions to ask yourself in the process of selecting a hypertext system. In the next chapter I'll show you some interesting hypertext applications.

NOTE: I won't attempt to rate the various hypertext systems based on these questions because the products are changing so rapidly. Apply the questions in this chapter to the products you are evaluating or considering.

7
Hypertext applications

In this chapter I will discuss some interesting applications of hypertext systems. These include:

- A hypertext program for improving personal productivity
- Book manuscript development with hypertext
- The *Oxford English Dictionary*
- KAS (Knowledge Acquisition System)
- Reg-In-A-Box
- PC memory-resident hypertext applications
- The *ComputorEdge* magazine as displayed by HyperRez
- A WordPerfect help system developed with HyperTSR
- Dr. Dobb's Journal in hypertext format
- Hypertext and museums
- A hypertext simulation
- Hypertext tutorials
- What makes music work
- Japanese Kanji exercises

Improving personal productivity

Because of their ability to manage a wide variety of resources, hypertext systems are useful for planning, setting priorities, managing projects and tracking accomplishments. EMPOWERment is a hypertext system designed specifically for personal management.

A planning node   When the program starts it checks the system date and consults a knowledge base to decide what to do. If EMPOWERment determines that the user has not yet accessed the planning node, it immediately updates a special history node and puts the user into that planning node.

Date buttons   When EMPOWERment goes to the planning node, it checks to see if deadlines are approaching and if so, displays a series of date buttons. These date buttons, then, only appear in the planning node if some deadline is approaching. To see the details about any approaching deadline, you just move the cursor to the date button and press F10. If any deadlines or appointments are scheduled they are highlighted on the calendar. You can mark a date button with an asterisk when you complete the task. The system will then move it into a history file for you automatically. See Fig. 7-1.

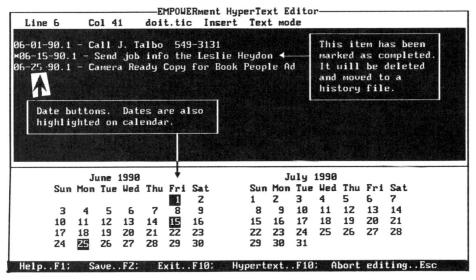

Fig. 7-1 EMPOWERment date buttons.

Action items Although EMPOWERment automatically displays date buttons, you can list related files as shown in Fig. 7-2. You can jump into a related file from the planning node by pointing to it with the cursor and pressing a hotkey. Also you can list "action items" in the planning node and mark these items so that the program can perform processing in a special way.

Notice that some action items are marked with an asterisk, some with a period, and some with a hyphen. When you first jot down an action item, you precede it with a hyphen. This enables the system to identify it as an incompleted action item. When you complete an action item, you let the system know this by marking it with an asterisk. If you carry out an item and you want to be reminded to do it again the next day, you can mark it with a period. Each day when you start EMPOWERment, it copies all of the action items to a history file for a permanent record. It also deletes items marked with an asterisk from the planning file. If you marked an item with a period, EMPOWERment resets the period to a hyphen to remind you to repeat the item.

Ensuring follow-through

A planned enhancement to EMPOWERment is to be an optional AI counseling mode. If EMPOWERment finds, upon checking its knowledge base, that you have marked certain

```
 Line 21    Col 1      doit.tic   Insert  Text mode
============================== DATE BUTTONS =============================

03-26-89.1 - Record expenses from Denver trip
04-28-89.1 - Send lit. to Donald Perrin & Susan O.
05-05-89.1 - Write to Yogesh
06-22-89.1 - Check page proofs for PRINT Shop


============================== ACTION ITEMS ========================

x  Call Carl Fischer   1-212-777-2550 about purchase order.
x Practice piano
- Research Turbo Debugger
. Call John Jackson 828-7896  (left msg)
. SBA 556-7784 called on 6/23/89  &  7/6/89 left message for Laura
. Work on Hypertext Book [sp]  HyperPAD 1-315-474-3400

^^^^^^^^^^^^^^^^^^^^^^^^^^^ RELATED FILES ^^^^^^^^^^^^^^^^^^^^^^^^^^^^^^^^
bs.tic
control.ctr
desk
dos.tic
history.tic
important.tic
  Help..F1;    Save..F2;    Exit..F10;    Hypertext..F10;    Abort editing..Esc
```

Fig. 7-2 EMPOWERment planning node.

action items as high priority and yet you have not worked on them, it will invite you to engage in a dialog. This dialog will help motivate you to move forward on your high-priority tasks.

Hypertext features   From within any deadline node or from within the main planning node, you can run other programs or jump into other text nodes. If you don't know the name of a file, you can include wildcards in your text button and the system will display a menu of files and subdirectories. You can view most text nodes even if they were created with another word processor. You can also edit such files although you cannot insert special control codes. To edit a file using the program that was used to create the node, you can create a command button that includes the program name followed by the file. For example, to edit a WordPerfect file using WordPerfect, you could create a command button such as:

(WP jongeward.doc)

Phone numbers also serve as hypertext buttons. If you put the cursor on the first character of a phone number and press F10, the system will dial that number (if a Hayes-compatible modem is connected).

EMPOWERment has other hypertext features: reference buttons, command buttons, customizable pull-down menus, automatic linking based on a keyword search, predefined nodes with built-in optional help, automatic backtracking, automatic fax dispatch via MCI Mail. A useful editing feature is the ability to search for, and access an external node and then merge just a part of that node into the current one.

Although EMPOWERment is good for organizing electronic documents and printing letters and memos, it is not a complete word processor, nor was it designed to be. For developing documents that ultimately are to be printed, a word processor is more appropriate. But what about combining hypertext with word processing. You might be wondering if there are any word processors that also have hypertext capabilities. Yes, you'll be happy to know they do exist, and I will discuss them soon.

Book development with hypertext

Tim Parker, a technical writer and systems programmer, reports in the May 1989 issue of *Computer Language* that he is using BlackMagic to develop book outlines. He puts notes to editors and to himself in separate nodes and links these notes to the outline. Tim goes on to say: "It seems doubtful that hypertext will replace standard word processors. . . ."

That's probably true, but as you will see in the next chapter, with Sprint it's possible to have a complete, full-featured word processor and a hypertext system. With a little programming know-how, you can customize the system to your liking. As mentioned earlier, in developing this book I used a special hypertext interface developed for Sprint called HyperSprint. Sprint enables you to have several files open at once. You can put each file into a separate window and switch from one file to another in a single keystroke. Figure 7-3 shows HyperSprint in action with three windows on the screen.

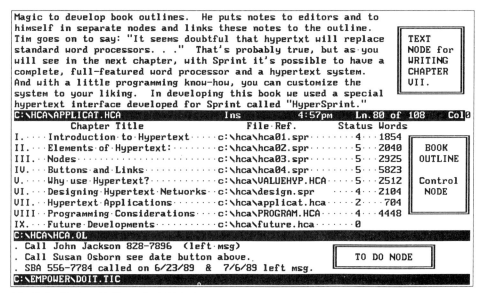

Fig. 7-3 Sprint with HyperSprint interface.

The top window contains some text that I am editing (the first draft for this chapter). The middle window is a control node; it contains an outline of the chapters along with other information. The bottom window contains a "to do" node, which helps me juggle my current writing activities with other miscellaneous tasks. At times it's really useful to have several windows on the screen at once. At other times it's sometimes distracting. But that is no problem. I can zoom any of the windows to full screen with a single key press.

When editing or writing text, I often zoom the top window to a full screen. If I need the other nodes, I "unzoom" the top window and the other windows reappear.

Notice in Fig. 7-3 that along with each chapter title, I list the file that contains it, the status of the chapter, and the word count for that chapter. A status of five here shows that I have finished the final draft for the chapter; a status of 0 shows I haven't yet started. The word count, which Sprint can produce automatically, helps me keep tabs on the length of the various chapters.

I would not want to work without being able to access the control node in the middle of the screen!

The control node helps me see the "big picture," gives me feedback on my progress, and enables me to immediately access any other chapter without losing my place in the current one. To access other chapters, I need not remember or type any file names—I just switch to the control node, move the cursor to the appropriate file reference, and press the hypertext hotkey. The control node also helps me keep track of other odds and ends related to the book: notes about conversations with the publisher, follow-up notes about changes and additions to chapters, notes about new hypertext software and so on. I'm really glad that these notes and chapters are linked to a central control node—not scattered on pieces of paper, or what is even worse, hidden in unconnected little files somewhere on my hard disk!

HyperSprint has other features, too, for example reference buttons, command buttons, insertion buttons, and a find-a-caption function. In the next chapter you will see that once you know how, very little source code is needed to enable hypertext using Sprint's macro programming language.

Sprint, like most modern word processors, has an impressive spelling checker and thesaurus. But it would be useful to have a full-fledged dictionary (not just a spelling checker) so that you could look up the meaning and usage of words on-line. It so happens that developers of stand-alone on-line dictionaries are not unaware of hypertext!

The Oxford English Dictionary

The Oxford University Press is considering publication of an electronic version of the *Oxford English Dictionary* (OED). Darrell R. Raymond and Frank Wm. Tompa evaluated a possible hypertext representation and reported their findings in the July 1988 issue of *Communications of the ACM*. They explain that the main reason for considering hypertext for the OED is to support browsing. Users find it enjoyable and fruitful to search for a word and then navigate from there, perhaps exploring synonyms.

One of the problems of converting the EOD to hypertext is deciding how to break it up into nodes. Why not just make each entry a node? This might work with the right software. But this approach is complicated by the wide variance in the size of entries. Entries range from a negligible one line for "Gig: see jig" to the nearly one-half megabyte of storage needed for the verb "set."

In developing the hypertext version of the OED, Raymond and Tompa have decided to support a kind of "dynamic fragmentation" where the user can control what information is presented in a node. Apparently, by some hotkey the user will be able to display different versions of the entry for a word. For example, one version might show the complete, detailed entry as it appears in the original OED. Another version of the node might show only the basic meanings of the word without example quotations. Another node might show quotations only, and so on.

Cross-references as hypertext buttons   The original OED is already replete with cross-references—explicit pointers to other entries. (It contains 569,000 cross-references, which is an average of 2.26 per entry.) However, the existing cross-references are not distributed evenly. It seems that editors were more likely to insert cross-references to sections of the OED currently in progress. It appears that the existing cross-references will be used as buttons, but that additional cross-references need to be added.

Lexical buttons   A *lexical button*, or lexical link, is simply a word within a definition that points to another definition. If you are reading a definition of a word and you come upon another word that you don't understand, ideally you should be able to zoom to its definition and then zoom back. But this is not as easy as it first looks. For example, the definition of "fossic" is (in part): "To search for gold by digging out crevices with knife and pick . . . ." Should the program search for "digging," "out" or "digging out." Should "digging" be cut to "dig"? Probably not because there is an explicit entry in the OED for "digging." Another problem involves linking a word to the appropriate definition—the one that fits the context in which it appears.

But lexical buttons need not explicitly link to the precise definition to be useful. The user can step through the various definitions and then select the appropriate ones.

Although the hypertext version of the OED was still under development at the time of this writing, INDUCTEL Inc. in Saratoga, California already has available several dictionaries with hypertext capability.

KAS (Knowledge Acquisition System)

INDUCTEL's on-line dictionaries include several McGraw-Hill dictionaries including dictionaries of: Computers, Electrical and Electronic Engineering, Physics, Biology, Chemistry, and Mechanical and Design Engineering.

Also INDUCTEL offers a hypertext version of the Funk and Wagnall's *Standard Desk Dictionary*, a five-digit zip code directory that includes streets and cities, and last but not least, *The Concise Dictionary of 26 Languages*.

The main program that searches the dictionaries is KAS (Knowledge Acquisition System). You can make KAS memory-resident by including the word "pop-up" on the command line when you start the program. The upshot is that every word on-screen in your word processor, or in any program, is a hypertext button that points to its definition! You just put the cursor on a word and press Alt-M. (The first time you do this you must select the dictionary you want to use. However, after you do this, KAS remembers the dictionary you have selected and takes you directly into it.) After you press Alt-M, the word you have selected is already at the KAS input prompt—so all you need to do is press the Return key to begin the search. KAS has a good search algorithm so the definition pops up in about one second or less, which meets the criteria of most hypertext aficionados. Often, but not always, KAS will find the word even if the word you have selected is not the root of the word. For example, if you are looking for the word "running," KAS might also show the word "run."

Lexical buttons KAS also supports lexical buttons as discussed earlier. If you don't know the meaning of a word that occurs within a definition, you can easily jump to the definition of that word by highlighting it and pressing the Return key. Highlighting is easy because as soon as you move the cursor, it immediately highlights the next word in the definition. You can keep browsing and exploring in this way without limitation. It can be quite enjoyable to explore the definition of related words without having to flip pages or even input words.

One drawback, though, is that you cannot backtrack automatically to the previous word. (This capability will probably be added in an updated version.) Figure 7-4 shows KAS in action. Notice that I have looked up the entry for the word time. Also notice, that I have highlighted the word hour within the entry for time. Figure 7-5 shows the destination node—the entry for hour.

The availability of a system such as KAS suddenly increases the value of having study materials, periodicals, trade journals, and even literature on disk. Not only can you build a global hypertext network of nodes, but you can look up the meaning of almost any word in a couple of seconds at the press of a hotkey. I've already had fun exploring words like vituperation, obdurate, ingenuous, sycophant, iconoclast, hegemony, and desultory.

If you can use hypertext to help look up the definition of words, what about using hypertext to clarify government regulations?

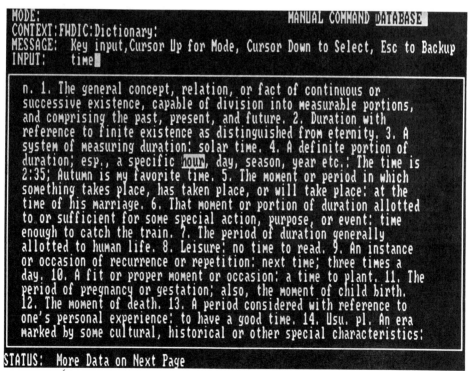

Fig. 7-4 KAS Funk and Wagnall's displaying a "parent node."

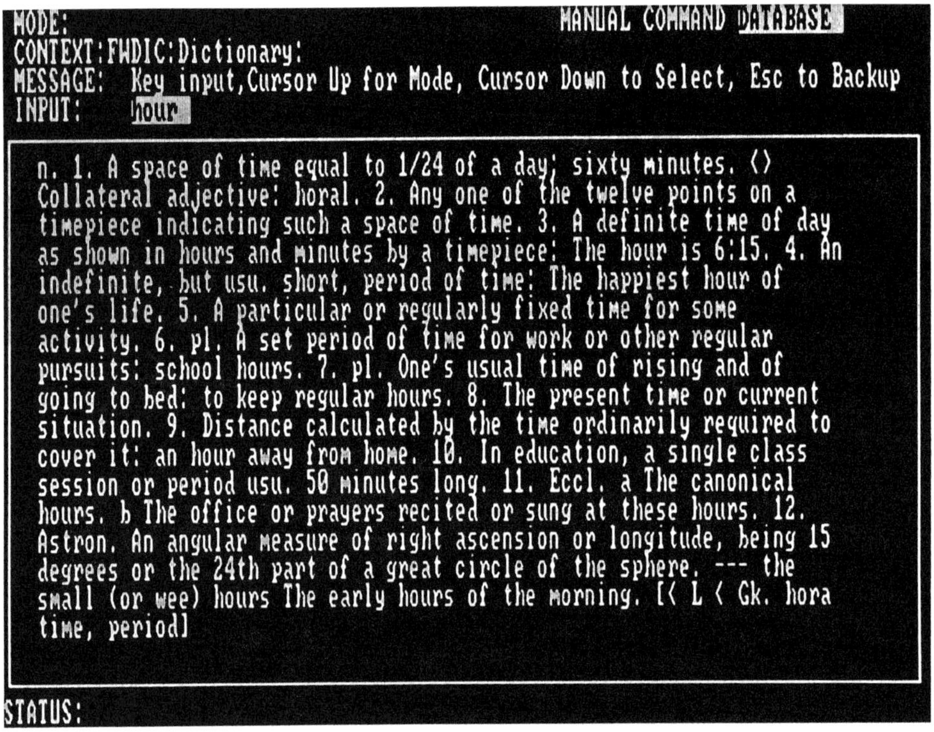

```
MODE:                                      MANUAL COMMAND DATABASE
CONTEXT:FWDIC:Dictionary:
MESSAGE:  Key input,Cursor Up for Mode, Cursor Down to Select, Esc to Backup
INPUT:    hour

  n. 1. A space of time equal to 1/24 of a day; sixty minutes. ()
  Collateral adjective: horal. 2. Any one of the twelve points on a
  timepiece indicating such a space of time. 3. A definite time of day
  as shown in hours and minutes by a timepiece: The hour is 6:15. 4. An
  indefinite, but usu. short, period of time: The happiest hour of
  one's life. 5. A particular or regularly fixed time for some
  activity. 6. pl. A set period of time for work or other regular
  pursuits: school hours. 7. pl. One's usual time of rising and of
  going to bed: to keep regular hours. 8. The present time or current
  situation. 9. Distance calculated by the time ordinarily required to
  cover it: an hour away from home. 10. In education, a single class
  session or period usu. 50 minutes long. 11. Eccl. a The canonical
  hours. b The office or prayers recited or sung at these hours. 12.
  Astron. An angular measure of right ascension or longitude, being 15
  degrees or the 24th part of a great circle of the sphere. --- the
  small (or wee) hours The early hours of the morning. [< L < Gk. hora
  time, period]

STATUS:
```

Fig. 7-5   KAS displaying a destination node.

Reg-In-A-Box

The Environmental Protection Agency is using the BlackMagic hypertext system to distribute complex regulatory information about storage tanks! Exciting? Well, allright, granted, the subject matter is not the best bedtime reading but the Reg-In-A-Box project does demonstrate that hypertext can be useful in clarifying government gobbledygook. Reg-In-A-Box consists of eight linked hypertext documents. Expert systems are even embedded in the system. Yes, hypertext provides a simple way to present most expert systems without resorting to an expensive inference engine. The hypertext nodes are presented with multiple-choice questions. As you work your way through the network answering the questions, the hypertext network is actually evaluating your situation and can pop up expert advice. Figure 7-6 shows a screen from Reg-In-A-Box.

The documents, like most government documents, are extensively cross-referenced. With the hypertext approach, you don't have to flip pages to check out the references. Other advantages include the ability to easily update the information and distribute it inexpensively. The EPA is distributing Reg-In-A-Box with pop-up a shareware run-time program. (See chapter 10 for more details.)

```
       Existing Steel Und
       Association Standa ┌──────────────────────────────────┐
       Extension of Exist │ 280.33(d)                        │
       Addition of Cathod │                                  │
                          │ Repaired tanks and piping must be tightness-tested │
◊Explain 280.33(b)◊       │ within 30 days after repair UNLESS: │
(b)  Repairs to fibergl   │                                  │
     manufacturers auth   │ 1. The tank is internally inspected; │
     practice developed   │                                  │
     independent testin   │ 2. You monitor the repaired part of the UST system │
                          │    monthly for leaks; or         │
◊Explain 280.33(c)◊       │                                  │
(c)  Metal pipe section   │ 3. You use some other test method authorized by your │
     result of corrosio   │    UST agency.                   │
     and fittings may b   │                                  │
     specifications.      └──────────────────────────────────┘

◊Explain 280.33(d)◊
(d)  Repaired tanks and piping must be tightness tested in accordance
     with △280.43(c)△ and △280.44(b)△ within 30 days following the date of the
     completion of the repair except as provided in paragraphs (d)(1) through
     (3), of this section:

(1)  The repaired tank is internally inspected in accordance with a code
Read: C:\USTREGS\REGINBOX.MAG                          Line:   13 Col:   17
```

Fig. 7-6 Screen from Reg-In-A-Box.

Dr. Dobb's Journal

The June 1990 issue of *Dr. Dobb's Journal*, which featured hypertext, was published in hypertext format using the HyperWriter Development system. It comes on two 360K disks with the data archived, along with a run-time version of HyperWriter. Figures 7-7 through 7-9 give you a sample of how the system works. Figure 7-7 shows the opening screen of an article about programming your own Hypertext system written by Rick Gessner. There are several hypertext buttons on this screen. Each button is delimited by pyramid characters. Notice that there is a button that leads to biographical information about the author. Also, important quotes from the article appear under the author's name. When you click on one of these quotes, you are zoomed to the place in the article where the quote appears so you can read it in context. You can retrace your steps by pressing Esc or clicking the right mouse button.

Another nice touch by the designer, Scott Johnson, was to embed these buttons at the top of each screen: Figures, Examples, Sub Headings, and Listings.

By clicking on the Figures button, you can get a list of all the figures in the article and then jump from there to any specific figure. The feature I like the best is the ability to click on the Sub Headings button. This gives you a list of all of the subheadings in the article as you can see in Fig. 7-8. In this figure notice that the mouse pointer is on Using the Hypr-Text Unit. (NOTE: HyprText is apparently spelled here without an ''e'' to conform to a name length limitation.)

When you click on, say, Using the HyprText Unit, the system immediately jumps to that point in the article as you can see in Fig. 7-9. In that figure I have the mouse pointer on a

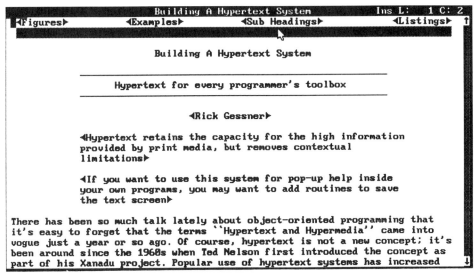

Fig. 7-7 An article in *Dr. Dobb's Journal* in hypertext format.

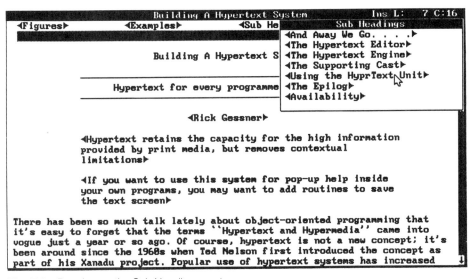

Fig. 7-8 Popping up the Sub Headings node.

button called Line 9. When I click on that button it takes me to a figure showing line 9 of the computer programming under discussion.

ComputorEdge magazine

The Byte Buyer, Inc. publishes *ComputorEdge*, San Diego's computer magazine in both conventional paper and electronic hypertext format. Readers can download the hypertext

```
character at a time, and detects when the user presses the Ctrl and Alt
keys.

Using the HyprText Unit
The code in ◄Example 7► shows how easy it is to use the HyprText unit in
your own programs. ◄Line 9► shows a call to the editor, Help_Editor, that
passes the name of the hyperdata file to be used. Once the user is finished
editing the file, the program calls the procedure Do_Help on ◄line 10►, and
passes to this procedure the name of the hyperdata file to be used. The
other parameters passed to Do_Help specify the starting and home page
numbers used to prime the stack (as described earlier).

If you want to use this system for pop-up help inside your own programs, you
may want to add routines to save the text screen before calling Do_Help, and
to restore the text screen once Do_Help terminates. Also, to keep the length
of the listing to a minimum, I omitted most of the error-checking steps that
a commercial application should have. You may want to add more
error-checking routines to meet your own needs.

The Epilog
Well, there you have it--a hypertext system that is simple to program and
simple to use. I hope that this system offers a useful addition to your
programming toolbox. I am sure that you can think of additional uses and
enhancements to this system.  What about converting this system to a
```

Fig. 7-9 Jumping to the "Using the HyprText Unit" subheading.

"stack" from "ComputorEdge On-line." (The communications number—not voice—is 619-573-1675.) Downloading an entire issue takes nearly an hour, but readers may also get a free copy by sending a self-addressed, stamped envelope (SASE) and a formatted disk to *ComputorEdge*. Editor Wally Wang says he is storing all articles on a hard disk and linking them with hypertext buttons for easy retrieval. That way, if a reader requests a reprint of an old article, he can easily access it and print it out. There's no charge for this reader service, but Wally asks that readers enclose the SASE and a few dollars for handling. *ComputorEdge* uses HyperRez (see chapter 10) to distribute the PC version of the magazine. HyperRez is a TSR program (terminate and stay resident), so you can pop it up when you get bored with your current database, spreadsheet or word processing program. Figure 7-10 shows the opening *ComputorEdge* screen.

Notice in Fig. 7-10, the highlighted button is < cover >. So if you press Return, the program will branch to the cover article by Dan Gookin.

Figure 7-11 shows the start of the "cover" node. It's called that simply because the DOS file that contains the text is named "cover." Actually, it's an article entitled "Looking Into Monitors" by Dan Gookin. You can scroll through this article using the Down arrow or automatically return to the opening screen by pressing the Left arrow. A help screen comes up if you press F1.

HyperRez also works with whatever you have on your current screen, even if the text was not created with HyperRez. For example, while writing this chapter, I popped up HyperRez and was amazed to see that my Sprint screen was not disturbed but that a file name in angle brackets was highlighted. HyperRez apparently looks for and highlights any text enclosed in angle brackets on the current screen, no matter what program is displaying that screen. When you press the Down arrow, HyperRez highlights the next angle bracket button. One limitation (in the version I was using) is that when looking for a file,

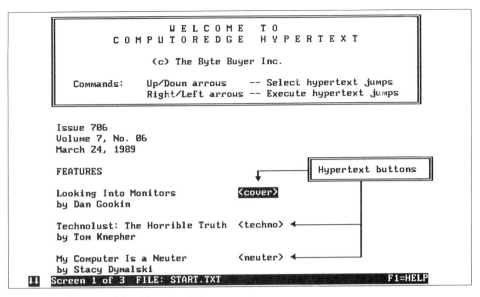

Fig. 7-10 *ComputorEdge* Magazine in hypertext format.

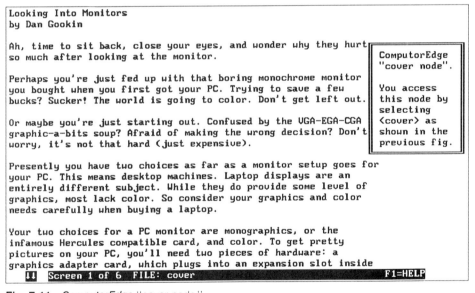

Fig. 7-11 *ComputorEdge* "cover node."

HyperRez always looks in the subdirectory in which it was first booted up. It cannot accept a path name or wildcard.

HyperRez is a shareware program and was produced by MaxThink. MaxThink also distributes PC-HyperText and other hypertext products. See chapter 10 for more details.

On-line help with HyperTSR

Another TSR hypertext program is HyperTSR. HyperTSR was written in Turbo C with the help of the Turbo C ToolBox from Blaise computing. The next chapter shows some of the C code used in HyperTSR. Unlike, HyperRez, HyperTSR stores all of its nodes in a single file. Buttons may include spaces and may be just about any length. However, only the first eight characters of the name are used to uniquely identify a node. Several different buttons may link to the same node, if desired. Users may search for a node by going through the usual hypertext control node, or they may search by entering a keyword. We, at Seyer Associates, are using HyperTSR to develop friendly help systems for various application programs.

Figure 7-12 shows what a HyperTSR node looks like when viewed by a developer, except I have added some comments enclosed in double-lined boxes. This particular node is from a network of nodes designed to act as on-line help for a popular word processor. Notice the keywords at the top of the node. Any number of these keywords may be listed. These keywords designate buttons that you may use in other nodes to point to this one.

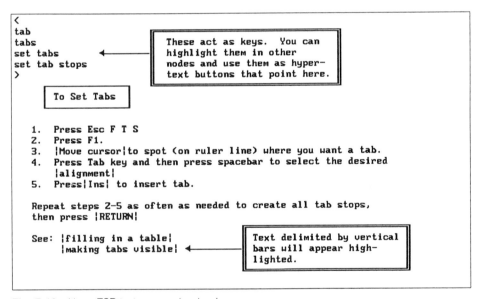

Fig. 7-12 HyperTSR text as seen by developer.

Figure 7-13 shows what the node looks like to a user. Notice that the words delimited with vertical bars are highlighted (shown in inverse video).

After a user is familiar with a node and knows the proper button, or keyword, to use to access it, the user might prefer to simply enter that keyword. HyperTSR enables this by supporting topic searches. As shown in Fig. 7-14, by pressing F10 the user can bring up a menu, select the Topic Search option, and then enter the appropriate keyword.

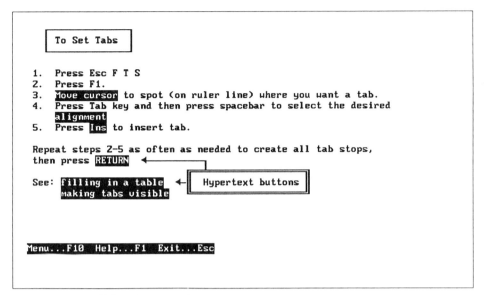

Fig. 7-13 HyperTSR node as seen by user.

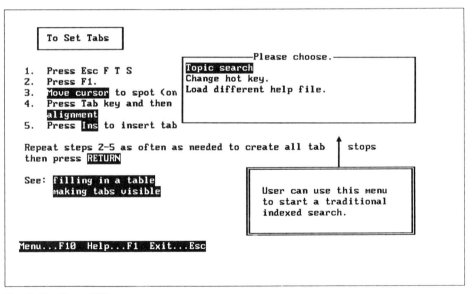

Fig. 7-14 HyperTSR menu.

Hypertext and museums

Hypertext is a natural medium of museums. For example, consider the electronic encyclopedia project for the upcoming New York City museum: "The Museum of Jewish Heritage." The purpose of the museum, which is scheduled to open in 1991, is to save for future generations information about the European Jewish culture that was destroyed in World War II. The hypertext system will be part of the museum's Hall of Learning; it will include 50 microcomputers with touch screens and interactive video. The network of nodes will include 3,000 articles! Also there will be thousands of photos as well as several animated video segments.

HyperTIES

The museum will be using HyperTIES, from Cognetics Corporation. HyperTIES will evolve as the project continues to evolve. The developers include a group from Cognetics, a programmer at the museum, and Professor Ben Shneiderman and his staff at the University of Maryland, and several scholars and writers. The developer will be facing problems like how to enable multiple levels of indexing and access time as the size of the database expands to 3,000 articles.

The system will enable users to get into the network in different ways: by maps of the exhibit areas, by timelines, by topics, and so on. Again, see chapter 10 for details on how to obtain HyperTIES.

A hypertext simulation

More and more, hypertext is finding its way into the educational community. An example is a hypertext network dedicated to the Election 1912. It runs on Macintosh models 512KE or better and uses Eastgate's Hypergate[tm] system. The network actually simulates the U.S. election of 1912, a close, exciting election that could have gone either way.

Users of the network can play around with the simulation, try different things and watch the outcome of the election. For example, the user can click on a certain button and get a map on which to plan a campaign trail. Or the player can go to a specific point in time and see how the campaigns were progressing on a state-by-state basis, by clicking on different states. The player can send telegrams to various leaders of the time to try to influence the election, and so on.

The developers say that to achieve a thorough simulation, they developed a new kind of link: a link from a procedure to a text node. Here, they are procedures written in C. To enable a simulation that would model the dynamics of the political process, many equations and databases were required. The procedures carry out the rather complex calculations and then—depending on the result of the calculations—pass information back to the main hypertext program, so it will know what to display next. Usually links work the other way and are embedded in text and launch programs or subprograms (procedures). But it is interesting to consider that the links can go the other way, too, as demonstrated by the Election of 1912. The audience for The Election of 1912 is said to be serious readers of all ages—not just hypertext lovers.

Hypertext/expert systems

KnowledgePro was used to develop a hypertext/expert system for use by aquaculture researchers. It's called Regis and was developed by NAL, the U.S. National Agricultural

Library, a division of the U.S. Department of Agriculture. Researchers can call up information about fish farming in various nations in Africa. To make it easier to access the information, the program displays a map of Africa as shown in Fig. 7-15. By clicking on a particular nation, the users can call up corresponding research data. Alternatively, users can work from a simple list of names in text mode. The system also includes an expert system designed to help users make technical aquacultural decisions. Hypertext is combined with the expert system so that users can branch off to get clarifications of key terms when needed.

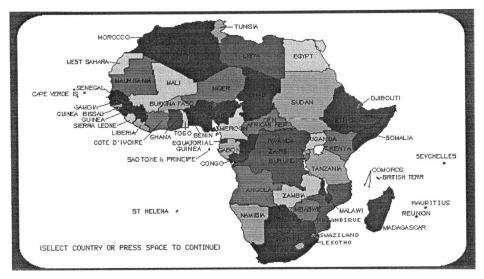

Fig. 7-15 Map of Africa where each nation is a button.

Hypertext tutorials

Music   Several hypertext tutorials are becoming available as hypertext matures. One such tutorial is one I am developing on music. It is based on a 256-page book entitled *What Makes Music Work*, originally published by John Wiley and Sons and now published by Seyer Associates. (You can find the book in quality music stores everywhere.) The hypertext version of the book will be highly interactive and will be available first for PC and then Macintosh systems. The book has hundreds of musical illustrations which, I am scanning and then merging into the hypertext program. (For an example of this, see Figs. 1-1 and 1-2 in chapter 1.) One problem, here, is disk space. How much disk space will I need to store an entire 256-page book? It appears that several megabytes will be required. To solve the disk space problem, I might need to represent some of the musical notation with modified ASCII characters. Alternatively, I might reorganize the book into three or four hypertext modules that could be distributed separately.

Because of the near omnipresence of HyperCard, there are many tutorials and learning exercises on various subjects available for Macintosh users. One interesting one is on Japanese writing systems. There are three basic writing systems in Japanese: Hiragana,

Katakana, and Kanji. The Kanji system was originally developed in China and grew out of pictographs. For example, the word for big resembles a person with his arms spread out to his sides as if gesturing "So big!" You'll see this Kanji character in a moment.

This HyperCard stack is called, aptly, Kanji Exercises and you can get it from Anonae Software in Berkeley, California. (See chapter 10 for detailed contact information.) HyperCard stacks are also available for studying Hiragana and Katakana, the two other Japanese writing systems. I might add, here, that the publisher is looking into converting the stacks into hypertext networks that will run on an IBM PC system.

The Kanji Exercises stack is really a sophisticated learning environment, not a tutorial. The program does not guide you step-by-step through a prescribed learning experience but rather provides you with many different learning tools. An excellent context-sensitive help system is built into the program and it shows in detail what the active buttons are in a given hypertext node. Figure 7-16 shows one of the help nodes. As you can see it explains where to click to activate various functions. For example, the box at upper left in the figure explains that you can get an expanded view of the Kanji and see the "stroke order" by clicking on the Kanji itself.

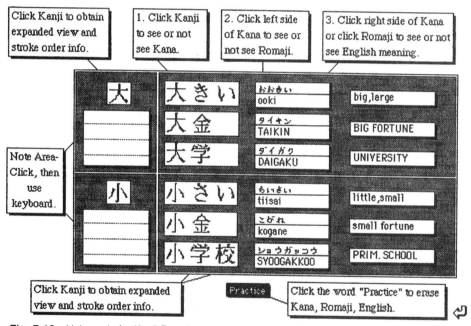

Fig. 7-16 Help node for Kanji Exercises.

When you write a Kanji character you make a number of strokes with your pen. The exact order in which you make theses strokes is called the *stroke order*. To the disciplined Japanese mind, this stroke order is crucial. You have not written a character correctly unless you have made the strokes in the prescribed order. (There is some sense to this, you know. It helps you remember the character if you always write it exactly the same way. And the characters tend to have the same "look" and are therefore easier to read.)

I decided to find the Kanji for the English word "big" because the pictograph is easy to remember. To find the node containing "big" I clicked on the appropriate search icon and entered big. The program searched through the network and then displayed the node shown in Fig. 7-17.

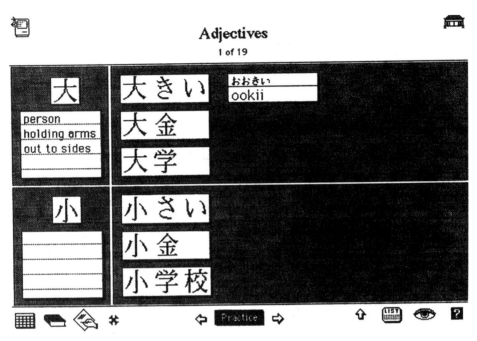

Fig. 7-17   Kanji for "big" (in top half of screen).

The Kanji for "big" appears at the upper left. Under the Kanji there is a blank field—an area the developer set aside to allow users to enter data. This is a spot where you can type in your own "memory joggers." The idea is to create hints that will help you remember the meaning or pronunciation of the Kanji. I typed in the words "person holding arms out to sides" as my memory jogger. At the upper right in Fig. 7-17, in the top row, you can see the same word written in Katakana, also referred to as Kana, for short and also in Roman letters (Romanji). Remember, each Japanese word can be written in several ways:

- Kanji (with a Chinese character)
- Kana (with Japanese phonetic symbols)
- Romanji (with Roman letters)

As explained in Fig. 7-16, you can make the Kana and Romanji appear or disappear by clicking on the proper buttons. This helps you test yourself. You can try to recall the Kana or Romanji and then confirm your responses by popping up the answer.

You can also pop up the English translation of the word by clicking on, say, the Romanji. Figure 7-18 shows how the English translation appeared when I clicked on ookii (the Romanji).

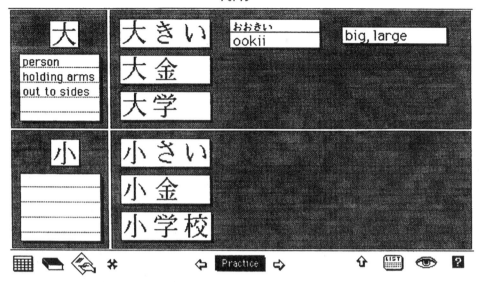

Fig. 7-18 Kanji for "big" with English translation.

When I clicked on the Kanji, itself, in the upper left corner, an expanded view of the Kanji appeared as you can see in Fig. 7-19.

Underneath the enlarged Kanji there are three interesting buttons. If you click on the "brush" button at the left, the program will write the character stroke-by-stroke. You can make the program write the character over and over until you've memorized the stroke order. By clicking on the cartoon of the speaking head, you can actually hear the Kanji pronounced by a native Japanese speaker! By clicking on the "eraser" icon at the right, you can erase the Kanji—the program erases the Kanji stroke-by-stroke to facilitate memorization.

There are several other active buttons in this node. Kanji characters often contain basic characters called *radicals*. For example, to see the program write just the radical part of the Kanji, you can click on the radical number. (Each radical is numbered.) To see a help node that explains all your options, you can click on the "eye" icon at the lower right. Figure 7-20 shows this help node.

The Kanji Exercises stack has several other features—for example, there is a quiz module that you can use to more directly test your mastery of the Kanji. I think the program is excellent. One limitation, is that to save space, not all of the meanings for the Kanji are presented. This is well-documented, though, and the developer advises you to use regular Japanese textbooks to study the Kanji along with his program. The current program teaches more than 300 Kanji and future stacks are planned so that eventually a learning environment will be available that contains the 2,000 Kanji identified by the Japanese government as being essential to learn.

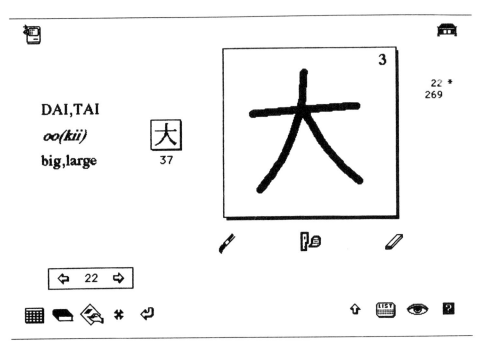

Fig. 7-19 Enlarged view of Kanji.

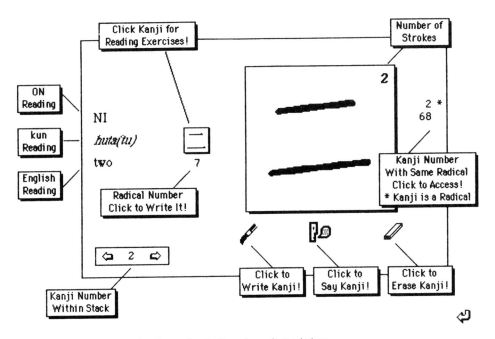

Fig. 7-20 Help screen showing active buttons for enlarged view.

Summary

Well, that completes this survey of hypertext applications. It just scratches the surface. If you have developed some hypertext applications yourself, I would be delighted to hear from you. Perhaps I can feature your application in the next edition of this book or in an article on hypertext. If you've enjoyed this chapter and hunger for more, you might want to take a close look at chapter 10, which lists names and addresses of hypertext companies and discusses additional hypertext projects which, for one reason or another I couldn't squeeze into this chapter.

In chapter 8 I will discuss hypertext programming considerations. You will learn how you can create and customize your own hypertext system as well as write scripts for a hypertext program someone else has developed. In fact, I will give you the complete source code for a handy hypertext editor!

<h1 style="text-align:center">8</h1>

Programming hypertext

There are at least three levels of hypertext programming. At the first, and simplest level, the developer may not, strictly speaking be a programmer. At this level the developer is simply setting up a network of nodes and ensuring that the proper links appear where they should. I've already discussed how this is done with several different hypertext systems. In this chapter I will continue this exploration, but focus on how to use existing systems for developing PC hypertext systems that can reside concurrently in memory with other application programs.

On another level, a programmer might be developing an original hypertext authoring system (which on PC systems has an .EXE or .COM extension). In developing such a program, the programmer might use a language such as C, BASIC, Pascal, assembly language, or Prolog. In this chapter I'll consider some tools that are available to you if you are interested in programming at this level.

A third type of programming involves writing a series of instructions that are interpreted by an existing hypertext system. These instructions are usually referred to as a script.

Probably the best known example of this kind of programming is that done in Hyper-Talk, a script language designed to allow Macintosh users to specify what will happen when a user selects a HyperCard button.

Scripting in HyperCard

Teaching all the details of HyperCard scripting is beyond the scope of this book. My intent, here, is just to give you a taste of HyperCard scripting, to whet your appetite and perhaps stimulate your thinking. Also, knowing a little bit about HyperCard scripting will help you learn and evaluate the scripting available in other programs.

NOTE: In this discussion I will be referring to various menus that are available in HyperCard. These are menus that you can activate with a mouse. You move the mouse pointer to the name of the menu at the top of the screen and press and hold the mouse button. See Fig. 8-1 which shows the Tools menu that drops down from the top of the

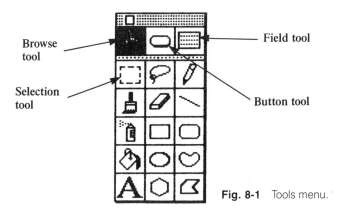

Browse tool

Selection tool

Field tool

Button tool

Fig. 8-1 Tools menu.

screen when you select Tools. The little images on this menu (*icons*) represent specific tools. In Fig. 8-1 I have labeled some of the important icons used in developing hypertext links.

Usually you think of a script as being a mini program that you can attach to a hypertext button. In HyperCard a script can be that, but it can be more than that, too. In HyperCard you can attach scripts to various kinds of objects, not just buttons. In HyperCard the fundamental objects are:

- Stacks
- Cards
- Fields
- Buttons

A *stack* is really just a hypertext network—a collection of nodes that have been organized into a whole. Each node in the network is referred to as a *card*. Cards, in turn, can have *fields*—specific named areas where text can be inserted by the user or by a script. Cards can also have buttons. These HyperCard buttons are hotspots on the screen that can be linked to other cards or to scripts. I might add here that fields and buttons can be placed on a special "background." Such fields and buttons will automatically appear on all cards in the stack. If a field is local to a card it is a card field. If a field is designed to appear on all cards, it is a background field.

I'd like to stress again that you can link a script to any HyperCard object. You can link a script to a stack, a card, a field, or a button. I'll show simple examples of such linking shortly.

HyperCard scripts are really small programs made up of what are called *handlers*. Each handler springs into action when a designated event occurs. For example, scripts can be attached to buttons so that when a user clicks on a button, a whole series of predefined commands will be executed.

Attaching a script to a button is easy once you know how. Assuming that you have created a button image on screen, you select the Tools menu and then select the Button tool. See Fig. 8-2.

Next, you hold down the Shift key and click on the button for which you want to create a script. When you do this, a script window will open. The structure for a simple script

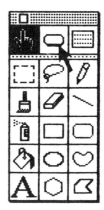

Fig. 8-2 Selecting the button tool.

will already be there. HyperCard automatically inserts on mouseUp and end mouseUp on separate lines and puts the cursor on a line in-between. Like this:

```
on mouseUp
|
end mouseUp
```

Notice, here, that there is a vertical bar on the line following on mouseUp. This represents the so called "I-beam" cursor that appears in addition to the mouse pointer. The cursor is already positioned indented under on mouseUp so you can begin entering your script commands. The on mouseUp simply specifies that the commands are to be activated when the user releases the mouse button. The end mouseUp line marks the end of the series of commands connected to the releasing of the mouse button. To create the script, just type in the commands that you want executed. Suppose you have created a button in the form of a sign that says "click here" and you want HyperCard to display "hello" in a pop-up node. Here is one way of doing it:

```
on mouseUp
put "Hello!" into message
beep
end mouseUp
```

Here message refers to a special message box that appears at the bottom of the screen. See Fig. 8-3 which shows the effect of selecting the Click here button.

Notice that the previous script handles the user's action of releasing the mouse button. The Hello! message appears only when the user releases the mouse button. When you think about it, selecting a hypertext icon actually consists of five actions:

1. Moving the mouse onto the icon.
2. Pressing the button.
3. Holding down the button.
4. Releasing the button.
5. Moving the mouse pointer off the icon.

Using various kinds of handlers you can specify that you want different kinds of things to happen at each stage in the process of selecting a hypertext button.

Hello

Fig. 8-3 Result of selecting the "Click here" button.

Figure 8-4 shows a simple script that displays different messages at each stage in the button selection process; it doesn't do anything useful, but it does show the fine control you can achieve with HyperTalk.

```
on mouseEnter
  beep
  put "Welcome.  Please press press the mouse button."
end mouseEnter

on mouseDown
   put "You pressed the mouse button."
   wait 1 second
end mouseDown

on mouseStillDown
   put "OK, please release mouse button."
end mouseStillDown

on mouseUp
   beep
   put "Thank you. Please move mouse pointer off button."
end mouseUp

on mouseLeave
   put "Thanks for visiting this button. Bye."
end mouseLeave
```

Fig. 8-4 Achieving fine control with a script.

Scripts and other objects

You've just seen how a script can be attached to a button and how it can handle different kinds of mouse activities with respect to a button. Now let's look at how scripts can be attached to scripts, cards, and fields.

Stack scripts If you want something to happen every time a user goes to a card in a stack regardless of which card it is, you attach a script to a stack. Suppose you have designed a stack where field 1 displays information and field 2 accepts information from the user. By default each time you go to a new card, you must explicitly click on field 2 before you can enter information. But you can attach a script to your stack so that the system will automatically press the Tab key twice. This will have the effect of moving the I-beam cursor to the second field. Such a script might look like this:

```
on openCard
    send tabKey
    send tabKey
end openCard
```

To create, or view, a stack script, just go to the Objects menu, hold down the Shift key and select Stack Info. A stack window will open. After entering your script, just script the OK button to exit back to your current card.

Card scripts   Card scripts are useful when you want a specific card to behave in a certain way. For example, you could pop up a message in the HyperCard message box at the bottom of the screen when the user goes to a specific card. To attach a script to a specific card:

1. Go to the card where you want to attach a script.
2. Select the Objects menu (at the top of the screen).
3. Select Card Info while holding down the Shift key.

A card script window will now open and you can immediately type in a script that will be tied to the current card. For example, to cause a message to pop up at the bottom of the screen when you go to a specific card, you could attach a script like this to that card:

```
on opencard
    put "Please enter your goals" to message box.
end opencard on closecard
    put empty into message box.
end closecard
```

Notice that this script has two handlers: one to handle the case where the user first opens (or goes to) the card and one to handle the case where the user closes the card (goes to another card). When the user enters the card a message appears in the message box. When the user leaves the card, the command put empty into message box has the effect of erasing the message. Notice that you can use upper- or lowercase characters on command words like opencard. Earlier I wrote it as openCard, but opencard works fine, too.

Field scripts   You can also attach a script to a field. For example, suppose you want the user to move the mouse into a certain field and enter some text. To encourage the user, you might want to pop up a message of some kind as soon as the user moves the mouse into the field. Here's an example of a script that you could attach to a field to make that happen:

```
on mouseEnter
    put "Yes! Now please enter your goals here!"
end mouseEnter
on mouseLeave
    put "empty"
end mouseLeave
```

In this script notice that I didn't tell exactly where to put the message. By default, the put command will put the string you give it into the message box at the bottom of the screen. To attach a script to a field, you just follow these steps:

1. Select the field tool from the Tools menu. (It's icon looks like a tiny rectangle with dots inside.)
2. Click on the field where you want to attach a script.
3. Go to the Object menu, hold down the Shift key and select Field Info.

In summary, keep in mind that HyperTalk gives you the ability to attach scripts to stacks, cards, fields or buttons. HyperTalk is a powerful language. In the next few paragraphs I will highlight some commands that are useful in developing hypertext applications.

Control structures and logical operators

Just like a traditional language, HyperTalk has an IF-THEN and IF-THEN-ELSE statements, as well as statements designed to control looping. Using IF-THEN statements you can test for certain conditions and a block of commands is executed only if the condition is true. Using a looping command called repeat you can make HyperCard repeat a series of commands over and over until a certain condition is true.

Go   The Go command lets you jump to any card in the current stack or even in another stack. You can attach a script to a card and specify in the script that when the user presses Enter, the user will be jumped to a specific card like this:

```
onreturnKey
    go to card 7 end returnKey
```

Find   If you don't know the specific name or number of a card, you can use the find command to search for a card that contains a certain string. With a simple command like:

```
find "expense"
```

the search begins with the current card and progresses through all fields on the card. By appending arguments to find you can specify that the search be done only on specific fields.

Field content modification

The content of fields can be directly modified with script commands. You can delete specific words, lines or characters with the delete command. For example:

```
delete third word of line 4 of card field 2.
```

Adding intelligence to nodes

You can add intelligence to a node (card) by attaching a script to it. Here is a simple example: Suppose on a certain card, you want to ensure that a user enters something in a field before moving on. Then you might write a script like the one shown in Fig. 8-5.

Notice the script in Fig. 8-5 has both an on opencard handler and an on closecard handler. When the user first accesses the card, the opencard handler is activated and the

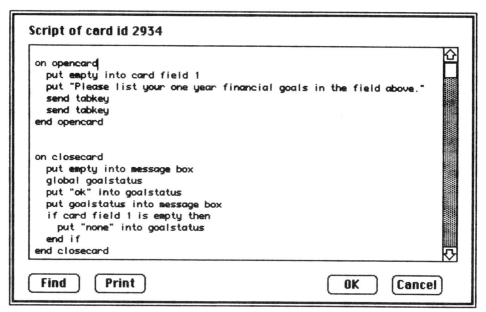

Fig. 8-5 Ensuring that a user enters data.

first card field is cleared with the put empty command. Then a prompt is displayed in the message box with the put command. (Remember, when no destination is specified for the put command, the message goes into the message box at the bottom of the screen by default.) Next, two Tab key presses are simulated with the send tabkey commands in the script. This has the effect of positioning the cursor in the first card field.

NOTE: It's a little difficult, here, to explain why it takes two Tabs to get to the first card field. The reason is that there are two fields in this card. The first field is a background field. The first Tab takes the cursor to the background field; the second, to the first card field. If this were hypertext, this comment would fit nicely into a note node wouldn't it?

The on closecard handler is more interesting. It clears the message box and declares a global variable called goalstatus. Declaring a variable as global makes it available to other cards in the stack. After declaring the variable, the script initializes it to "OK." Next, if the user has failed to enter anything into the first card field, the script sets the goalstatus variable to "none." Now, when the user goes to the next card, that card can know whether the user made an entry on the previous card. Consequently, the next card can then react differently depending on the contents of the goalstatus variable. Figure 8-6 shows the script for this card.

Notice that this script also declares goalstatus as a global variable. This is necessary otherwise goalstatus would be regarded as a new variable known only to the current card—not the goalstatus declared earlier. After declaring that goalstatus is a global variable, the script checks to see if it is set to "none." If it is set to "none" the script has the Mac beep twice, display a new message in the message box, and then jump back to card 1.

This script shows how you can process data in a field when a user leaves a node in a hypertext network. More complex processing is certainly possible. For example, the user

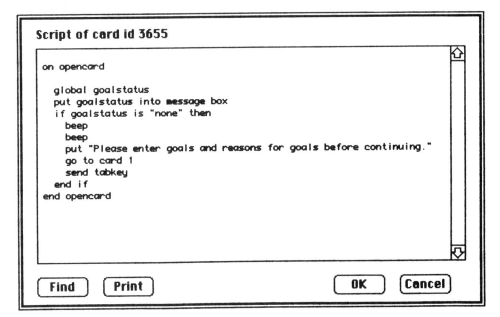

```
Script of card id 3655

on opencard

  global goalstatus
  put goalstatus into message box
  if goalstatus is "none" then
    beep
    beep
    put "Please enter goals and reasons for goals before continuing."
    go to card 1
    send tabkey
  end if
end opencard
```

Find   Print   OK   Cancel

Fig. 8-6   Reacting to contents of global variable.

might be branched to one of several cards depending on the status of two or three global variables. These variables might have been set to different values by users earlier in their travels through the network.

As you can see from this brief discussion, it's possible to do a lot with HyperTalk, but I haven't covered everything. It's possible to:

- Read information from fields
- Sort cards by field contents
- Animate objects
- Play musical tones
- Carry out math functions
- Dial phone numbers
- Expand HyperCard's functionality by adding special programs (as resources)

Details about all of this is beyond the scope of this book. For more information, you might want to refer to one of the books about HyperTalk mentioned in chapter 10.

Scripts and PC programs

When HyperCard first came out many PC users were envious. Until recently few IBM PC hypertext programs had the ability to recognize and interpret scripts the same way as HyperCard. Recently, though several such PC programs have appeared that have scripting capability. The ones that come to mind now are: HyperPAD, Plus, Hyperdoc, HyperWriter, and LinkWay. Let's look at some scripts from these programs and consider what you can do with them. I'll start with HyperPAD.

Scripting in PADTalk

HyperPAD's scripting language is called PADtalk. In HyperPAD terminology, a network is called a *pad*. A pad is analogous to a stack in HyperCard or a document in HyperWriter. A pad is a collection of "pages" of related information stored in a file. HyperPAD uses an object-oriented message-passing system. Pads contain various objects: buttons, fields, pages, and backgrounds. Messages can be passed among the various objects. A pad contains at least one page and one background. The background stays the same from page to page. When you put a button or field on the background, it stays the same from page to page. Fields are places on the pad where you can enter text. (Sound familiar?)

The basic objects, in HyperPAD, then, are pads, buttons, fields, pages, and backgrounds. Each object has its own distinguishing characteristics: color, size, position, message handling capability, etc. Once you create an object you can copy it into different places.

Every object in a pad has a script. You can write these scripts yourself. Like other programming languages, PADtalk has if statements, loop control structures, and math and I/O operators. Here is an example of a simple PADtalk script for an object on the screen:

```
handler select;
begin
   go to the next page;
end;
handler help;
begin
   go to pad "MYHELP";
end;
```

If the user selects the object that this script is associated with, the script goes to the next page. If the user presses F1, the designated help key, the user is taken to a pad called MYHELP.

Figure 8-7 illustrates a more complicated HyperPAD script. This script shows how you might develop a kind of "intelligent hypertext" where the system knows that certain key tasks are required and reminds the user to deal with these tasks when entering text.

```
handler select;
--
--      This button first asks a person for his/her job title.
--         Then based on that information it will select  the
appropiate
--      background to go to.  Next the button asks the user for
some
--      information and puts it into the appropriate fields.
--      Then it sorts the background.
--
begin
     ask "What type of job do you curently Hold?";
     put it into fld "prevjob";

--   Find  out  previous  position  held.   Put  it  into  field
"prevjob";
```

Fig. 8-7   A more complicated HyperPAD script.

Fig. 8-7 Continued.

```
        put "Worker" into title;
        find whole "President" in field "prevjob";
        if the result is "found" then put "big cheese" into title;
        find whole "Manager" in field "prevjob";
        if the result is "found" then put "Small time" into title;

-- Find out employee's level.

    case title of

        "Worker": begin
                  go to pg 1 of background "worker";
                  domenu "new page";
                  process_info;
                  end;

        "President": begin
                     go to pg 1 of background "President";
                     domenu "new page";
                     process_info;
                     end;

        "Manager": begin
                   go to pg 1 of background "Manager";
                   domenu "new page";
                   process_info;
                   end;
            end;
-- Send user to the appropiate background based on the
information in
--    the title field, then ask for information.


    end;


handler Process_info;
begin
-- Ask for information and put it into correct fields.

ask "Please enter your full name";
put it into fld "Name";

ask "Please enter your company name.";
put it into fld "Company_Name";

ask "What is your street address?";
put it into fld "street_add";

ask "What is your City?";
put it into  fld "city";

--   After getting the correct info, send a select to a sort
button.

Send "Select" to background button "Sort";

end;
```

Scripting with LinkWay

IBM LinkWay has a fairly well developed scripting language complete with variables, DOS I/O, screen I/O, string handling, functions, If statements, subroutines, external program execution, string search, printer control, mouse input, node jumping control. You can use this language to build intelligence into a hypertext network. For example, you can develop a computer-based training program that asks questions and branches to the user to different nodes depending on the answer given. Figure 8-8 shows a simple example. It is from a tutorial on reading and writing the Japanese Hirigana.

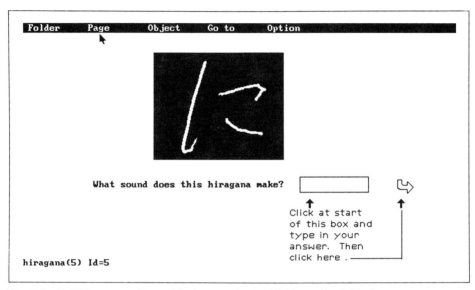

Fig. 8-8 LinkWay page with graphic, input and output fields, and script button.

The purpose of this node is to test the user's memory of the sound of the Japanese character displayed at the top of the screen. To enter data into a LinkWay node, the user must first click on a field. So here I provided a boxed field for the user to type in an answer. To check the correctness of the answer, the user then clicks on the arrow to the right of the input box. This activates a script attached to that hypertext button; you can see this script in Fig. 8-9. I've added line numbers to the script to make it easier to refer to specific commands, but you wouldn't use such numbers when entering the script into LinkWay.

The statement VAR A(10) in line 1 of the script just declares a variable called A and specifies that it can hold 10 bytes of information. It's necessary to declare each variable before you use it in LinkWay. Previously, I had named the user's input field answer. So in line 2, the script moves the current contents of the answer field into variable A. In line 3 the script clears the contents of the answer field by setting it to an empty string (""). In line 4, I check to see if the user typed in the correct answer, "ni" (which is pronounced "knee"). The command that does this is the If statement in line 4: if A = "ni". If A does equal "ni", the script clears any hint that might currently be displayed in the node and jumps to the next node in sequence. The command that enables this jump is the go seq + 1

```
1    VAR A(10);
2    set A = answer;
3    set ans = "";
4    if A = "ni" {
5        set nihint = "";
6        go seq+1;
7        }
8    else {
9        beep;
10       set nihint "Imagine a joint that connects
11       the upper and lower parts of the leg.  Try again.";
12       }
```

Fig. 8-9 LinkWay script.

in line 6. In LinkWay, seq is a function that returns the current node number. So seq + 1 will return the number of the next node in sequence.

If the user does not enter "ni", then the statements beginning at line 9 will be executed: the system will beep and the script will display a hint in a field called nihint. Figure 8-10 shows the node with the hint displayed. The curly braces in the script are used to group together several statements so they are treated like a single unit.

The example, here, is quite simple and just touches the surface of what you can do with LinkWay scripting. LinkWay has about 43 script commands and 17 functions.

The Hyperdoc action language

Hyperdoc is an industrial strength development system with a hefty price tag. One of its most powerful features is its built-in scripting. The Hyperdoc Action Language, as it is called, has about 61 command words and 17 functions.

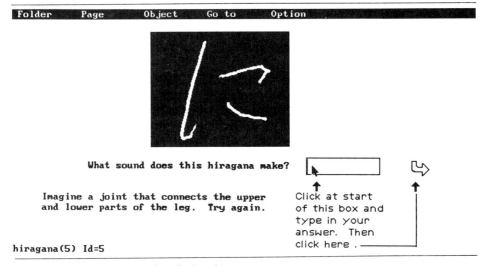

Fig. 8-10 Node with hint being displayed.

A function typically takes a number that you give it and processes that number in some mathematical way. For example, if you give the SQR function a number, it will return its square root.

Command words usually carry out some action. Some of these Hyperdoc commands are quite powerful. An interesting example is the Hyperdoc DBASE command. Using this command you can go into a dBASE file, search for a specific record and extract data from selected fields. For example:

```
&dbase, &dbrecord, 0, "CUSTOMER", "L", "BOST431", 2;
```

The first word on the line, &dbase, is the command. The following words are called arguments to the command. The second word, &dbrecord, is the name of the variable that will receive the information that will be extracted from the dBASE file. Next comes 0; it specifies that the search will begin with record number 1 (the search always begins with the next record). "CUSTOMER" is the name of the dBASE file to be read. "L" is an arbitrary code that tells Hyperdoc to read the file (there are other options, too). "BOST431" is a string that we want Hyperdoc to look for in the second field as it reads each record. The final 2 at the end of the line is what tells Hyperdoc to compare the target string with the second field.

Another powerful command in Hyperdoc is VIDEO, which you can use to control a videodisc reader. This command works with some special software called MIC (Multimedia Interactive Control) and a special board referred to as a DVA4000, available from Videologic Inc. Using the DVA4000 you can do multitasking—run Quattro in one window, a video clip in another, and ProComm in a third reportedly with no slow down in processing speed. MIC allows for many of the special effects you see on TV: fades, dissolves, repositioning of images and windows, image distortion, frame freezes—all in real time. I presume that you can do all this from Hyperdoc with the VIDEO command, although I haven't tried it. You can pass the VIDEO command different arguments depending on your purpose. A sample command might be:

```
%video, "init;video on;play", &frame;
```

which initializes the videodisc for playing, turns it on and starts play at a specific frame address.

Guide scripts

In Guide, you attach scripts to "command buttons." When you click on a command button, Guide compiles the script into an intermediate machine language, and then interprets it and executes it. (This all happens in one step and the details are hidden from the user.)

Guide's script language is called LOGiiX. LOGiiX is a full-blown programming language—it has more than 160 functions you can use to build rather complex programs. It is complete with:

- Arithmetic and logic operations
- String functions
- Looping constructs (WHILE...DO)
- File input/output

Also, LOGiiX let's you communicate with a user using dialog boxes. Special functions like Answer and Ask are provided for this purpose. In addition, with LOGiiX you can access Guide menu commands and objects in Guide documents. And LOGiiX has support for MS-Windows Dynamic Data Exchange feature (DDE), which allows you to pass data to other programs operating in the Windows environment.

Creating a LOGiiX script   To create a LOGiiX script, you first create a command button (I covered this earlier, but in short, you type a word or phrase that you want to use for the command button. Then you highlight it, go to the Make menu and choose Command Button). After making the button, the next step is to create the definition for it. One way to do this is to:

1. Move the mouse pointer over the button.
2. Hold the Shift key and press and hold the mouse button. A pop-up menu appears.
3. Choose Make Definition from the menu.
4. Enter the text of your LOGiiX program.

To identify a definition as a LOGiiX script, you put #LOGiiX on the first line. This tells Guide to pass the rest of the definition to LOGiiX (a separate .EXE program) for execution. LOGiiX programs are a lot like Pascal programs. For example, they have routines called "functions" and each function must begin with the word "begin" and end with the word "end." Every LOGiiX program must have a function called "main." The basic skeleton for a LOGiiX program is:

```
#LOGiiX
function Main( )
begin
end
```

This skeleton doesn't do anything, but it does contain all of the requirements for a valid LOGiiX program.

Guide comes with a file containing several sample LOGiiX programs. One such program automatically creates a new document, inserts some text into it and then automatically creates a "note button." You can view the script for this program. Here's how:

1. Open the file called LOGiiX.GUI.
2. Move the mouse pointer over the button that says "Note Button and Definition."
3. Hold down the Shift key and press and hold the mouse button. A pop-up menu appears as you can see in Fig. 8-11. Choose Show Definition from the menu.
4. After you choose Show Definition the LOGiiX script will appear as you can see in Fig. 8-12.

The code in Fig. 8-12 is somewhat hard to follow at first, but by referring to the comments in braces and looking up each of the commands in the LOGiiX reference manual, you can see how the program works. The program insets some text into a node using a special function called InsertText. Then the program creates the definition for a pop-up node with a function called MakeNew like this:

```
MakeNew(DefA, 14, "\nGuide files are called Guidelines.\n");
```

Notice that MakeNew takes three arguments. The first argument is the "handle" for the

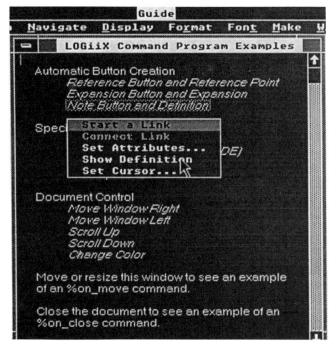

Fig. 8-11 Guide Pop-up menu.

Fig. 8-12 Guide LOGiiX script.

definition window of the current document. In this case, a *handle* is simply an integer that refers to a document or a window of a document. Here DefA is a variable that holds the handle. Previously, DefA was set to the proper handle by another function. The number 14 is an arbitrary code that tells MakeNew to create a definition rather than, say, a button. The string in quotes is what you might type into a definition window if you were creating a pop-up node manually. The \n, you might recognize, is a specification for a new line character.

At this point, the definition is not linked to anything so it is ambiguous. The next command in the program:

```
DoMenu("Start a Link");
```

Automatically selects the Start a Link option from the Definitions window. This starts the process of linking the text in the Definitions window to some buttons in the document.

At the bottom of Fig. 8-12 you can see that the Find command is embedded in a "while" loop so that the entire document is searched for the word "Guideline." Thanks to an IF-statement, each time the program finds the word "Guideline," it executes these two commands:

```
Make(docA,13);
ConnectLink(docA);
```

The Make command in LOGiiX can create a number of different objects: buttons, reference points, expansions, and so on. Whatever text is selected at the time will be converted to an object. If you are wondering about what text is selected, just know that, in this example, the word "Guideline" will be selected whenever the Find command succeeds. Notice that Make takes two arguments. The first argument names the document in question, the second tells what kind of object is to be created. Here, 13 means create a "note button." The variable docA, by the way, is a document handle that was returned earlier by the new command in the first line of the program.

The Make command just makes an object, but it does not link it to anything. The command ConnectLink links the previously defined, but unlinked, button to the previous text that was identified as a definition node by the Start a Link menu option. (If this seems hard to follow, keep in mind that it is easier to understand after you have created and linked a few buttons manually.)

Again, I don't have space here to give you more than just a taste of what you might do with Guide scripting, but I hope you see some possibilities. Now let's look at one more hypertext program that has a built-in language: KnowledgePro. KnowledgePro is especially good for creating expert systems.

KnowledgePro

KnowledgePro has a full-blown language especially designed for creating expert systems with hypertext capability. Its built-in language has about 120 commands. It includes commands for list manipulation, string operations, screen and file input/output, debugging, and logic and arithmetic operation. In addition it has some special functions for returning values from what are called "topics." A *topic* in KnowledgePro is a kind of amorphous object that can behave in different ways. A KnowledgePro topic can:

- Hold commands, like a procedure
- Store values, like a variable
- Return values
- Inherit values
- Be linked into a hypertext network

An interesting feature of KnowledgePro is that when you ask a question of the user in the process of working through a decision tree, you can easily mark certain words or phrases as hypertext buttons. If the user selects the hypertext button, by pressing F4, KnowledgePro will search for a topic with that name. That topic, in turn, can ask other questions and branch off in a different direction. The user however, can backtrack in hypertext fashion by pressing the Spacebar or Esc.

Here's a simple example from an expert system on bidding in contract bridge. It shows the use of the ask command, which automatically throws up a prompt and a menu of options that the user can select from using arrow keys.

```
ask ('Do you have an #mopening hand#m?',hand,[Yes,No]).
topic 'opening hand'.
window( ).
say ('An opening hand should normally
contain at least 12 high card points.').
close_window( ).
end.
```

The phrase opening hand will appear highlighted because it is delimited with #m in the string passed to the ask command. If the user presses F4 with opening hand highlighted, the system will immediately branch to the opening hand topic. Here this topic just presents information, but it could branch off to another series of questions or linked hypertext nodes.

Figure 8-13 shows the code for the beginning of an expert system for helping managers analyze employee performance problems. It's based on some ideas from the book *Analyzing Performance Problems* by Robert Mager and Peter Pipe published by Lake Publications.

NOTE: The code shown is just a sample. A full-blown program, which the authors call "smart system" rather than an "expert system" is also available from Lake Publications.

In Fig. 8-13 notice how I used the #m delimiter to mark certain words as hypertext buttons. Before answering a question posed by the expert system, the user can press F4 to branch off to an explanatory node. When the user presses F4, the system searches for a topic whose argument matches the selected word or phrase.

Figure 8-14 shows one of the screens generated by the code in Fig. 8-13. Notice how the word punishment is highlighted in this figure showing that it is a hypertext button. When the user presses F4, the system jumps to the screen shown in Fig. 8-15. When the user presses the Spacebar or Esc, the system retraces its steps and the screen in Fig. 8-14 reappears.

```
(* File name: ANALYZE.KB                                    *)
(* This is the start of an expert system to help managers    *)
(* analyze employee performance problems.  It is not a complete *)
(* program--just the start of one.  It is presented to        *)
(* show how hypertext can be used to clarify terms.          *)
(* The idea for this expert system comes from the book       *)
(* "Analyzing Performance Problems" by Mager and Pipe,       *)
(* published by David Lake. A complete expert system is      *)
(* available from David Lake.                                *)

ask ('#nIs this problem due to the employee''s #mlack of ability#m?',
lackskill,['Yes--employee lacks ability',
'No--employee has ability']).
do (?lackskill).

    topic 'Yes--employee lacks ability'.
    ask ('#nCould the employee perform OK in the past?',
    pastok, [Yes,No]).
    do (?pastok).

        topic 'Yes'.
        say('Performed OK in past.').
        (* More question would appear here *)
        end.
        topic 'No'.
        say('Never performed OK previously').
        (* More questions would appear here *)
        end.
    end. (* employee lacks ability *)


    topic 'No--employee has ability'.
    ask('#nDoes the desired performance lead to #mpunishment#m?',
    punish,['Yes','No']).
    do (?punish).
        topic 'Yes'.
        say('#n#n  Performance leads to punishment.#n#n',
        '  Once you realize this is the case, the solution is clear:',
        '#n  Find a way to remove the unpleasant consequences to',
        '  desirable performance--on the flip side, look for ways',
        '  to help the employee feel good about doing well.').
        end.

        topic 'No'.
        say('Performance is not punishing.').
        (* More questions would be inserted here *)
        end.
    end. (* employee has ability*)



    (* Follow topics are hypertext nodes for clarifying *)
    (* meaning of key terms used in questions *)
    topic 'lack of ability'.
    say('#n#n  To decide whether the employee really lacks the',
    '  ability to perform as desired, ask yourself:#n#n',
    '    - Could the employee do it in a life and death situation?',
    '    - Are the employee''s present skills enough?').
    end.
```

Fig. 8-13 Beginning of expert system for managers.

```
topic 'punishment'.
say('#n#n  By punishment, here, we do not necessarily mean formal',
' punishment such as a reprimand, fine or penalty.  To decide',
' whether the performance is punishing, ask yourself:#n',
'     - Is the job boring, or unpleasant?',
'     - Are there undesirable consequences to good performance?',
'     - Does the employee associate performance with either physical',
'       or emotional pain?').
```

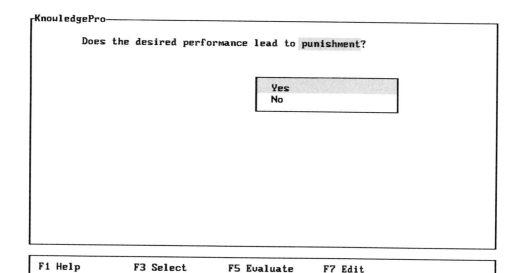

Fig. 8-14 Hypertext button "punishment."

ToolBook

A late arrival in the PC hypertext world is ToolBook—that's why I haven't discussed it much in previous chapters. ToolBook is a HyperCard-like development system for Windows 3.0. ToolBook has a powerful scripting language called OpenScript. OpenScript appears to hold the record for the most developed language—it has about 180 different command words. OpenScript is complete with If statements, DO/UNTIL, and many special effects commands like, say, fsDissolve, which causes the current node to dissolve to black, gray, white or another page. Here is an example from the OpenScript manual. Notice that it uses DO/UNTIL and If statements.

```
to get otherDistrictTotal
    local OtherDistricts, NumberOfDistricts
    set OtherDistricts to 0
    set NumberofDistricts to the pageCount of this book
--Perform the loop for each district
Do
        if text of field "ZipCode" contains 98001
```

```
              increment OtherDistricts--adds 1 to OtherDistricts
          end if
          go to the next page
          decrement NumberOfDistricts
      until NumberOfDistricts = 0
      return OtherDistricts
  end otherDistrictTotal
```

By the way, the ToolBook documentation is excellent—the best I've seen! It appears to draw on the Information Mapping techniques I've discussed earlier. These techniques improve readability and make it easy to find information quickly.

Plus

Another HyperCard-like product for PCs with a scripting language is Plus. Although I haven't seen it, others have reported that Plus will be useful if you want to make Hyper-Card stacks with heavy scripting (hypertext networks) available on PCs. If you're planning to do this, I recommend you consider ToolBook as well. Programs that automatically translate HyperCard scripts are reportedly being developed and will probably be available by the time you read this.

As you can see from the various examples I've presented, hypertext scripts can add substantial power to a hypertext authoring system. I'd like to caution you, though, that once you get into scripting you are investing a lot of time and effort. The results can be gratifying but you must consider whether that is the kind of investment you want to make. Let's turn now to another approach that does not require scripting. This approach allows you to develop hypertext systems that can reside with other DOS programs on the PC.

Setting up memory-resident hypertext systems

Hypertext is especially suited for help systems. As you've seen, several programs such as Lotus 1-2-3, Quattro Pro, and Turbo C already come with built-in hypertext help. But often companies are so busy developing their products that they don't have enough time or energy to develop thorough and easy-to-use on-line help. Also, sometimes the help that is needed may be very specific to the procedures that have developed in a specific company. That's why it is useful to be able to develop memory-resident customized hypertext help—help that people can access immediately without having to shut down the program they are currently working on. There are now several good memory resident hypertext development systems. I've already discussed one of them, HyperRez, in chapter 7. Here I'll discuss three more:

- PC-Browse
- xText
- HyperTSR

PC-Browse

PC-Browse is a shareware program developed by Steven Levy of Quicksoft, Inc., the company that developed the popular and powerful PC-Write, a shareware word processor.

Steven is an interesting guy who has been programming off and on since the late 1960s. During his off times, he was Artistic Director of an Off-Off-Broadway theater. He also played in several rock-and-roll bands. While programming he developed educational programs as well as computer-based training materials for retail stores and AI think tanks.

Using PC-Browse you can build hypertext help systems with little, if any, programming; although some definite setup work is required. In addition to some simple hypertext features, PC-Browse lets you do strings searches. You can also "grab" text from a file and paste it into your foreground application program. Let's look at the hypertext features and see how to implement them.

Reference buttons PC-Browse let's you create reference buttons, buttons that allow you to jump to a reference point in the same or different file. PC-Browse is like PC-Write in that it is highly customizable. Unlike most hypertext systems, PC-Browse allows you to decide how you are going to identify buttons and distinguish them from ordinary words in a text file. There are several other items you can customize: what colors to use, if any; how many lines to use in your display; and which kinds of files to search. There are other parameters you can set as well. This power comes at a price, though. You have to spend extra time figuring out how to create simple hypertext buttons. But once you've learned how, it's relatively easy. Here, I'll focus on showing you how to tell PC-Browse what hypertext buttons look like.

In PC-Browse, a hypertext button is called a *trigger*. When you pull the trigger, so to speak, the hypertext jump is activated. There are different kinds of triggers. The simplest and easiest to use is a *linear search trigger*. To define a trigger you delimit a word or phrase with some special characters. You have to tell PC-Browse what those characters are. You can do this in four different ways:

- You can put the information in a special control file called BR.DEF.
- You can define a DOS environment variable called BR.
- You can put the information on the command line when you start PC-Browse.
- You can put the information on the first line in any text file by inserting the command [BR =].

The most direct and reliable method is to put the delimiter information directly in the file you plan to use as a hypertext look-up file. To specify what characters you will use to delimit the linear search trigger, you first write [BR = , then a forward slash, a capital J, the ASCII code for the opening delimiter, a colon, and then the ASCII code for the closing delimiter. Then you close the whole thing with "]". For example, to specify that you will use " < " as the opening delimiter and " > " as the closing delimiter, you could start by writing:

[BR = /J:60.62

Notice that the closing bracket is missing. That's because I'm not done yet. Hold on. I'll get to that in a moment. First let me explain the J. The J, here, is arbitrary. You might remember it by thinking of the "J" in the phrase "hypertext Jump." The 60 is the ASCII code for " < ". The 62 is the ASCII code for " > ".

To complete the specification, you also need to tell PC-Browse what delimiters will mark the destination of the hypertext jump. To do this, you start with "/I" and follow the

```
┌─KnowledgePro────────────────────────────────────────────────────┐
│                                                                  │
│  By punishment, here, we do not necessarily mean formal          │
│  punishment such as a reprimand, fine or penalty.  To decide     │
│  whether the performance is punishing, ask yourself:             │
│                                                                  │
│    - Is the job boring, or unpleasant?                           │
│    - Are there undesirable consequences to good performance?     │
│    - Does the employee associate performance with either physical│
│      or emotional pain?                                          │
│                                                                  │
│                                                                  │
│                                                                  │
│                                                                  │
│                                                                  │
│                                                                  │
│                                                                  │
│                                                                  │
└──────────────────────────────────────────────────────────────────┘
┌──────────────────────────────────────────────────────────────────┐
│  F1 Help                    F5 Evaluate     F7 Edit    Pg 1 of 1   │
│  Space Cont.                F6 Display KB    F8 DOS     F10 Quit    │
└──────────────────────────────────────────────────────────────────┘
```

Fig. 8-15   Destination node for jump from "punishment."

same pattern. For example, to specify that an asterisk is the delimiter for the destination text, you might finish off the control statement like this:

[BR = /J:60.62/I:42.42]

Again, the /I is apparently just an arbitrary code that programmer Steven Levy picked out of a hat. In any case, the /I always means that what follows after the colon is the ASCII code for a the first "linear search target" delimiter. The 42 is the ASCII code for "*". Notice that in the example 42 appears twice. That's because this line specifies that an asterisk is to be used for both the opening and closing delimiter. The complete specification in the BR.DEF file, then, might look like this:

/J:60.62/I:42.42

As I mentioned earlier, you can also specify the delimiters you want to use on the command line when you first start up PC-Browse. A good way to do this is in a batch file so that you can just give a command like, say, BROWSE without having to remember the setup details. When you start PC-Browse in this way, you can also specify a file that you want PC-Browse to read. For example, because I provide job referral information to a local professional society, I set up PC-Browse so it can read a job information file. This way, I can easily pop up the job information even if I am running another program. To make it easy to start PC-Browse, I made a batch file called BROWSE.BAT and put this command line in it:

BR c:\nspi\nspirep.txt /C /J:60.62/I:42.42

Here, BR is the DOS command to launch PC-Browse. The rest is the DOS command line tail. The first argument, c:\nspi\nspirept.txt, is the file to be loaded by PC-Browse. The /C tells PC-Browse that I am using a color monitor. The J:60.62 specifies that " < " will be used for the opening trigger delimiter and that " > " will be the closing trigger delimiter. The /I:42.42 tells PC-Browse that * is the delimiter for the "target string."

Figure 8-16 shows PC-Browse (in the lower part of the screen) popping up over HyperSprint. The top part of the screen is a control file in HyperSprint, which I discussed earlier. The bottom part of the screen is a PC-Browse window.

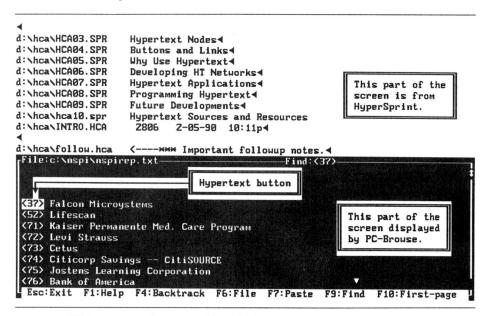

Fig. 8-16   PC-Browse popping up over HyperSprint.

In Fig. 8-16 I have annotated the hypertext buttons, or triggers as they are called in the PC-Browse documentation. Here, I am using numbers for hypertext buttons. These numbers correspond to record numbers in a traditional dBASE file. I like to use dBASE to initially enter the data because it provides a structure that helps to ensure that I don't forget to gather key information. Also, using dBASE I can easily generate various kinds of reports with the information arranged in different ways. However, for quick access of single records, I like to use hypertext because it's faster and more convenient. I don't try to access the dBASE file directly with PC-Browse. Instead, I use dBASE to prepare a report which I dump to an ASCII file. Notice in Fig. 8-16 that <37> is highlighted. You can move the highlight bar in PC-Browse by pressing the Tab key or the Arrow keys. When you move the highlight, it jumps to the next available hypertext button. You don't have to drag the cursor slowly through the text. In this example, when I press Return or the gray plus key, PC-Browse does a linear text search for *37* in the same file. Because the file is relatively small, the hypertext jump is nearly instantaneous. Even in large files, the jump is fast! Figure 8-17 shows the node that I jumped to, when I pressed Return with the highlight on <37>.

Notice that PC-Browse offers a brief status line menu at the bottom of its window. As you can see, F4 is the key that you use to backtrack to the previous node. If you press F10, you jump to the beginning of the file. If you press Esc, you instantly exit PC-Browse and

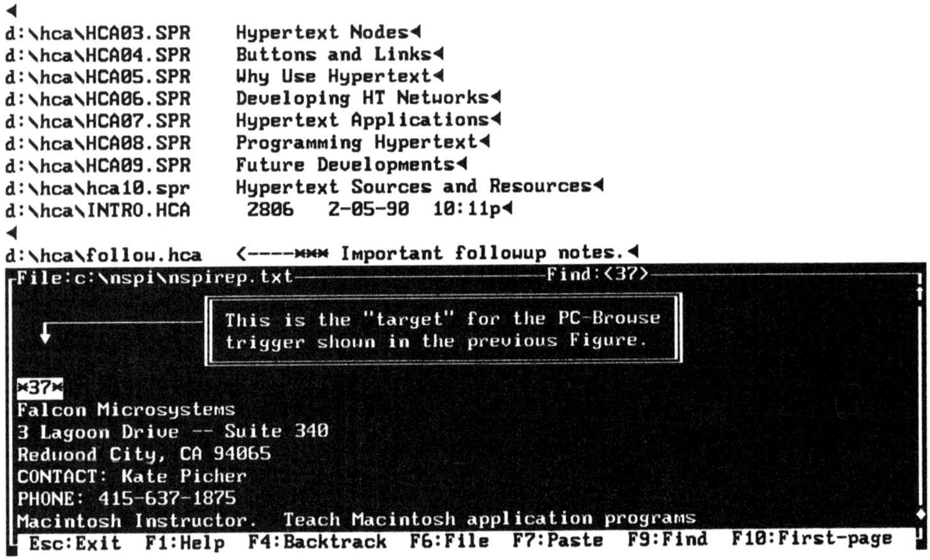

```
◄
d:\hca\HCA03.SPR    Hypertext Nodes◄
d:\hca\HCA04.SPR    Buttons and Links◄
d:\hca\HCA05.SPR    Why Use Hypertext◄
d:\hca\HCA06.SPR    Developing HT Networks◄
d:\hca\HCA07.SPR    Hypertext Applications◄
d:\hca\HCA08.SPR    Programming Hypertext◄
d:\hca\HCA09.SPR    Future Developments◄
d:\hca\hca10.spr    Hypertext Sources and Resources◄
d:\hca\INTRO.HCA      2806   2-05-90  10:11p◄
◄
d:\hca\follow.hca   <----*** Important followup notes.◄
┌File:c:\nspi\nspirep.txt─────────────────────Find:<37>─────────┐
│                      ┌─────────────────────────────────────┐  │
│          ↓           │ This is the "target" for the PC-Browse│  │
│                      │ trigger shown in the previous Figure. │  │
│                      └─────────────────────────────────────┘  │
│                                                                │
│*37*                                                            │
│Falcon Microsystems                                             │
│3 Lagoon Drive -- Suite 340                                     │
│Redwood City, CA 94065                                          │
│CONTACT: Kate Picher                                            │
│PHONE: 415-637-1875                                             │
│Macintosh Instructor.  Teach Macintosh application programs     │
│ Esc:Exit  F1:Help  F4:Backtrack  F6:File  F7:Paste  F9:Find  F10:First-page│
└────────────────────────────────────────────────────────────────┘
```

Fig. 8-17 Destination node in PC-Browse.

pop back to your foreground program. F7 is the paste key, which you can use to capture information in the PC-Browse window and paste it into your foreground program.

Ensuring hypertext capability In my work with PC-Browse, when I start it from a batch file, everything works fine. But then if I switch to a different file using the F8 function key and then return to the file that I first loaded, the hypertext functionality is gone. To solve this problem, it seems that the best solution is to include the hypertext button specifications directly in the hypertext file. Each time PC-Browse loads a file it looks in that file for any special customization parameters. By putting a line such as [BR = /J:60.62/ l:42.42] at the top of the file, you can ensure that the hypertext buttons appear highlighted as expected.

NOTE: In the rest of this discussion, I assume you have previously defined " < " and " > " as the delimiters for linear search triggers and "*" as the character for marking the target string. I also assume you have defined the asterisk as the delimiter to use for marking a destination point or target string.

Jumping to other files PC-Browse also lets you make hypertext jumps to specific destinations in other files. To create a hypertext button that makes PC-Browse jump into another file, just enclose the file name in square brackets after trigger text. For example, to create a jump to *Kumiko* in the \ empower \ phone.tic file, you might write a button like this:

    < Kumiko > [\ empower \ phone.tic]

Although this works well, such a button might be somewhat hard to read because of the inclusion of the file name and subdirectory path. This is not a problem, however, because you can ask PC-Browse to hide the file name. To do this, just put a question mark in front of the file name immediately after the left square bracket, like this:

    < Kumiko > [? \ empower \ phone.tic]

If you write the button like this, the user will see only:

    < Kumiko >

< Kumiko > will appear to be boldfaced or in a different color if you are using a color monitor and you have included the /C switch on the control line. When the user selects the < Kumiko > button, it will be highlighted in inverse video.

If you don't like the angle brackets, you can get rid of them, too. To do this, you need to use different delimiters for your linear search keyword delimiter. One method is to use ASCII code 22 to delimit your hypertext buttons. PC-Browse doesn't display this code. If you use this approach you might want to include a control line like this at the beginning of the file:

    [BR = /I42.42 /J22.22]

You can put this line at column 90 or so on the first line; that way, the user won't see it when PC-Browse displays the file. I hope this gives you a good feel for the capabilities of PC-Browse. It has several other capabilities besides those I've just discussed. You can leave bookmarks in files, run external programs, pop-up extra windows, and more. Although it is a shareware program, it is a solid product and you get a nicely bound, detailed manual when you register.

You might be wondering if you could develop and market your own hypertext applications using PC-Browse. The answer is yes, but there are some qualifications. I'll discuss those qualifications shortly. (See "Distributing Your Own Hypertext Applications" in this chapter.)

Now, let's move on to another excellent product, xText.

xText

The xText Toolkit is a PC system produced by Flambeaux Software that lets you develop and distribute your own hypertext help systems. The help can be accessed from DOS in the usual way or a user can pop up the help while using some other application program. You can also attach the help to a specific program so that when the user exits the program, memory-resident help is also removed from memory.

To author a hypertext document with xText, you first prepare a source file, which you later process with the xText compiler, XTC. The xText compiler compresses the text and links the various hypertext nodes together into a hypertext network.

A separate program, HELP.EXE, referred to as the Help! Engine actually displays the help file after it has been compiled by xText. To prepare a source file, you can use any editor or word processor that can create a standard DOS file. In addition, you can use the output from certain word processors, such as WordPerfect. (More on that later.) Typically, things won't go perfectly the first time. If you've ever written a compiled program, you know what I mean. The compiler will flag various syntax errors, which you will have to fix before you can use your hypertext network.

Creating a source file   When you create a source file for xText, you break it up into separate nodes called *pages*. In this process you specify that certain keywords are hypertext buttons by surrounding them with tildes (~). To mark the word subdirectory as a button or "hyperword" you would write it like this in an xText source file:

subdirectory

I might add, here, that xText offers another more convenient method for specifying hypertext words, which I'll discuss shortly.

The xText program recognizes "dot commands" reminiscent of WordStar. For example, to specify that you want a new page, you start a new line with a period followed by a capital P, followed by a page name. To start a new page called "Subdirectories," you would write:

.P Subdirectories

Every xText source file must have at least three pages. It's easier to explain the structure of an xText file if I first show you a simple example. See Fig. 8-18. In Fig. 8-18 notice that the file starts with .N. A line that starts with .N gives a name to the document. You can have multiple compiled help files in the same directory. If you press F4 while the Help! Engine is active, you will be presented with a menu of document names. Notice that the document name can be different from the name of the compiled help file.

The .N line need not be at the start of the file but that is a good place for it. The line that starts with the .P logo marks the beginning of the logo page. This is a page that normally appears only when the user first invokes the program. (You can change this.) The logo page is a good place to put any copyright notice or other message that you want to appear only once on start-up. If you want to use the default setup, you need to put your copyright notice at exactly lines 19 and 20. That's because, by default, the Help! Engine will draw a box around these screen lines. The box will be animated, like a neon sign. It's a nice effect, but you have to put your copy exactly on lines 19 or 20 or you'll have an empty neon box sitting above the Flambeux Software copyright notice. That's the reason for all of the blank lines at the top of Fig. 8-18.

The next dot command in the example is .C. This command simply marks a line as a comment. Comment lines are ignored by the compiler—they are just there for the benefit of someone reading the source file.

The second "page" in Fig. 8-18 is an Auto-Lookup Page. This page is required in all xText source files, although it might be blank. On this page you list all the topics that you want a user to be able to look up from the DOS command line. For example, because directory is listed as a topic on the Auto-Lookup Page, the user could get to the "Directory" page from DOS by entering the command:

help directory

I've called the third page in this sample source file the "Main Menu." You can call this third page anything you like; you don't have to name it "Main Menu." This third page is actually the first page that the user will see after the logo page appears. The user can also access the Main Menu page at any time by pressing F2.

At the end of the source file notice that there are lines starting with ".A." A line that

.N DOS
.P logo

Greetings and welcome to HyperDOS Help

Copyright 1990 Seyer Associates

.C --- .P Auto-Lookup Page
    ~directory~
.C --- .P Main Menu
  ~Files~
  ~Subdirectories~
  ~Programs~

  ~Exit Help~

  Move cursor to selection and press RETURN to select.
  When finished, select Exit Help.
.C--- .P Files
There are two basic kinds of files: program files and data files...etc.
Files may be stored and protected in ~directories~. .C---
.P Subdirectories
A subdirectory is a place on the disk where ~files~ may be stored.
.C--- .P Programs
A program is a series of instruction to the computer which may be stored in a ~file~.
.C--- .A ~File~ Files
.A ~directory~ Subdirectories
.A ~directories~ Subdirectories
.A ~Exit Help~ __EXIT

Fig. 8-18 Simple xText source file.

starts with ".A" is an "alias line." This means that it specifies an alternate name and links
that name to a standard page name. For example the line:

    .A directory Subdirectory

specifies that directory is an alias for subdirectory. This means that directory can serve as a hypertext button that takes the user to the subdirectory page.

xText has other dot commands, but those are the basic ones. Figure 8-19 shows the Logo Page that appeared when I ran my sample xText help system. Notice that my copyright notice appears in a box at the bottom of the screen. What you can't see in the illustration is that the box is "magically" animated. When the user presses any key, the "Main Menu" page pops up instantly with the first hypertext button already highlighted.

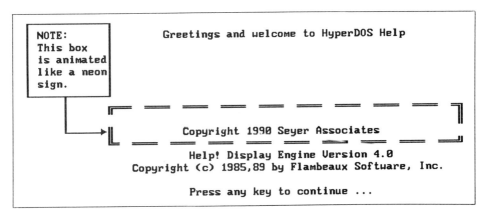

Fig. 8-19 xText logo page.

Notice that the tildes, which were used to delimit the hyperwords in the source file do not show up when the compiled file is displayed. To select the directories button I just move the highlight down to it by pressing the Down arrow key and the Return key. When I activated the directories button the Help! Engine displayed the subdirectory page. Again, this worked because directory was declared as an alias for subdirectory with an .A command.

When I first compiled this example, it didn't compile correctly because I had made some syntax errors. For example, earlier, I had referred to a page called "Erase" on the Auto-Lookup page, but I had not defined such a page. To see an explanation of any errors, you need to include /V on the DOS command line when you give the XTC command. I redirected the output to another file called NOTES, so I could read the "verbose error listing" as it is called. Here is the command line I used:

```
XTC /V DOSHELP > NOTES
```

Using a word processor xText also lets you prepare source files with certain word processors, such as WordPerfect and Microsoft Word. The advantage of using a word processor is that it is easier to format your text and you don't need to fool with tilde symbols to delimit hypertext buttons. Instead, you just boldface such words; each boldfaced word then becomes a hypertext button. Another advantage to using a word processor is that you can insert certain special characters that are not usually provided with an ASCII editor. Also, with a word processor you can use its line drawing, spell-checking, and so on. To use a word processor, though, you have to follow a different procedure.

The basic steps for using, say, WordPerfect are:

1. Install a special WordPerfect printer driver (that comes with xText). Make this printer driver "the current printer."
2. Create your document in the word processor's normal document mode.
3. Print your document to a file. In WordPerfect, to do this you need to set the output port of the printer to a file name. In WordPerfect 5.0 the keystrokes for this are:

    Shift-F7 SEPfilename <Enter>

    where filename is the name of a file you want to create.
4. Exit to DOS and process the file that you created in step 2, using the XTC program. For example, if you created a file called DOSHELP.PRN, you could issue the command:

    XTC DOSHELP.PRN MANUAL.H! /T

Here, XTC is the name of the xText compiler program. DOSHELP.PRN is the name of the file created by WordPerfect. MANUAL.H! is the final output file, which can be read and displayed by the Help! Engine.

Launching the Help! Engine   The Help! Engine is quite flexible. You can start it from DOS as a primary foreground application program, or you can install it as a memory-resident program and then activate it with a hotkey even though you are running another application program. To install help! as a memory-resident program, you just add /X to the command line. For example, you start it like this:

help /X

By default the Help! Engine will immediately load the first compiled help file that it finds in the current subdirectory. You can specify that you want a specific on-line help "manual" loaded by adding /M = filename.h! to the command line, where filename.h! is the actual name of the file containing your compiled hypertext network. For example to load a hypertext network stored in a file called baseball.h! and make the whole thing memory resident, you would start the Help! Engine like this:

help /X /M = baseball.!h

If you start help with the /X option, then you can remove it from memory by entering EXIT at the DOS command line.

Once you install help as a memory-resident program, you can pop it up with either Alt-L or Alt-H. If you use Alt-L to pop up help, it will immediately start to look for a page name or alias that corresponds to the word that the cursor was on (or to its right). The beauty of this is that each word in your foreground application can serve as a hypertext button! However, this approach doesn't work with all applications. Some applications don't use the BIOS cursor, whose location is checked by Help!

There is yet another way to launch Help! Although this method is rather involved, it involves setting CPU registers and executing an Interrupt, it does give you a lot of control. You can specify exactly when, where, and what to pop up over the foreground program. You can find the details on this method in the xText manual under the heading "The INT 2Fh Interface Technique."

Like PC-Browse, xText is quite flexible and customizable. For example, you can include an .O (set Options) command in a source file and control such things as whether:

- the "neon box" appears on the Logo Page.
- colored text and backgrounds will appear.
- your credit lines will be seen when the user presses F8.

One problem is that the syntax for using the .O option is rather difficult. You have to understand binary notation and how to turn specific bits on and off. Flambeaux reports, however, that this dot command might be simplified in a future release.

Besides the .O command, which you embed directly in a source file, you can also customize your hypertext system somewhat by using command line switches. You've already seen how you can use /M to specify exactly which compiled hypertext network you want to use on start-up. Some other option switches include:

Switch	Description
/K	Lets you specify the hotkey that will pop up the system.
/Q	Suppresses the display of the Logo Page on start-up.
/Qn	Allows you to specify whether you want a half or full window screen and whether it should be positioned at the top or bottom of the screen. You set n to either 0, 1, or 2. A 0 specifies a full window; 1 specifies a half window at the top of the screen; and 2 specifies a half window at the bottom of the screen.

I discussed the /X option earlier as a way of making the HELP.EXE program memory resident. You can also use it in another way to simultaneously start a separate application program and load your help system. For example, if you give this command:

```
help /X = wp
```

you will start up WordPerfect and make the HELP.EXE program memory resident. When you exit from WordPerfect, HELP.EXE will also be unloaded from memory.

You've now seen at two ways to create memory-resident hypertext systems: PC-Browse and xText. Now, let's look at a third: HyperTSR.

HyperTSR

The TSR in HyperTSR stands for "terminate and stay resident." The HyperTSR system is rather unique because nodes can be associated with multiple keywords, by putting the keywords between angle brackets, like this:

```
<
bold
boldface
bold face
font
>
```

The " < " indicates that a series of keywords will follow. Notice that each keyword is on a line by itself. When listing a series of keywords to be linked to the node, be sure to use lowercase letters, because HyperTSR converts all buttons to lowercase before doing a hypertext jump.

It is not necessary to combine the file that holds the network of nodes. As soon as a hypertext file is created, it is ready to be displayed by HyperTSR—the only requirement is that the hypertext file must be named HELP.EMP and be in the same subdirectory as the HyperTSR.EXE file. When you first invoke HyperTSR, it reads the entire help file and builds an index table that shows the location of each of the nodes in the file. (Note that in this system, one huge file holds all of the nodes in the network.)

Highlighting words on screen   To show which words you want to be hypertext buttons, you delimit them with vertical bars. For example, the word "boldface" would be highlighted in the following sentence:

It is easy to |boldface| words.

In highlighting keywords, the program reads a line and then checks that line for a "|". If the program doesn't find a "|", it just displays the line. If it finds a single "|", it continues to search the line and builds a data structure that contains all the positions in the line that contain "|". The program then uses this information to highlight the keywords on that line. As well as highlighting the appropriate words, the program also stores the row and column number of each highlighted word. The program uses this information to enable it to jump to the next hypertext button when an arrow key is pressed.

When the user selects a hypertext button, the system jumps to the appropriate node. The user can then automatically backtrack by pressing the PgUp key. After packing up several nodes in the current path, the user can then go forward again by pressing the PgDn key.

Designating the Menu node   The Menu node is the one that first appears when you press a hotkey to invoke HyperTSR. You identify the Menu node with the keyword @menu@, like this:

```
<
@menu@
>
```

Figure 8-20 shows the Menu node that pops up when a user activates HyperTSR with a WordPerfect hypertext help file installed. Notice how one of the hypertext buttons has been selected.

Figure 8-21 shows the node that appears when this button is activated. Notice that the HyperTSR node appears as a small window popping up over the WordPerfect screen.

A useful feature of HyperTSR is that you can bypass the usual hypertext search procedure and directly enter a keyword to search for. To do this, you press F10 and choose Topic Search from the menu that appears. Then at the prompt, you enter the keyword or phrase. The system will immediately jump to the first node it finds that has a key that matches the topic you have entered. If the system finds a node, but not the one you wanted, you can press N to go to the next node linked to that key. Because you can easily link any number of keys to a node, searching for a node in this way can be highly effective.

Once you reach the desired node, you can still explore the hypertext network by selecting any hypertext links embedded in that node.

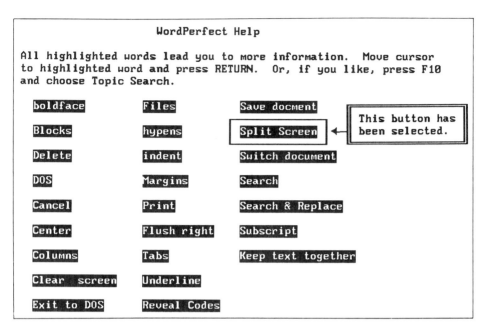

Fig. 8-20 HyperTSR displaying WordPerfect Help.

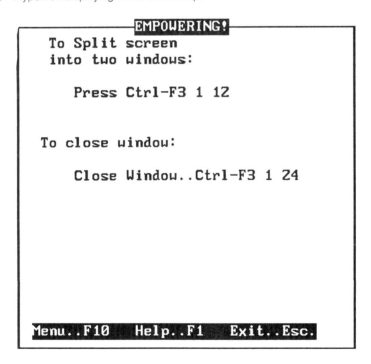

Doc 1 Pg 1 Ln 1i Pos 1i

Fig. 8-21 HyperTSR destination node.

There you have it—a description of three PC systems that let you build memory-resident hypertext networks. But wait, there's more. Exwells Software in Berkeley California offers an on-line Information Manager called Xhelp. Xhelp is extremely fast and uses little memory. For more details you might want to see the discussion about it in chapter 10.

Distributing your own hypertext systems

All of the programs I have discussed allow you to distribute your own help systems. In each case, you must distribute some kind of hypertext "engine" that allows the user to browse your hypertext files. The policy of each company varies.

PC-Browse If you want to distribute PC-Browse along with your own hypertext files, you need to contact QuickSoft and work out a payment method. You can either pay a reasonable flat fee based on the number of copies you think you will distribute, or you can work out a royalty schedule and pay as you go. (You can distribute PC-Browse freely in the United States as long as you do not distribute it with any of your own hypertext files.)

xText You can distribute unlimited copies of the Help! Engine from Flambeaux Software at no charge as long as you always distribute along with it some hypertext network file that you have created with XTC, the xText compiler. You cannot, however, distribute XTC, the xText compiler.

HyperTSR You can distribute unlimited copies of HyperTSR available from Seyer Associates as long as you distribute along with it a hypertext help file that you have designed to be used with it. Users could conceivably use the program to create their own networks as well as use the ones they've created.

HyperWriter You can distribute unlimited copies of the HyperWriter run-time program free of charge. (Nice policy, don't you think?) This engine allows users to annotate nodes by putting comments in pop-up nodes. User's can't create their own networks.

Hyperdoc There is a fee for each hypertext network that you distribute. One price quoted to me was $90 per shot. For the latest price information I suggest you contact Hyperdoc Inc. (See chapter 10.)

LinkWay Amazingly enough, IBM allows you to distribute unlimited copies of a run-time program at no charge. Users can annotate the network (if you have programmed it that way), but they can't generate original networks.

For information about how to contact QuickSoft or Flambeaux Software see chapter 10. To contact Seyer Associates about HyperTSR, see the order card in this book.

Developing original hypertext applications

The languages I have found useful for programming original hypertext applications include C, Turbo Prolog, and Sprint's macro programming language. HyperTSR was developed in C, EMPOWERment in Turbo Prolog and HyperSprint in Sprint's macro programming language.

Turbo Prolog

Turbo Prolog, available from Borland International, is especially good for developing hypertext applications because it has a full-featured editor built into the language. Also an enhanced version of Turbo Prolog with even more features suitable for hypertext development is available under the name PDC Prolog from the Prolog Development Center.

To edit a string of characters in memory with Turbo Prolog or PDC Prolog, you need only issue a call like this:

```
edit(InputString,OutputString)
```

The InputString variable holds a string (of characters) that you want to edit. This command (called a predicate in prolog) immediately puts the users into a powerful editor. When the user exits the editor, by pressing F10, the OutputString will contain the text that the user created while in the editor.

The InputString can be taken from a file that you have read from the disk. To read a file from the disk, you just use the file_str predicate.

```
file_str(DosFileName,FileString)
```

In using this predicate you set DosFileName to the name of the file you want to read. When the predicate finishes, the variable FileString will contain the contents of the disk file.

To enable a hypertext system with prolog, you can use a more advanced edit command, which has many arguments. You might call the advanced edit predicate like this:

```
edit(InputString,OutputString,Heading,SaveName,Msg,Pos,
Helpfilename,EditMode,Indent,Insert,TextMode,RetPos,RetStatus)
```

All these arguments give you a lot of flexibility in using the built-in Turbo Prolog editor. The Heading argument lets you specify a heading at the top of the screen. SaveName specifies the name the file will be saved under when the user presses F2. Msg lets you put a temporary message at the bottom of the screen. (This message goes away as soon as the user presses a key.)

Pos specifies the exact byte location in the file where you want the cursor positioned. This is important for hypertext applications because you can easily instruct the editor to jump to a specific location in a file. Helpfilename specifies the help file that will pop up if the user presses F1 and selects the Show Help File option. Using this feature you could write a program that would recognize hypertext buttons with help specifications. That is, a button could not only specify the node that would be accessed, but also a related help file. The user could access the help file by pressing a help key, such as Shift-F1. For example the hypertext button might look like this:

```
< shipping /h ship.hlp >
```

This might specify a link to a file called SHIPPING along with a help file called SHIP.HLP. The /h in this example might specify that the following item is the name of a help file.

NOTE: This is not the exact Turbo Prolog code you would write to parse the hypertext button and execute the appropriate call to the edit predicate. I am just suggesting the possibility.

EditMode, another argument to the edit predicate, lets you specify whether the user can actually edit InputString or just browse through it. In some cases you might not want users to be able to modify a node. Especially if you are developing a help system. Indent tells whether you want the automatic indentation feature on or off. Insert sets the editor to either insert or overwrite mode. Textmode tells whether automatic word wrapping will occur. When creating programs or files for sending via telecommunications, it is better to make the user press Return at the end of every line to ensure that a pure ASCII file is created.

RetPos is an important argument of the edit predicate. It tells exactly where the cursor was in the file when the user exited from the editor. With this knowledge, you can determine which word or phrase the user was pointing to with the cursor. Once a program knows this, it can parse the string (analyze it structurally) and then decide what it should do next—jump to another part of the current file, dial a phone number, execute a program, or perhaps jump into an external file.

The RetStatus argument shows which key the user pressed to end the editing session. If RetStatus equals zero, the user pressed F10. If RetStatus equals 1, the user pressed Esc.

Prolog is especially well-suited to parsing (analyzing and categorizing) text strings. Also, Prolog stores data as knowledge rather than as isolated bits of information. That is, along with each piece of information that you store in a Prolog knowledge base, you can easily store "typing" information. For example, if you peek into a dBASE file you might see a string of numbers, but unless you have knowledge of the structure of the database, you might not know what the numbers represent. In a classical Prolog knowledge base, however, what the data represents is stored directly with the data.

```
personaldata(Name("Maria Hashim ",age(24), married("yes")).
```

Notice that you can easily read this data without having to refer to any structural definition of the data.

This makes it easy to store information that a program can use to activate a hypertext button. For example suppose you want the program to jump into a file called CURPROJ .MAN if the user exits the editor with the cursor on <Current Projects>. To accomplish this, you can put this fact into our Turbo Prolog knowledge base:

```
reps("Current Projects","curproj.man").
```

In English this means "Current Projects" represents the file name CURPROJ.MAN. If a variable called String is set to "Current Projects," it's easy for us to get the name of the file to go to. You just make this statement in Prolog:

```
reps(String,FileName).
set to "Current Projects"
```

In making this statement, String is an input argument because it has already been set to "Current Projects". But FileName is an output argument—initially it is not bound—that is, it is not set to any value.

When you make this simple declarative statement, Prolog checks to make sure that it is true. That is, it automatically searches the knowledge base to see if it is true that there is a button fact such that the first argument is "Current Projects." When it finds the fact, it binds FileName to "curproj.man." You can then pass that file name to the edit predicate and presto, you can view and edit the hypertext file.

A complete hypertext editor   Figure 8-22 shows the complete source code for a hypertext editor written in Turbo Prolog. It illustrates what I have just discussed.

```
/*******************************************************************
```

HE.PRO (Hypertext Editor)

```
USE:   Demonstrate how you can create a hypertext editor
       with Turbo Prolog in just a few lines of code.

              Copyright 1989 Philip C. Seyer
```

Commented Out Code

```
At the beginning of the program, there is a line that is
commented out. This line retracts a fact that may be left over
from a previous run of the program. This is only for convenience
when testing the program within the Turbo Prolog Environment.
When you start the program from DOS there will be no such fact in
memory.
```

How Program Begins

```
The program begins by loading an external knowledge base into
memory. Borland's documentation refers to it as a database.

The statement needed in this program to load an external
knowledge base is:

      consult("buttons.kba" - external)

The knowledge base is contained within a file called
"buttons.kba". This file might contains facts such as:

      reps("<Telephone list>","phone.lst")
      reps("<Autoexec.bat file>","\\autoexec.bat")
      reps("<Important Projects>","projects.tic")

In prolog, we call the first item on each such line a functor.
Often we structure facts so that the functor works like as a verb
does in English. In this example, you might think of "reps" as
the verb  "represents."  Here, we can view the first string after
the  opening parenthesis, as the subject of a sentence. So the
first  fact means:

      "<Telephone list>" represents "phone.lst".

(NOTE: We don't always interpret Prolog facts like this.)

As you will see, these facts give us a simple way of handling a
nonstandard DOS filename within a text file.
```

Fig. 8-22   A source code for hypertext editor in Turbo Prolog.

Checking the Filename

After consulting the file, the program grabs the command line argument, which we assume is the name of a file to be edited. Next the program declares checks this filename by calling a predicate called "checkname". (Predicates in prolog are sort of like subroutines.) The checkname predicate carries out several checks. First it checks to see if it was passed a name of some sort. If it finds that it was not passed a name, but just an empty string, it returns a default filename called "work". This enables you to start the program by giving the command HE with no arguments and go immediately into a file called "work". You can use this file as a "top level control node" from which you can access other files. In this "work" file you can list all the files that you need to access frequently. It's easily, too, in this work file, to document the purpose of the various other files (or nodes as they are called in hypertext terminology.)

If checkname determines that it was passed the name of a file that exists, it just returns. If it finds wildcards in the filename, it throws up a menu of files for you to choose from. If checkname finds that it was passed a name, but that the file does not exist, it asks the user whether he wants to create the file, search for a similar file, or just return.

After checkname finishes its work, control returns to the main predicate. Main now declares that the name returned by checkname is an existing file. The declaration in Turbo Prolog is:

        existfile(FileName)

If prolog determines that this declaration is false, the first clause of main predicate fails and control passes to the second clause. The second clause of main just displays an error message and returns control to DOS. But if the file does exist, the main predicate create a window for the editor to use:

```
makewindow(31,7,7,
  "From \"Hypertext Concepts & Applications\"",
          0,35,18,45),
```

I won't go into detail about the meaning of these arguments, here, except to comment that "0,35,18,45" means put the window in the upper right corner of the screen. This allows you to see most of what is on the previous screen while editing a file. If you want, you can easily zoom the small window to a full screen by pressing F5.

Creating a List of Files

After making the window, we put the filename at head of a list with this statement:

        assert(filelist([FileName])),

Then we call the editit predicate, which edits the file whose name appears at the head of the list. Just before editing the file, the editit predicate asserts the name of the file to the prolog knowledge base. Later, the program will use this knowledge to write a report of all of the files accessed during the editing session.

Fig. 8-22. Continued.

We use the list of files to keep track of the multiple files that the user may be editing. The program can retrieves the file list with the statement:

```
filelist(FileList).
```

Whenever the "editit" predicate executes, it grabs the head of the FileList and uses it as the name of the file to dit.

Hypertext Jumps

As a user, when you are inside of a file, you can select another one just by pointing to a filename that is delimited with angle brackets. For example, in my work file, I have a list like this:

```
************** System ************
<c:\autoexec.bat>  System file
<c:\config.sys>    Configuration
<c:\util\*.bat>    Batch files

*********** Administrative ********
<c:\empower\*.tic> Administrative
<c:\hyp\*.*>       Hypertext notes
<c:\sa\*.ltr>      Letters
{Mailing List}
{Important Things To Do}
{Critical Incidents}
{Telephone List}
```

etc.

I can jump into any of the files by putting the cursor on the "<" in front of the filename and pressing F10. Notice that some files are designated with descriptions in curly braces. For example {Telephone List}. You can also jump into such files. Just put the cursor on the opening curly brace, the "{", and press F10.

Exiting from a File

To exit from a file, press F10 when the cursor is NOT on a "<" or "{". Whenever you press F10, the program looks at the string pointed to by the cursor. If the first character is "{", the program extracts the description from with the braces and uses it to retrieve the proper filename from its knowledge base. We do this easily with the statement:

```
reps(HyperName,FileName).
```

If the cursor is on "<" the program just extracts the symbol delimited by the angle brackets takes it as a filename. After getting the filename, the program verifies that it exists with the statement "existfile(FileName)".

The program then adds the filename to the head   The program then adds the

Next, the program declares that the file list is empty with the statement:

```
filelist([])
```

This statement will fail since the file list is not empty! When this failure occurs, prolog backtracks and executes the repeat predicate. Turbo Prolog then continues with the rest of the predicates in editit in an effort to make it all the way through the editit predicate without a failure. Since the file the user picked is now at the head of the filelist, the program edits that file.

If the user presses F10 and the program is not able to come up with a filename, it removes the filename currently at the head of the list of filenames. The file that was the second element in the list now becomes the head of the list. (This is sort of like "popping the stack.") This way, when the editit predicate repeats, the user will return to the previous file.

If you keep pressing F10, without selecting a file to jump into, eventually filelist will be empty. When this happens, the statement "filelist([]) will be true and prolog will not need to backtrack. Consequently the editit predicate will succeed and return control to the main predicate.

Saving the Trail

The main predicate then opens a file called "trail.he" in the root directory. This file will contain the user's hypertext trail, that is, it will contain a list of the all files that the user visited in the course of each editing session. The "trail.he" file also lists the date of each session. If the "trail.he" file does not yet exist, it will be created and opened for writing. If it exists, it will be opened for appending data. IMPORTANT: this file will grow and grow. You may want to archive it from time to time or just delete it if the hypertext trail is not important to you.

After opening the "trail.he" file and setting itself to write to the "trail.he" file, main calls the writetrail predicate. The writetrail predicate gets the system date and writes it to the "trail.he" file. This way you can look back and see which files you accessed on which dates. Next the writetrail predicate retrieves all the facts from the knowledge base about the files that were accessed, one-by-one, and writes the filenames into the "trail.he" file. Notice how easy it is to do this in prolog, which has a built-in backtracking algorithm.

After writetrail finishes, control returns to main, which closes the "trail.he" file and then ends the program.

Editing Features

HE has many editing features. For help on how to use them, press F1. The "Show Help File" option in the Help Menu will display a file called "HE.HLP" in the root directory. You can customize this help file to your liking.

You may not like having the BUTTONS.KBA, HE.HLP and TRAIL.HE files in your root directory. I did this just for simplicity. If you want, you can change the prolog code so that these files are stored in a subdirectory of your choice. Just remember to use "\\" to specify a backslash when setting up a pathname to a subdirectory.

Fig. 8-22. Continued.

The rest of this figure contains the source code for the program.

Source Code for Hypertext Editor (HE)

```
********************************************************************/

DOMAINS
   file = outfile
   STRINGLIST = STRING*
   CHARLIST   = CHAR*

PREDICATES
   main
   process(CHAR,STRING,STRING)
   fileSpec_fileName(STRING,STRING)
   ask(STRING,STRING)
   getfname(STRING,STRING)
   checkname(STRING,STRING)
   checkdefault
   consultknowledge
   editit
   opentrail
   writetrail
   setfilelist(STRING)
   findobj(STRING,STRING)
   oneline(STRING,STRING)
   getHypNAME(STRING,STRING)
   extractname(STRING,STRING)
   /* pause(STRING,STRING)  /* use for testing */   */
   errorpredicate(INTEGER)
   wildcard(STRING)

/* Utility predicates */

   unfold(STRING,CHARLIST)
   n_member(INTEGER,CHAR,CHARLIST)
   n_member(INTEGER,STRING,STRINGLIST)
   repeat
   listwords(STRING,STRINGLIST)
   searchright(STRING,CHAR,INTEGER,INTEGER)
   getchar(STRING,INTEGER,CHAR)
   parsepath(STRING,STRING,STRING)

DATABASE
   filelist(STRINGLIST)
   f(STRING)    /* Stores name of file accessed */
DATABASE - external
   reps(STRING,STRING)

GOAL
   MAIN.



CLAUSES

/*************************** main  ***************************/

/* USE: this the top level predicate in the program.   */

   main if
```

```
       /* retractall(  filelist(_)),  Use only when testing.      */
     consultKnowledge,    /* Consult knowledge base file.        */
       /* Argument = "test",   /* Use only when testing. */       */
                           /* in the Turbo Prolog Environment.    */
     comline(Argument),               /* Get command line argument */
     checkname(Argument,FileName),   /* Handle file selection     */
     existfile(FileName),             /* Make sure file exists    */
     makewindow(31,7,7,"From \"Hyptext Concepts and Applications\""
                 ,0,35,18,45),  /* Make window for editor         */
     assert(filelist([FileName])), /* Put filename at head of list */
     editit,                           /* Edit the file(s) */
     opentrail,                        /* Open file for saving trail */
     writedevice(outfile),      /* Output now goes to trail file.  */
     writetrail,                /* Write list of all files accessed */
     closefile(outfile), !.

  main if
     write ("Sorry, error in filename."),
     exit(0), !.

/******************************** opentrail *********************/
/* USE: open file that will hold a list (trail) of all files
        accessed by this program.  If file exists, we open it
        for appending data.  Otherwise, we open the file for writing.
        This creates the file.  Notice that we put the file into
        the root directory.  You may want to change this.  Be sure
        to use double backslashes when specifying a subdirectory
        path.
*/

opentrail if
   existfile("\\trail.he"),
   openappend(outfile,"\\trail.he"), !.
opentrail if
   openwrite(outfile,"\\trail.he"), !.

/******************************** writetrail *********************/
/* USE: write a list of all files accessed during this session */
writetrail if
   date(Year,Month,Day), /* Get the system date */
   Y = Year-1900,        /* Adjust year for only two digits */
   write(Month,"-",Day,"-",Y),nl,
   f(FileNAME),          /* Get FileName fact */
   write(FileName),nl,
   fail.                 /* Force backtracking so we write all facts */

writetrail if !.         /* We come here and succeed after writing   */
                         /* all FileName facts. */

/*********************** consultKnowledge *********************/
/*
   USE: consult knowledge base file if it exists.  If it doesn't
        exist just return. If knowledge base is incorrectly
        structured, report an error.  The knowledge base contains
        information that links non-standard file names to standard
        DOS file names.  It could also be modified to contain
        information about link types.

   Never fails.
  NOTE: you may wish to keep the buttons.kba if a subdirectory.
        If so, change "\\buttons.kba" to show pathname.  Be sure
        to use double backslashes in the pathname as in:
            \\UTIL\\BUTTTONS.KBA
*/
   consultKnowledge if
```

Fig. 8-22. Continued.

```
      existfile("\\buttons.kba"),
      trap(
            consult("\\buttons.kba",external),
            Error,
            ErrorPredicate(Error)
           ), !.
   consultKnowledge if !.

/*********************** ErrorPredicate(Error) ********************/

/* USE: display error message if user's button.kba file is
        incorrect.  Never fails.
*/
errorpredicate(E) if
  write("\nPlease note: format of \\util\\buttons.kba is incorrect."),
  write("\nProlog error No. ",E," Press RETURN to continue."),
  readchar(_), !.

/*************************** checkname **************************/
/*
USE: Check filename.  Adjust filename if it doesn't exist.

   If filename is "", ensure that default file exists and return
     name of default file.
   If file exists just return.
   If user entered wildcards, throw up menu and check menu selection.
   If still unable to locate file, throw up menu of all files that
   start with first letter of filename.

Fails if unable to verify file name.
*/

/* No filename, so use default file in root directory. */
checkname("",FileName) if
     FileName = "\\WORK",    /* You may want to put default file in */
     checkdefault, !.        /* a subdirectory */

/* File exists */
checkname(FileName,FileName) if
     existfile(Filename), !.

/* If user entered wildcards--throw up menu. */
checkname(F,FileName) if
     getfname(F,FileName),  /* throw up menu if wildcard in name */
     existfile(Filename), !.

/* If can't find filename, ask user if she wants to search
   for filename (based on first letter and wildcard), create
   file or just return.   */
checkname(F,FileName) if
   not(wildcard(F)),  /* no wild cards in F */
   ask(F,FileName),   /* Ask user to choose what to do */
   existfile(FileName), !.

/*************************** ask ********************************/
/*
USE: Search for file, create file, or just return depending
     on user's response.  Returns name of File to edit.
Fails if unable to identify filename.
*/
ask(F,FileName) if
   makewindow(10,7,7,"",10,10,10,60),
   concat("\nDid not find ",F,Msg),
```

```
      write(Msg),
      write("\nSearch, Create, or Return  (S, C or R?) "),
      readchar(T),
      upper_lower(R,T),
      process(R,F,FileName),   /* process user's response */
      removewindow, !.

/* Just remove window setup in previous clause.  Then fail. */
ask(_,_) if
      removewindow,
      fail.

/***************************** process ****************************/
/*
USE: process response of user in "ask" predicate.
      If first argument is S, search for F (filename)
      If first argument is C, create file F.
Fails if first argument is neither S or C.
*/

process('S',F,FileName) if
      parsepath(F,Path,File),     /* Separate subdir from file name */
      frontstr(1,File,F2,_),      /* Get first letter of file name.*/
      concat(F2,"*.*",F3),        /* add *.* to first chart of filename */
      concat(Path,F3,F4),         /* add Subdir to filespec */
      getfname(F4,FileName),
      existfile(FileName),!.
process('C',FileName,FileName) if
      file_str(FileName," "), !. /* Create file */

/*************************** checkdefault ***********************/
/*
USE: if default file does not exist, create it in root directory.
      You may wish to change this so default file is in a subdir.
*/

checkdefault if
      existfile("\\WORK"), !.                /* File exists--just return */
checkdefault if
      file_str("\\WORK","WORK FILE\n"),!.   /* Create the work file */

/*************************** getfname ****************************/
/*
USE: If Spec contains wildcard, then call fileSpec_fileName, which
throws up a menu of files that match the file Spec.  Just return if
no filename.  Never fails.
*/

getfname(Spec,FileName) if
      wildcard(Spec),
      fileSpec_fileName(Spec,FileName), !.

/* There is no wildcard--just return */
getfname(FileName,FileName) if !.

/*************************** wildcard ****************************/
/*
USE: check for * or ? in string.  Fails if wildcard not found.
*/

wildcard(S) if
      findobj(S,"*"), !.
wildcard(S) if
      findobj(S,"?"), !.
```

Developing original hypertext applications   185

Fig. 8-22. Continued.

```
/********************** fileSpec_fileName ************************/

/*
   USE: Displays menu of files.  Should be called only with filespec!
   Never fails.  If user presses Esc from menu, the wildcard
   spec is returned to the caller in the second argument.

   Never fails.
*/

fileSpec_fileName(S,F) if
   disk(Path),
   makewindow(10,7,7,"",0,0,25,15),
   dir(Path,S,F, 1,1,1),
   removewindow, !.
/* If user escapes from menu */
fileSpec_fileName(S,S) if
   removewindow, !.


/****************************** findobj ************************/
/*
Find a "token" in a string.  A token, here is a word or a special
character like '*' or '?'

Fails if it cannot find token in string.
*/
   findobj("",_) if
      fail.
   findobj(Line,Object) if
      fronttoken(Line,T,_),
      T = Object,!.
   findobj(Line,Object) if
      fronttoken(Line,_,Rest),
      findobj(Rest,Object).


/***************************** editit ************************/
/*
   USE: edit the file that is the head of the List in the fact
        filelist(List).

   NOTE:--this predicate keeps repeating until the FileList
   is empty.  That is, until the statement "filelist([])" is true.
 */

   editit if
      repeat,
      filelist([FileName|_]), /* Get the head of the list */
      clearwindow,
      file_str(FileName,Instr), /* Get contents of file */
      window_attr(7), /* set color of window */

      assert(  f(FileName)),  /* keep trail of files accessed */

      edit(Instr,Outstr, "Zoom-F5 Help-F1 Save-F2 Exit-F10",
              FileName,
              "For source code call (415) 687-7778",
              0,  "\\HE.hlp", 1,  0,  1,  1,  RetPos,_),
      frontstr(RetPos,Outstr,_,Rest), /* Get string at cursor pos. */
      oneline(Rest,Line),             /* Take only 80 characters    */
      getHypNAME(Line, HyperName),    /* Extract filename */
      setfilelist(HyperName),         /* Put name at head of list */
      filelist([]), !.  /* If FileList is empty, program ends. */
```

```
/************************** setfilelist ***************************/
/*
USE:  If incoming argument is a valid filename, or if we can convert
      it to a filename, add the filename to front of list.
      Otherwise, if HyperName is an empty string, we remove head
      of file list.  If HyperName is not a space, we just return
      without modifying filelist(List).
Never fails.
*/

setfilelist(FileName1) if
   FileName1 <> "", /* HyperName is not empty string */
   checkname(FileName1,FileName2),     /* validate filename */
   filelist(List),              /* Get filelist fact */
   retractall(filelist(_)),        /* Retract old filelist fact */
   assert( filelist([FileName2|List])), !.  /* assert new fact */
/* We come here if HyperName is empty.  This happens when user puts
   cursor on space or newline exit exiting file.  In this clause
   we remove head of the filelist. This allows editor to return
   to previous file.
 */
setfilelist("") if
   filelist([_|TailofList]),   /* Get filelist fact */
   retractall(filelist(_)),    /* Retract old filelist fact */
   assert( filelist(TailofList)), !.
setfilelist(_) if !. /* leave filelist unchanged. */


/*************************** oneline ********************/
/* Flow pattern: i, o */

/* USE: Extract first 80 characters from string */

   oneline(Rest,Line) if
      frontstr(80,Rest,Line,_), !.

   /* Line has less than 80 characters, just return line */
   oneline(Line,Line) if !.

/************************** getHypName ********************/
/*
USE: String contains the string that cursor was on when user
     exited from edit. If string starts with "<", return a
     filename or a name that may serve as a filespec.  If
     string does not start with "<" return empty string.

*/
/*  We can extract a filename and it exists. */
   getHypName(String,Name) if
      trace(on),
      frontchar(String,'<',_),
      extractName(String,Name),
      existfile(Name), !.

/* We can extract a name that matches a fact in knowledgebase */
   getHypName(String,FileName) if
      frontchar(String,'{',_),
      extractName(String,Name),      /* We can extract name */
      not (wildcard(Name)),          /* Name does NOT have wildcard. */
      reps(Name,FileName),
      beep, !. /* HyperNames represents Filename */

/* We can extract a name */
   getHypName(String,Name) if
      extractName(String,Name), !.
```

Fig. 8-22. Continued.

```
/* We cannot extract name.  Setting name it to "" */
   getHypName(_,"") if !.


/*************************** extractname ***********************/
/*
USE: Returns XXX when given inside of {XXX} or <XXX>
*/

extractname(String,Name) if

   frontchar(String,'{',Rest1), /* First chart is "{" */
   unfold(Rest1,CharList),     /* Convert "XXXXXX} XXX" to charlist */
   n_member(P1,'}',CharList),    /* Find position of '}' */
   trace(on),
   P2 = P1-1,
   frontstr(P2,Rest1,Name,_), !.

extractname(String,Name) if
   frontchar(String,'<',Rest1), /* First chart is "<" */
   unfold(Rest1,CharList),     /* Convert "XXXXXX> XXX" to charlist */
   n_member(P1,'>',CharList),    /* Find position of '>' */
   trace(on),
   P2 = P1-1,
   frontstr(P2,Rest1,Name,_), !.

/*************************** repeat ***************************/
/*
USE: allow a predicate that fails to repeat itself
*/
repeat.
repeat
   if repeat.

/* *********************** unfold *************************** */
/*
USE: unfold a string into a list of chars
*/
   unfold("",[]) if !.
   unfold(Word,[H|T]) if
      frontchar(Word,H,Rest),
      unfold(Rest,T).

/*************************** n_member ***********************/

/* USE: Extract the n'th member of the list */

   n_member(1,X,[X|_]) if !.
   n_member(N,X,[_|Y]) if
      n_member(M,X,Y),
      N = M + 1.



/*********************** listwords ***********************/

/*
USE: turn string into a list of words
*/
   listwords(String,[Head|Tail]) if
      bound(String),
      fronttoken(String,Head,Rest),
      !,
```

```
        listwords(Rest,Tail).

        listwords(_,[]) if !.


/***************************** parsepath *************************/
/*
USE: Input: Pathname set to, say, "C:\util\test"
     Output: Path = "C:\util\"  File="test"
*/

parsepath(Pathname,Path,File) if
    str_len(Pathname,Len),
    searchright(Pathname,'\\',Pos,Len),
    frontstr(Pos,Pathname,Path,File), !.


/********************** searchright ***************************************

    searchright -- search from right to left for a character in a
                   string.
    Example:  searchright("ABADAF",'A',Pos,Length)
        ...returns Pos bound to 5 since the first 'A'
        encountered on a search from right to left is at position 5
    Input: String=String to search
           Target=char to search for
           L= Length of String
   Output: Position of char as found in a left to right search
*/

    searchright(String,Target,Pos,L) if
      getchar(String,L,CH),  /* first time get last char of string  */
      CH<>Target,!,          /*   We have not yet found char  */
      L2 = L-1,
      searchright(String,Target,Pos,L2).

    searchright(_,_,Pos,Pos) if !. /*   We come here when we have    */
                                   /*    found the character         */


/************************* getchar *************************** */
/*
USE: extract the character at a specific position in a string

*/

    getchar(String,Num,Char) if
      X = Num -1,
      frontstr(X,String,_,Rest),
      frontchar(Rest,Char,_).


/*** (pause is commented out.  Use it for testing.)
/*********************** pause **********************************/

/*  USE: This is a handy predicate for inserting debug statments into
       a program that uses windows. It pops up a debug window and
       displays two arguments.  You can use one argument for a
       literal and the other for a variable.

       Example:  pause("Filename=",Filename)
*/

pause(A,B) if
```

Fig. 8-22. Continued.

```
  makewindow(1,7,7,"",18,0,5,80),
  write(A,B), nl,
  readchar(_),
  removewindow, !.
***/


/************************* buttons.kba ***************************/
/*
USE: buttons.kba is an external knowledge base file stored in
     the root subdirectory.  We use it to store facts about
     buttons. A button, here, is a non-standard representation
     of a DOS filename. (Symbolically, when you "press a
     button," you start editing a file.)

     The first object of each fact contains the button text.

     The second object contains the filename
     represented by the button text.

     Note: we use double backslashes when specifying
           subdirectories (\\) because a single
           backslash is reserved for special use as in

           "\n", which means "newline character"


Here are some examples:

reps("<Writer Control File>","\\sa\\writer.ctr")
reps("<Telephone list>", "\\empower\\phone.tic")
reps("<Critical Incidents>","\\empower\\critical.tic")

External files that we consult follow rigid structural
rules:

   Note: no period at end of line.  No extra spaces allowed
   between objects.  For example this is wrong:

reps("<Telephone list>", "\\empower\\phone.tic").
                      /\                    /\
                      ||                    ||
          space here is not allowed.    no period allowed.
*/
```

If you have Turbo Prolog, you can type in this program and compile it to an .EXE file. I suggest the name HE for hypertext editor. You can use HE to write programs, batch files, and organize notes, reports, memos, and so on. You might be wondering why you would want to use it instead of your usual word processor or editor. Let's take a look at how it works. If, at the DOS prompt, you enter:

```
HE \ autoexec.bat
```

HE will load the AUTOEXEC.BAT file and you can immediately start editing it. By default HE starts with a small window as shown in Fig. 8-23. But you can zoom it to a full screen by pressing F5. The small window is handy because it allows you to see what is on the DOS screen while you are editing. (You can move the window around and precisely resize it by pressing Shift-F10.) If, at the DOS prompt, you just enter:

```
HE
```

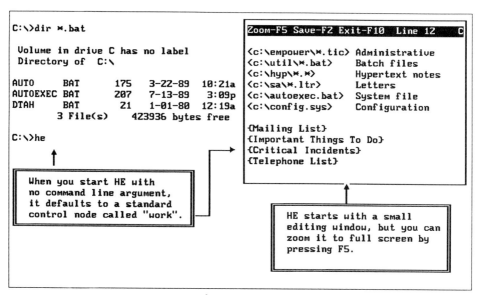

```
C:\>dir *.bat                        ┌─────────────────────────────────────────┐
                                     │Zoom-F5 Save-F2 Exit-F10  Line 12     C│
 Volume in drive C has no label      │<c:\empower\*.tic> Administrative       │
 Directory of  C:\                   │<c:\util\*.bat>    Batch files          │
                                     │<c:\hyp\*.*>       Hypertext notes      │
AUTO     BAT     175   3-22-89  10:21a│<c:\sa\*.ltr>      Letters              │
AUTOEXEC BAT     207   7-13-89   3:09p│<c:\autoexec.bat>  System file          │
DTAH     BAT      21   1-01-80  12:19a│<c:\config.sys>    Configuration        │
         3 File(s)    423936 bytes free│                                       │
                                     │ {Mailing List}                         │
C:\>he                               │ {Important Things To Do}               │
                                     │ {Critical Incidents}                   │
                                     │ {Telephone List}                       │
                                     │                                         │
                                     │                                         │
                                     │                                         │
                                     └─────────────────────────────────────────┘
```

When you start HE with no command line argument, it defaults to a standard control node called "work".

HE starts with a small editing window, but you can zoom it to full screen by pressing F5.

Fig. 8-23 HE's small default editing window.

the program will immediately go into a default node called "Work." You can use this Work node as a kind of menu or control node from which you access many different files. Whenever you create a new memo, program or report, you can link it to the Work node and add a line or two describing the purpose of the new node. Then you will be able to access it quickly without having to remember in which subdirectory you put it. Later you can just enter HE at the DOS prompt and browse through the work node. You can jump into any node simply by pointing to its name and pressing F10.

In the Work node, any reference to a file enclosed in angle brackets is actually a hypertext button. For example:

< \autoexec.bat>

is a hypertext button that allows you to go into the AUTOEXEC.BAT file in the root directory. If you put the cursor on "<" and press F10, HE will go into that node. (In this system a node can be a file of any length up to 64K.) Once you go into any node, you can branch to another one. You can keep branching into different nodes (files) in this way as long as you like. As you skip from node to node (actually file to file), HE keeps track of your trail. Then when you press F10 and the cursor is not on a button, you will automatically return to the previous node. HE allows you to update the current node. To save any changes you have made, you just press F2 before leaving the current node.

Nonstandard DOS file names   As discussed earlier, you can set up a hypertext button so that it contains more than just a simple DOS file name. For example, you can have a hypertext button that looks like this:

{Telephone Directory}

To access the telephone directory node, you would put the cursor on { and press F10.

Notice, here, that braces {} surround the nonstandard DOS file name Telephone Directory. So HE can understand what Telephone Directory means, you need to put an appropriate fact in a knowledge base. HE consults a knowledge base stored in a file called BUT-TONS.KBA. (The .KBA extension stands for "knowledge base.") To be able to use Telephone Directory as a button, you might include this fact in the knowledge base:

> reps("Telephone Directory","C:\data\phone.dir")

With the knowledge that "Telephone Directory" represents the DOS path name "C:\data\phone.dir", HE can access the "phone.dir" node when you select "Telephone Directory".

Wildcard buttons   Although HE is primarily a teaching example, it has many practical features, thanks to the power of Turbo Prolog. For example, I frequently find that I want to access a node but I don't remember its exact name. (In well-designed hypertext, you should always be able to find the node you want in ten keystrokes. But this is not always the case!)

To help me overcome the problem of finding misplaced or "floating nodes," I developed the wildcard button. For example, if you want a menu of all nodes that end with the .LTR extension in the SA subdirectory on drive C, you can set up this button:

> <c:\SA*.LTR>.....Business.Letters

Figure 8-24 shows the menu that HE produces when you activate this kind of button.

Automatic wildcard insertion   If you think you know a node name, but misspell it, HE will automatically switch to a wildcard search at your request. For example, suppose I want to access a node dealing with a proposal I wrote to an editor named Thiagi. I know

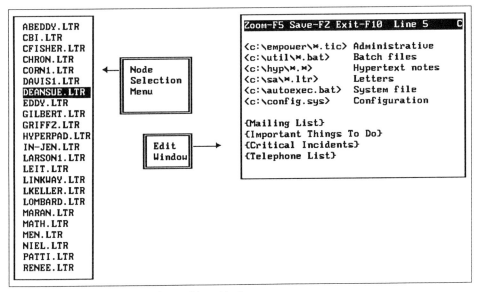

Fig. 8-24   HE menu resulting from wildcard button.

the node is in a subdirectory called NSPI so I might make a button that looks like this:

< \ NSPI \ THIAGI.PZL >

But when I activate the button, the message shown in Fig. 8-25 appears. Now I can press S for a wildcard search, C to create a new node, or R to return to the parent node.

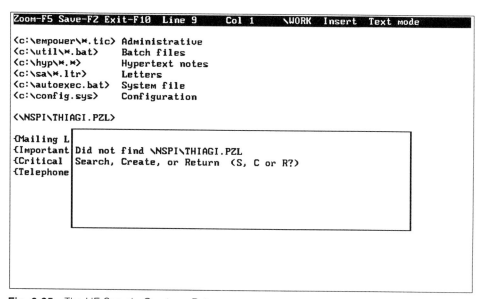

```
Zoom-F5 Save-F2 Exit-F10  Line 9      Col 1      \WORK  Insert  Text mode
<c:\empower\*.tic>  Administrative
<c:\util\*.bat>     Batch files
<c:\hyp\*.*>        Hypertext notes
<c:\sa\*.ltr>       Letters
<c:\autoexec.bat>   System file
<c:\config.sys>     Configuration

<\NSPI\THIAGI.PZL>

 Mailing L ┌──────────────────────────────────────────────────┐
{Important │ Did not find \NSPI\THIAGI.PZL                    │
{Critical  │ Search, Create, or Return  (S, C or R?)          │
{Telephone │                                                  │
           │                                                  │
           │                                                  │
           │                                                  │
           └──────────────────────────────────────────────────┘
```

Fig. 8-25 The HE Search, Create or Return menu.

Figure 8-26 shows the menu that popped up when I pressed S for a wildcard search. As you can see, I was mistaken in thinking that the file name ended with a .PZL extension. There are two THIAGI files, but neither of them has an extension.

If you would like to design a routine to do such an automated wildcard search, note that these are the basic steps:

1. Parse the button into path and file name, where Path is the subdirectory path and Filename is the name of the target file.
2. Take the first letter of the file name and add *.* to it.
3. Concatenate the original path specification with the wildcard specification. For example, the button < \ NSPI \ THIAGI.PZL > would result in a file specification of \ NSPI \ T*.*

Linking and creating nodes You can avoid, for the most part, the problem of incorrect node names by always creating the button before the node. When you press the create button first, you are actually linking the new node to the current node. After creating a new button, put the cursor on the " < " and press F10. When HE shows the Search/Create/ Return message, just press C to create the new node. Then type in the contents of the node and press F2 to save it. When done, press F10 to exit to the parent node.

If you are interested in using HE, be sure to read the documentation that appears in Fig. 8-22. Note that HE has a built-in help system. If you press F1, a rather detailed help

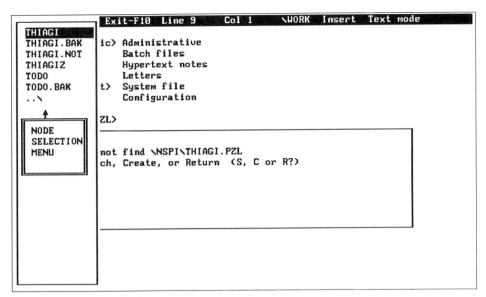

```
        Exit-F10  Line 9      Col 1     \WORK  Insert  Text mode
┌─────────┐
│THIAGI   │ ic>  Administrative
│THIAGI.BAK│       Batch files
│THIAGI.NOT│       Hypertext notes
│THIAGIZ  │        Letters
│TODO     │ t>   System file
│TODO.BAK │        Configuration
│..\      │
│   ↑     │ ZL>
├─────────┤
│ NODE    │
│SELECTION│
│ MENU    │ not find \NSPI\THIAGI.PZL
└─────────┘ ch, Create, or Return  (S, C or R?)
```

Fig. 8-26 HE node selection menu.

menu appears. The help system explains how to copy and move blocks of text, copy a block to the printer, delete and undelete blocks and so on. As mentioned earlier, a useful feature is the ability to resize the edit window. By default a small node pad like window appears. This allows you to see what is on the DOS screen while you edit. You can zoom the window to the full screen by pressing F5. You can also make the window virtually any size you want by pressing Shift-F10. These features are all built-in to the Turbo Prolog editor.

If you don't have Turbo Prolog, but would still like to try HE, you might be able to find it as shareware on your local bulletin board. You may also get a copy by sending a blank formatted disk in a stamped, self-addressed disk mailer and $3.00 to Seyer Associates, 1015 Cadillac Way, #5-201, Burlingame, CA 94010. Mark the envelope "HE shareware."

PDC Prolog

Turbo Prolog is good for developing proprietary hypertext engines and systems, but PDC is even better! That's because Borland, the publisher of Turbo Prolog has stopped enhancing it and has returned the rights to the original developer. Consequently, a new Prolog has emerged for PCs and compatibles called PDC Prolog. It's available from the Prolog Development Center in Atlanta, Georgia. PDC Prolog is compatible with Turbo Prolog, yet it adds some powerful new features that, among other things, enable you to customize the built-in editor. For example, you can define custom predicates that will be called when the user presses one of eight "application keys." You can easily define these application keys from a setup menu provided in the PDC Prolog development environment.

Once you have defined the eight application keys, PDC Prolog will detect when the user presses one of these keys while in the editor and execute a specific clause of a predicate called "edithook." This predicate can have "knowledge" of the state of the editor at the time that the user pressed one of the designated application keys. This knowledge includes:

- The application key that was pressed.
- The current text in the editor.
- The cursor position.
- The starting position and length of any selected block of text.
- Whether a block was marked.

The edithook predicate also allows you, the programmer, to process the edit text in various ways. For example, you can:

- Specify a new cursor location.
- Mark a different block of text.
- Turn block selection on or off.
- Delete a block of text.
- Insert text from the "paste buffer."

Figure 8-27 shows one clause of a simple edithook predicate. The clause shown will execute when the user presses Application Key 1 while in the editor—that's because the first argument of the head of clause is "1." The job of this clause is to grab the word that the cursor is on and display a message to that effect in yet another edit window. This is just a simple example to demonstrate how the edithook predicate works; you could do many other interesting and useful things. However, identifying the word the cursor is on is usually one of the first steps in hypertext programming.

Figure 8-28 shows how the sample edithook predicate might work. In creating this example, I moved the cursor to consistent and pressed Alt-F1, 1, which I had previously defined as "Application Key No. 1." Notice that the user is still in the editor, even though a secondary editing processing is going on in the smaller window.

Many additional enhancements besides the edithook predicate have been added to Turbo Prolog. For example, there is support for OS/2, improved string handling, im-

```
        ┌─────────────────────────────────────────────┐
        │ The "1" here means "activate this clause only │
        │ when the user presses Application Key 1."     │
        └─────────────────────────────────────────────┘
                    │
                    ▼
edithook(1,TXT,CP,_,_,MM,CP,0,0,MM,0,0,CP):-
    NCP=CP-1,                   /* CP=current cursor position. */
    frontstr(NCP,TXT,_,END),    /* Extract text from cursor pos. */
       fronttoken(END,Word, _), /* Get first word of text.*/
       concat("The cursor was on: ",Word, Text),  /*Build msg */
       makewindow(10,7,7,"",10,10,10,40),
       edit(Text,_),            /* Put user in new edit window */
    removewindow,!.
```

Fig. 8-27 Using the edithook predicate.

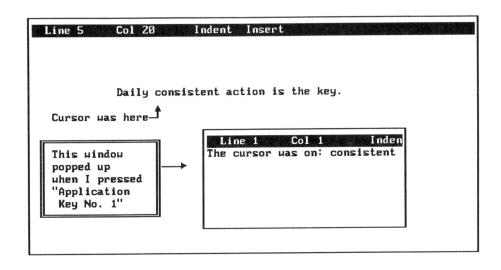

```
 Line 5     Col 20        Indent  Insert



           Daily consistent action is the key.

   Cursor was here ┘

  ┌──────────────┐       ┌─────────────────────────────────┐
  │ This window  │       │ Line 1    Col 1        Inden│
  │ popped up    │  ──►  │ The cursor was on: consistent   │
  │ when I pressed│      │                                 │
  │ "Application │       │                                 │
  │  Key No. 1"  │       │                                 │
  └──────────────┘       │                                 │
                         │                                 │
                         └─────────────────────────────────┘



 F1-Help  F2-Save  F3-Load  F5-Zoom  F6-Next  F7-Xcopy  F8-Xedit  F10-End
```

Fig. 8-28   How the edithook predicate might work.

proved window control, and improved control over configuration. If you want to do serious Prolog programming on a PC, definitely consider PDC Prolog. I might add, here, that the Prolog Development Center also offers a Professional User's Guide that shows how to write a memory-resident Prolog program that uses only 12K of RAM! Also included in this guide is information about mixed language programming, overlay managers, and moving Prolog programs to C, plus some interesting application programs.

Prolog is fun to work with once you get the hang of it, and it is mind expanding. If you would like to explore hypertext programming and write problem-solving programs, you might want to get Safaa Hashim's book, *Exploring Hypertext Programming: Writing Knowledge Representation and Problem-Solving Programs*. The book comes with the complete source code for MicroIBIS, a hypertext system for problem-solving along with detailed explanations of the theory behind its use. It also has an extensive bibliography on hypertext and problem-solving issues. With Hashim as a consultant, the MIS department at the University of Texas is using MicroIBIS and modifying it for group problem-solving on a local area network.

If Prolog is not for you, you might want to consider taking an existing word processor and adding hypertext capability to it. You can do that with a customizable word processor called Sprint.

Hypertext programming with Sprint

The Sprint word processor has a complete built-in programming language. The language has many different macros that you can use to:

• Display menus

- Control the cursor
- Jump into external files
- Execute other programs
- Access PC hardware

If you already have a powerful word processor, you have a big headstart in developing hypertext authoring tools. For example, you don't have to write code to highlight text on screen. Using Sprint's Typestyle menu you can easily make text stand out by assigning it to different typestyles. In fact, you can use one of five different typestyles. If you have a color monitor, you can assign a different color to each typestyle.

Figure 8-29 shows a simple example that just touches the surface of what you can do with Sprint. This macro reads a boldfaced word or phrase from the screen and then executes it as a DOS command. Notice how little code is needed in Sprint to create a command button. This is because Sprint comes with a powerful macro programming language complete with variables, math operations, If statements, loop control functions, and so on. In addition, the language has a number of special built-in variables and commands designed to help you manipulate text—just what you need to create your own hypertext system!

```
; FILEAME: COMMAND.SPM
; MACRO NAME: Command    Copyright 1989  Philip C. Seyer
;
; USE:  Allow user to execute a program by pointing to
;       bold-faced text and pressing Alt-O.  You can easily
;       assign this macro to a different hotkey see ~O at
;       the end of this listing.
;
Command:

  if (curatt = 0) ; If cursor is not between control characters
     {
       bell          ; Sound a warning tone and display message:
       message "Please put cursor on bold-faced program name."
       abort          ; Return control to user.
     }              ; Otherwise, we continue.
  set QP ""        ; Clear the QP register.

; The "r" command declares that the next command will move
; cursor in REVERSE direction.

  r to isopen    ;  Move point up to typeface open deliminter.
     setmark     ;  Set a "mark" at this position.
     to isclose  ;  Move point forward to closing delimiter (^N)
     copy tomark QP      ; Copy area between the point
                         ; and the mark to the Q4 register.
     16 call "command /c" QP   ;Call the DOS command processor
                               ;specified by the COMPSEC variable
                               ;and pass it the program specified
                               ;by the QP register.

~O: Command       ;Specify that Alt-O will be the hotkey
                  ;that will execute the Command macro.
```

Fig. 8-29 Creating a command button with Sprint.

Fig. 8-29 Continued.

```
; Technical notes:
; ---------------
; The "point" is an imaginary position in the text between
; two characters.  The point is always just to the left of
; the cursor. The 16 in front of "call" is an argument that
; is passed to the call macro.  In Sprint macro programming,
; when a number (or variable containing a number) appears in
; the code, it is always passed to the next command.

; Here, the 16 tells Sprint to overlay the called program on
; top of itself.  Sprint then occupies only 3 K of memory.
; This allows Sprint to call large programs without running
; running out of memory. When the called program finishes,
; Sprint restarts itself. The "command /c" means:
; "call the program specified by the DOS COMSPEC variable
; and pass it the command that follows.
```

Programming with the Sprint macro programming language is not exactly the same as writing a script because you need to compile the source code that you write into a binary file. Still, you're not developing a stand-alone system, but rather an interface to Sprint. (Sprint can load various binary files and interpret them.)

If you have Sprint, you can easily compile the macro in Fig. 8-29. As soon as you compile it, you can immediately use it. To compile the macro, follow these steps:

1. Make sure you are using Sprint's Advanced User Interface.
2. Type the macro into a file that has an .SPM extension. I suggest you use COMMAND.SPM as the file name. Inside the file, be sure the macro name command: appears flush left and that the other lines are indented.
3. With the text of the macro on screen, press Shift-Alt-R. This will compile the macro.

To use the macro, boldface some text that you would normally enter at the DOS prompt. Then put the cursor anywhere on that boldfaced text and press Alt-O (the hotkey). Sprint will exit, free up all but 3K of memory, and then call the external program. When the external program finishes, Sprint will reactivate itself.

So that's one way you can enable command buttons with Sprint. Now let's look at a couple of other kinds of hypertext tricks you can do with Sprint.

Insert buttons   Figure 8-30 shows how you can enable insertion buttons using Sprint's macro programming language. Using Sprint, you can compile this code in the same way as explained before. An insertion button, as I use it here, is simply a DOS file name enclosed in angle brackets. For example:

> < C: \ filename >

If you put the cursor on an insertion button and press a hotkey, the text contained in the external node will be inserted into the current node below the button.

The insertion button may include a path name and wildcards:

> < C: \ empower \ * .tic >

```
; FILENAME: getnode.spm
; HOTKEY: Alt-G
; MAIN MACRO: Getnode
; USE: Read an external node into the current node.  Node must be
;      filename enclosed in angle brackets as in <filename>.  Put
;      cursor on filename and press Alt-G.

; Copyright 1989 Philip C. Seyer
; ************************* Submacros *****************************

; The following two macros are called by Getnode.  They must be
; declared here.
Getname:
MyInsertFile:

;**********************************************************************
;**************************** Getnode *****************************
;**********************************************************************

;  USE: this macro gets the filename that the cursor is on and
;       moves it into the QD register.  Then it does a carriage
;       return and reads that file into the current edit buffer.
;       If the file specification contains wildcards or if the
;       Sprint cannot locate the file, Sprint displays a menu of
;       files.

Getnode:
    Getname        ; move filename into qd register
    MyInsertFile   ; insert named file into current file


;**************************** Getname *****************************

Getname:

; Read the underlined expession from the screen and put
; it in the Q0 register.  NOTE: we assume user has put the
; cursor on a filename
; ----------------------------------------------------

        set Q0 ""  ;clear Q0 register before loading
        r ('<' csearch)         ;reverse search for "<"
        c                       ;go forward filename
            setmark             ;set a mark
        '>' csearch             ;forward seach for ">
        copy tomark Q0          ;Copy region from point to mark
                                ; into Q0
        c                       ;Move cursor past ">"

 ; *************************** MyInserstFile **********************

; USE: insert the file named in the Q0 register into the current
;      file.  Throw up menu if Q0 contains wildcards or if
;      file named does not exists.

MyInsertFile :
        ; if file found, put it into QD, if wild cards are present
        ; throw up a menu of files.
        if (! 2 set QD flist Q0)  ; Get filename or throw up menu.
           {set QD flist "*.*" }  ; Throw up a menu of all files
                                  ; if previous flist command failed.
```

Fig. 8-30 Code for an insertion button macro.

Fig. 8-30 Continued.

```
if exist QD                ; If file exists,
    {
    "\n"                   ; insert carriage return into file
    read QD                ; read in the file
    }
else
    {message "Sorry, could not find file."}

;HOTKEY
~G: Getnode       ; assign Getnode to Alt-G
```

Figure 8-31 shows how a menu pops up when you press a hotkey with the cursor on an insertion button that contains a wildcard. When the menu appears, the user can select one of the nodes and its text will be inserted into the current node.

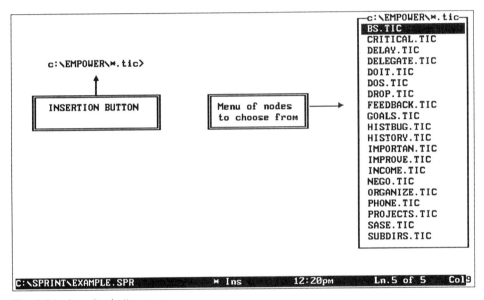

Fig. 8-31 Insertion button menu.

Figure 8-32 shows yet another Sprint macro. This one searches the current node and expands all insertion buttons to the text that they contain. A master node might contain nothing but insertion buttons. By arranging the insertion buttons in different ways, you can easily change the sequence of the nodes in the final document.

Notice that these programs use simple DOS file names in the buttons. A useful enhancement would be to allow users to use longer, descriptive names in the buttons as in the Turbo Prolog example shown earlier. This would be fairly easy to do given Sprint's programming capabilities. You could keep the knowledge about nonstandard file names in a Q register.

For more information on Sprint macro programming, you might want to see *Mastering Sprint Macro Programming* by Eddy Conway and Philip Seyer. If you can't find a copy, please let me know! (Scott Foresman, and Sons, 1989).

```
; FILEAME: COMMAND.SPM
; FILENAME: Insert.spm
; HOTKEY: Alt-I
; MAIN MACRO: InsertNodes
; USE: Expand all insertion buttons within a node.  For example,
;       a node that contains these node references:

;           <Intro>
;           <Body>
;           <Conclu>

; will be expanded so that it contains the complete text of
; all the nodes referred to.

;                 Copyright 1989 Philip C. Seyer
;
; The following include directive compiles the macros in the
; getnode.spm file.  As listed here, the getnode.spm must exist
; in a subdirectory named SPM.  If you have previously compiled
; the getnode.spm file, you can comment out this include statement.

#include "c:\\spm\\getnode.spm"

;********************************************************************
;************************ InsertNodes   *****************************
;********************************************************************

InsertNodes:
    r to isend          ; go to top of file
    while (! isend)     ; while not end of file
        {
        if ('<' csearch) ; search for "<"
            {            ; if we find '<' then...
            c            ; move cursor forward one position
            getnode      ; insert node (getnode macro compiled earlier)
            }
        else
            return       ; exit current macro
        }

;HOTKEY
~I: InsertNodes         ; assign InsertNodes to Alt-I
```

Fig. 8-32 Macro for activating all insertion buttons.

Programming hypertext in C

Programming hypertext in C is more difficult than in Prolog and in Sprint because you have to do more of the detail work yourself. There is no built-in editor. You must define each procedure yourself. You can't just make a declarative statement (as in Prolog) and expect the system to verify its truth for you as in Prolog. There are advantages, though. Programs written in C are more compact. And using C you have more flexibility and, depending on your programming skill, it might be easier to debug a program written in C. Prolog has its own built-in algorithms and if you don't understand how Prolog "thinks" you can really get confused. In C, you write your own algorithms and you can trace execution step-by-step.

Programming tools   Libraries of C routines that you can incorporate into your own programs are available. You can even buy the source code for a complete WordStar-like editor called SUPERTEXT from Zortech Inc. You can make a C program memory-resident by using functions from a special library called Turbo C Tools, available from Blaise Computing, Inc. (See chapter 10 for names and addresses.)

Figure 8-33 shows the C code I used to enable highlighting of buttons (words or phrases) on-screen in the HyperTSR program discussed earlier. This code uses functions from the Turbo C Toolbox available from Blaise Computing. I present it here just to give you an idea of what is involved in just highlighting words on-screen using Turbo C.

Fig. 8-33 Highlighting buttons in C.

```
/***************************** hilight ****************************/
/*
    USE: Display one line of text and highlight any hypertext buttons,
    which are delimited with vertical bars in the text file.
    Keep track of row and col position for each highlighted area
    and put this info in "hpos" structure. Keep a count of the
    total number of highlighted areas and put this value in the
    "harea" variable.

    Earlier a line of text was read into a buffer pointed to by
    "lineh".

    NOTE: this code is presented for illustrative purposes only.
    It will not run as is. It needs the Turbo C Tools functions and
    certain variables such as hpos must be defined.

*/

hilight()
{

    char *pline;
    int num;
    int hl = 1;
    int i;

    fore = norfore;   /* norfore contains value for normal forground */
    back = norback;   /* norback contains value for normal background */
    findLOCS('|',&lineh); /* Find location of vertical bars in string */
    pline = lineh;    /* let pline point to beginning of string */
    i = 0;
    num = locs[i];    /* Set num to first element of the locs array. */

    /* If num = -1, no vertical bar found, so print line & return */
    if (num == -1)
        {
        num = 0;
        /* wnwrstr (from Turbo C Tools) lets you to write a string to */
        /* a window & specify the foreground and background colors    */
        wnwrstr(pline,norfore,back);
        }

    else   /* vertical bar found */
        {
        /* Line has some hyperwords; hl initialized to 1 */
        while(1)   /* Keep looping until break encountered */
            {
            /* if hl is an even number */
            if ((hl % 2) == 0)
                /* Highlighted text cannot be first string in line */
                {
                wncurpos(&grow, &gcol)     /* Get hyperarea cursor position */
                harea++;                   /* harea = count of highlighted areas */
```

```c
            hpos[harea].hrow = grow; /* save row & column positions */
                hpos[harea].hcol = gcol;

                /* set up variables for highlighting */
                fore = hifore;
                back = hiback;
                }
            else
            /* we are on an odd number so display text normally */
                {
                fore = norfore;
                back = norback;
                }
            hl++;
            num = locs[i];
            i++;

            /* If num set to -1 there is no more hypertext in line */
            /* so we break out of this loop */
            if (num == -1)
                {
                wnwrstr(pline,fore,back);
                break;
                }

            /* This actually displays the string fragment! */
            /* wnwrstrn is a function from Tubro C Tools */
            wnwrstrn(curwin,pline,num,fore,back,CHARS_ONLY);

            pline = pline + num + 1;
            wnprintf(" ");
            }  /* Finished printing line with hyperwords */

        }  /* ending for first if statement in function */
    }

/*************************** findLOCS ***************************/
/*
USE:    find all the locations where the target (an ASCII value
        expressed as an integer) is found in the string "line".  Put
        these locations into an array named "loc"
*/

findLOCS(char target, char *pline)
{
int pos;
int i = 1;

/*
/* NOTE: stschind (from Turbo C Tools) finds a character within
   a string and returns its position.  If stschind does not find
   the character, it returns -1.  Here, target is the character
   we are searching for and pline points to the string.
*/
    pos = stschind(target,pline);
    i = 0;

/* Repeat loop until character not found */
    while (pos != -1)
        {
        locs[i++] = pos;            /* Set array element to position */
        pline = pline + pos + 1;    /* Increment string pointer */
        pos = stschind(target,pline);  /* Search next part of string */
        }
    locs[i] = pos;
}
```

String searches and automatic linking If your hypertext system uses ASCII files and does not provide a string search, you can easily add a comprehensive search function by using a library of C functions called POWER SEARCH available from Blaise Computing, Inc. I say comprehensive because POWER SEARCH can search for what some people call regular expressions. A *regular expression* is a special way of expressing a character string pattern. For example, you can use a dollar sign ($) to specify that a pattern must appear at the end of a line before it meets your search criteria. For example, if you say you are looking for:

    Seyer$

the search program would find "Kristina Seyer" only if this string appeared at the end of a line of text.

    If you want to specify a class of characters in a search string, you can easily do that by putting each of the characters in that class in brackets. For example, the expression:

    D[aiou]n

will match Dan, Din, Don, or Dun.

    You can also specify a range of characters. To specify a pattern that will match any digit 0 through 9, you would use this expression:

    [0 – 9]

The expression:

    B[0 – 9]

would match B0, B1, B2, B3, B4, B5, B6, B7, B8, or B9.

    Several other pattern-matching rules are included in what are called regular expressions. For example, a period matches any character. If you use a caret (^) as the first character, you create a negative class. For example, the expression:

    [^aeiouAEIOU0123456789]at

would match strings like bat, cat, or dat.

    In other words, the first character could be anything that is not a vowel or a number.

    A period will match any character except for a line break. It's similar to the ? wild-card character in DOS.

    POWER SEARCH comes with some sample programs with source code included. You can use these programs as a starting point for developing your own string search utilities. One such program, BFIND, will search multiple files for multiple regular expressions. To see how well BFIND might work to help do some automatic hypertext linking, I obtained some files that listed all of the shareware available from a local computer store, UC Computers in Berkeley, California. This store has an extensive collection of shareware. Even though the store offers a well-organized printout of their shareware collection, the printout is not completely up-to-date. Also I found it extremely time-consuming to read through it and make notes of software that I might want to purchase. I found BFIND highly effective in helping me build a hypertext control node and ultimately enabling me to jump immediately to items of interest in the software listings.

    I got seven ASCII files from UC Computers: LIST1, LIST2, LIST3, up to LIST7.

Each file contained a different category of software. For example, database-related programs were in one file, graphics in another, and so on. My goal was to create a control node that I could use to instantly jump into the proper spot in each file to read about a particular topic. I chose the topic "hypertext" so I could find out what shareware hypertext programs were available. I decided to do a simple search for the string "hyper" so that I would also locate a word like "hyperguide." (I found that I didn't really need the power of regular expressions here.) The command I gave at the DOS prompt was:

```
bfind /o hyper list*.* > hyper.ctr
```

Here, bfind just invokes the BFIND program. The rest of the command line contains the arguments to BFIND. The /o is a command modifier. It tells BFIND to display its output in a format that is similar to GREP (a string search program available in UNIX).

The next word, hyper, is the target search string—the string I am looking for. Next comes list*.*. This tells BFIND to search through all files whose names begin with "list."

The " > " symbol is a standard DOS symbol that means "please send the output of this program to the following file." (namely "HYPER.CTR").

After creating the HYPER.CTR file, I loaded that file into an enhanced version of HE (the hypertext editor I presented earlier in this chapter). Figure 8-34 shows a HE screen with the HYPER.CTR file loaded. The screen shows a listing of all the lines that contained the word "hyper" in the seven files that were searched.

Notice that BFIND, when invoked with the /o option, always lists the name of each file along with the contents of the line where it found the search string.

For example, in Fig. 8-34 the file name in the first column on the left can serve as a hypertext button. By moving the cursor onto the "L" of "LIST7" and pressing F10, I can jump directly to the proper spot in the LIST7 file. Figure 8-35 shows how HE jumps directly to line 252 in the LIST7 file, which contains the phrase "World magazine issues;".

```
────────From "Hyptext Concepts and Applications"────────
Zoom-F5 Help-F1 Save-FZ Exit-F10  Line Z     Col 1     hyper.ctr  Insert

LIST1   DU-199  MANUAL - is a semi-hypertext indexing program which
LIST1   DU-214  CABLE DESIGNER V.1.03 - this is a hypertext-type tutorial
LIST1   ED-158  HELPSB - the most comprehensive hypercard-type DOS on-line
LIST1   hypertext program contains complete information of any DOS commands
LISTZ   ED-100  HYPEIT - a text-oriented hypertext program for C language
LISTZ   programmer; the program let you can create your own hypertext data
LISTZ   ED-104  C++TUTOR - is a hyperguide to C++ language which is an
LISTZ   ED-130  TP 5.5 HYPERGUIDE - is a hyperguide to Turbo Pascal 5.5
LISTZ   TP 5.5 and object-oriented implementation, etc; hypertext browser
LISTZ   hypertext system with the Prolog programming language; it allows
LIST7   hypertetxt system for graphical images; Windows 2.1/MOUSE/640K of
LIST7   World magazine issues; it applies hypertext system which can let
LIST7   hypertext systems of files, graphics and programs.
LIST7   W-024  HYTEXT V.2.5 - a simple-to-use hypertext environment which
LIST7   uses simple codes imbedded in any document to create hypertext
LIST7   W-032  HYPER HELPER V.1.1a - a hypertext compiler enables you to
LIST7   construct custom hypertext help for application programs and readme
LIST7   W-043  HYPERSHELL V.2.5 (2 disks) - is a hypertext control system;
```

Fig. 8-34 File created automatically by BFIND.

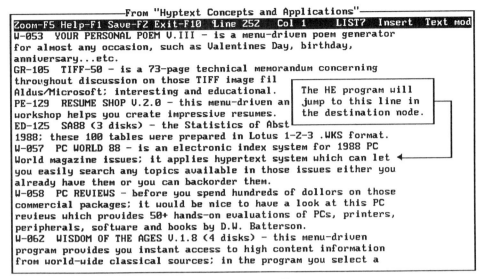

```
Zoom-F5 Help-F1 Save-F2 Exit-F10  Line 252   Col 1       LIST7  Insert  Text mod
W-053  YOUR PERSONAL POEM V.III - is a menu-driven poem generator
for almost any occasion, such as Valentines Day, birthday,
anniversary...etc.
GR-105  TIFF-50 - is a 73-page technical memorandum concerning
throughout discussion on those TIFF image fil ┌──────────────────────┐
Aldus/Microsoft; interesting and educational.  │ The HE program will  │
PE-129  RESUME SHOP V.2.0 - this menu-driven an│ jump to this line in │
workshop helps you create impressive resumes.  │ the destination node.│
ED-125  SA88 (3 disks) - the Statistics of Abst└──────────────────────┘
1988; these 100 tables were prepared in Lotus 1-2-3 .WKS format.
W-057  PC WORLD 88 - is an electronic index system for 1988 PC
World magazine issues; it applies hypertext system which can let ◄───
you easily search any topics available in those issues either you
already have them or you can backorder them.
W-058  PC REVIEWS - before you spend hundreds of dollors on those
commercial packages; it would be nice to have a look at this PC
reviews which provides 50+ hands-on evaluations of PCs, printers,
peripherals, software and books by D.W. Batterson.
W-062  WISDOM OF THE AGES V.1.8 (4 disks) - this menu-driven
program provides you instant access to high content information
from world-wide classical sources; in the program you select a
```

Fig. 8-35 HE jumps directly to "World magazine issues;"

To make this work, HE reads the file name from the screen along with the line of text to the right. Next, HE searches for the line of text much like you would do in WordStar with Ctrl-Q, F or with F2 in WordPerfect. I did this by stuffing the keyboard buffer with a built-in Turbo Prolog predicate called unreadchar. When you stuff the keyboard buffer, it's like having a phantom typist at the keyboard. This kind of programming is rather tricky and it helps to have a source of reliable information. In this case, the idea came from a helpful technical support analyst at Borland. Another source of such information is in publications like *PC Magazine*, *PC-Resource*, *Programmer's Journal*, and *Dr. Dobb's Journal*.

Dr. Dobb's Journal

In the previous chapter I presented some sample screens from an electronic hypertext version of Dr. Dobb's Journal created with HyperWriter 2.0. The main focus of that issue, aptly, was on hypertext. If you are interested in programming your own hypertext systems, I highly recommend you get a copy of that issue (June 1990). Besides being full of information on techniques for programming hypertext, it's fun to read because it is a hypertext document. You don't need the HyperWriter development system to read it because it comes with a run-time version of HyperWriter. You can download the issue from the DDJ CompuServe forum (GO DDJ), the Bix hypertext forum (J hypertext/listings), or from NTERGAID's HyperBoard (203-366-5698). You can also order it direct from NTERGAID for a $15 handling fee.

NOTE: There are two versions of the document: an abbreviated one with just the key articles and an unabridged version with all articles listings, figures, etc.

Summary

In this chapter you've seen that there are at least three different levels of hypertext programming. At one level, you are programming if you link nodes together in a network. At another level, you are programming if you write special scripts that add intelligence to nodes. At a deeper level, you can develop original proprietary hypertext engines and compile them to machine language.

You've seen how to use a complete hypertext editor using Turbo Prolog and how you can add even more control with PDC Prolog. You've also seen how you can transform a powerful word processor into an even more powerful hypertext system with complete word processing capability. You have been exposed to some of the considerations involved in writing a memory-resident hypertext system in C.

Now, let's take a look at the future of hypertext.

9

Future developments

Although the idea for hypertext/hypermedia has been around since at least 1945, it seems that the technology is still in its infancy. Every day more and more new hypertext products and development systems are emerging. Now let's explore hypertext of the future as well as some emerging technologies related to hypertext/hypermedia.

New pointing devices

Hypertext depends on the ability of the user to point to a button and select it. As hardware continues to improve, there will be more and more convenient ways of selecting hypertext buttons. In the future, pressure-sensitive screens could become commonplace and enable users to select buttons by actually pressing them. Or imagine Christine, a super-user of the future. Christine looks at a specific word on the screen and raises her eyebrows. The system instantly zooms to the node she has selected. This doesn't sound so farfetched when you consider that the Stanford Research Institute is now testing a prototype system that can track eye movements and carry out programs in response to those eye movements. Other pointing devices are under development, too: special gloves, goggles, and head orientation sensing devices.

What about a system that tracks your blood pressure or galvanic skin response? What about a system that measures changes in brain waves?

Voice input might be widely used in the future. In some hypertext systems if you press, say, the Tab key a selection bar jumps to the next hypertext button. When you press Return the selected button is activated. Using voice input, you might just say "Next" to move the selection bar to the next button and "Go" to activate the button. Such a system is possible now using existing technology such as Intro Voice VI and the VOICE MASTER KEY SYSTEM (see chapter 10). So imagine what the future will bring!

New media

New types of media will emerge. Whatever emerges will have the potential of becoming a node in a network. Perhaps someday we will be able to activate holographic images by selecting hypertext buttons. Speech nodes are already possible as described earlier using devices such as the SPEECH THING. Currently speech nodes do not contain buttons, but that would be possible. For example, if the user presses a hotkey upon hearing certain emphasized words the program might branch to another node. A program called Smooth Talker can already automatically switch the pitch of its voice when it comes to text that has been boldfaced.

Compact disk interactive

A relatively new kind of media is CDI (Compact Disk Interactive). CDI extends compact disk technology by including audio, still and motion pictures, animation, text, and data. These different media can be manipulated in real time. The disks will store 660 megabytes of memory. Enough for 7,000 still photographs or 8 hours of stereo sound.

Elastic music

CDI will enable elastic music to become a reality. The name elastic music was coined by Dwight Marcus. *Elastic music* is music that can be shaped by the listener. By selecting various options, the listener can shape the music and control various musical elements such as the featured soloists, the musical instruments, and the volume of various musical parts. Recorded music will no longer have to be a static linear piece. Hypertext will be used to allow users to access an electronic jacket. If they want, they will be able to see pictures of the recording artists, the composer—or see the lyrics, production credits, technical specifications and so on. Consumers will be able to store their favorite versions of a piece and recall them later by pressing a hypertext button. AIM (American Interactive Media, Inc.) is committed to making elastic music a reality for the average consumer.

In addition I believe that ultimately people who do not necessarily have musical training also will be able to collaborate with their CDI player and compose outstanding and significant new music. For example, the player will suggest a motif (musical theme). By clicking a mouse or other selection device without leaving his or her couch, the composer/ listener will show acceptance or rejection of the system's suggested motif. The system will then expand the motif based on the specifications selected by the composer/listener. Or perhaps the user will be able to enter a motif—by keyboarding it, playing it on a musical instrument, or even humming it. The system might then, at the user's option, vary this motif. After the user approves the variation, the system will unfold it into a complete musical phrase and again wait for approval or rejection from the user. Other options will allow for harmonization of a melody or the addition of counter melodies—melodies that sound simultaneously, with the main melody, fit into the song and produce a pleasing effect.

Systems that approach this are already available, but only for musicians and composers. For example, a program called M for the Macintosh and a similar program from Voyetra Technologies for PCs are available for helping composers generate new musical ideas. (See chapter 10.) I have also created similar programs in my research laboratory using Turbo Prolog. I believe it's only a matter of time before such programs are in the hands of music listeners who themselves will become composers.

User seduction

Entertainment HyperMedia of the future will seduce you. When you start a program, it will give you options, but if you don't take them it will create a unique story on its own. If you just put the disk in and turn on the system, it will do something interesting. If you interact with the the system, it will do something more interesting. Hypermedia will be super friendly. It will be easy to use. You will be able to:

- Install it in a minute without a manual.
- Learn to use it within 10 minutes.
- Use it for years without it crashing.

Hypertext and telecommunication

Currently telecommunications services such as BIX, CompuServe, AppleLink Personal Edition, and Prodigy offer a wide variety of information. But they don't use hypertext. In the future, though, instead of having to give a command like GO BORLAND and then wade through several menus, you will be able to select a hypertext button and move immediately to your area of interest.

The media lab

Research on new media is going on full force at the media lab at MIT. The lab is divided into several groups. The Electronic Publishing group (using about $1 million from IBM) is researching electronic books and self-personalizing newspapers, magazines and TV broadcasts. In the Speech group, the focus is on such things as intelligent phones that know your friends and can talk to them for you.

(Actually, I am doing this now. I create hypertext buttons that launch WATSON, an inexpensive, programmable voice message system for PCs. WATSON can then make multiple calls for me or call specific individuals. To a certain extent WATSON can converse with callers. WATSON, however, does not yet understand human speech so my associates have to answer by pressing the touch tones on their phones. They can leave recorded messages, but WATSON cannot yet respond interactively to those messages.)

Anyway, returning to the media lab at MIT, the Spatial Imaging group is exploring holography with grants amounting to about $500,000 per year. A lot of this comes from General Motors, which is probably why the first projected holograph image is that of an 18-inch Camaro parked in midair. For more information on this kind of research, you want to see Steward Brand's book *The Media Lab* published by Viking Penguin, Inc.

Hypertisements

In a traditional linear advertisement there are a lot of limits on what you can do but possibilities open up when you think about advertising with hypertext. For this to work we probably need hypertext on a telecommunications service. Companies will be able to register items they want to sell and add nodes to a network of hypertisements. Control nodes will allow users to get a quick overview of what is available in certain industries.

Different levels of information will be available. Readers will be able to zoom in on technical detail if they want it. A query system will allow users to create webs (subnetworks). For example a reader might say: "Give me a control node that lists all compact cars selling for under $30,000 that get at least 50 miles per gallon." Such a query will produce a control node from which the reader can begin browsing. Order buttons will surely be available. When you select an order button the system will prompt you for your method of payment and so on. General Motors has already begun to explore hypertisements. They've noticed that hypertext/hypermedia users tend to have high discretionary income.

Hypertext of the future

Greg Shaw writing in *HyperMedia* (Summer, 1988) describes his vision of a hypertext system of the future. Greg uses the term "Hyperpad," a name later adopted by Brightbill Roberts for its hypertext product HyperPAD. The Hyperpad that Greg describes here is not HyperPAD, the software product for PCs, but rather Greg's vision of what is to come.

"Imagine an object the size of a notepad. You detach the pen fastened to its side; from then on, until you re-attach the pen, your Hyperpad is listening, recording every sound you utter, recording every word or scribble you draw with the pen on its writing surface, recording with full motion every scene you point the Hyperpad lens surface toward. If, after you have done nothing intelligible, the Hyperpad says "Hello?" In three modes simultaneous; verbally, through a small speaker on the side; visually, appearing on the writing surface which doubles as a display surface; and tactually, in Braille, using a set of pins on the side that function like an oversize dot-matrix printer.

Further inactivity on your part prompts the Hyperpad to begin teaching you how to use it, constantly adjusting its instruction to a level appropriate to the savvy you demonstrate.

Within a few minutes, you learn how to record and play back multimedia notes, discovering in the process that the Hyperpad is connected by cellular telephone technology to a network of all other hypermedia stations in existence, so you can send and receive multimedia notes to anyone so equipped.

The Hyperpad also teaches you how to find out what topics are available in all of the world's hypernotes, and how to hyperjump around, looking at just those portions of the notes pertaining to the topics of interest to you, assembling a perspective on all the world's hypermedia information that illustrates your personal viewpoint."

Shaw goes on to point out that the technology to make this happen is a few years down the road. But he wisely points out that now is the time to start dreaming about such things, because such dreams will help us "lay a global foundation of compatible multimedia communications." Only with the proper foundation will we be able to build the HyperPAD of the future.

Ted Nelson's dream

As you might know, Ted Nelson, who coined the term "hypertext" predicts that someday we will have an electronic hypertext publishing system which will include all documents in the world! As soon as you ask for a document, it will be fed to your screen and royalties will immediately be allocated to the various owners of the document in proper proportions. There will be a royalty on every byte transmitted, which will be, say, 1/1000 of a cent. If you publish something, then you will get a royalty when someone reads it directly or whenever someone reads a quotation from your work.

You will be able to make new documents by creating an annotated collage of other documents. When your document is read, royalties will go to you and the other authors based on how much new material you created with your annotations and how much material you quoted. If you quote material from the public domain, such as a work by Shakespeare, then the royalty will go to an Author's Fund. (Perhaps this fund will go to an annual Christmas party for contributing hypertext authors or perhaps it will go to starving hypertext writers.)

Does all of this sound a bit farfetched to you? It does to me at times, but the future is ours to form. Who knows what will happen?

Hypertext and world hunger

The Hunger Project in San Francisco (founded in 1977) is a consciousness-raising group dedicated to making the end of world hunger a major priority. We have the resources and the technology to end world hunger now. But we are not yet making it a priority in the world of politics and business. Perhaps hypertext—if it helps to link us together globally as one people—can help play a part in making that goal a reality. If we can instantly call up and read a document created by a farmer in Africa, we might be more interested in working together to eliminate world hunger. Actually under Nelson's system, just reading such an article might help because the system will automatically calculate the royalties and allocate them to the proper account!

I invite your help

If you are like me, you enjoy exploring hypertext/hypermedia and creating new kinds of buttons and nodes, links, networks, and hypertext development systems. Because the imagination of users is always greater than that of developers, I invite you to write and share your needs with me. What features would you like to see in the hypertext of the future? Perhaps we can work on a project together or with your permission, I can quote you in the next edition of this book. In the meantime, "happy hypering."

<h1>10</h1>

Hypertext sources and resources

This chapter lists hypertext/hypermedia resources and is organized into these categories:

- Hypertext programming tools
- Node design methodology information sources
- PC hypertext development systems
- Macintosh hypertext systems and related programs
- The "HyperCard" for the Apple II
- Hypertext for the Amiga
- HyperCard on the Atari
- Hypertext applications
- Articles, magazines, newsletters
- Books
- Organizations
- Graphics, video, sound, and animation
- Miscellaneous products of interest to hypertext users

Let's begin with hypertext programming tools.

Hypertext programming tools

4C A hypertext editor designed for programmers working with C and Pascal. The 4C editor makes it easy to explore source code. It includes a point-and-shoot zoom key that locates any function, global variable, structure definition, #define statement, etc. See Fig. 10-1. The 4C editor is available from:

TRI-TECHNOLOGY SYSTEMS INC.
1225 S. Elgin
Forest Park, IL 60130
Phone: (312) 366-7595

POWER SEARCH A library of C functions designed to search for character strings or

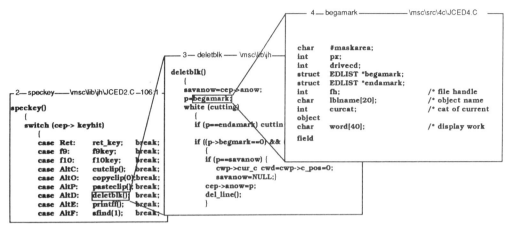

Fig. 10-1 The 4C hypertext editor for programmers.

"regular expressions" in DOS or OS/2 applications. If you program in the C language you can integrate POWER SEARCH into your own program and pay no royalties. POWER SEARCH is particularly effective for searching huge volumes of data. That's because for each search pattern, the system creates custom-optimized machine code—optimized for searching for the particular pattern specified by the user. You can include place holders to match a class of characters. For example, $d matches any decimal digit, $u matches any uppercase letter, $l, any lowercase letter, $x any letter, and so on. You may use several other special characters in a file search. For example, if you know that a string appears at, say, the beginning of a line, or the end of a line you can give that information in your search specification. Versions are available for Turbo C, Quick C, and Microsoft C. Cost: $149.00. These utilities would be invaluable in creating routines that do automatic linking or that enable the user to query a hypertext network. Sample C programs are included to show how to search for multiple patterns in disk files. Available from:

BLAISE COMPUTING INC.
2560 Ninth Street, Suite 316
Berkeley, CA 94710
Phone: (415) 540-5441

KeyPilot   A program that lets you run PC programs and feed them keystrokes. You can record the keystrokes automatically while using a special learning mode and store those keystrokes in a data file. KeyPilot works by calling an application program and "tricking" the program into taking its input from the data file. When the application program terminates, KeyPilot drops out of memory as well. You might use KeyPilot to create complex command buttons. For example, just by clicking on a button, a user might be able to start up a spreadsheet program, load a particular spreadsheet, and print out a specific report. KeyPilot is available from Blaise Computing (see address above). The cost is about $50.

ProBAS HyperHelp ToolKit   A hypertext engine designed to be called from Quick BASIC. Can be used to build terminate-and-stay-resident help systems. Requires the Pro-

BAS Library. Available from:

HAMMERLY COMPUTER SERVICES, INC.
9309 Jasmine Court
Laurel, MD 20707
Phone: (800) 343-7484

SuperText Toolkit Source code you can use to create your own word processor or to develop your own hypertext application. The cost is about $49.95. Available from:

ZORTECH INC.
361 Massachusetts Avenue
Arlington, MA 02174
Phone: (617) 646-6703

Tech Help! A memory-resident hypertext help system for IBM PC programmers. This is like having several technical reference books available on-line. Extensive hypertext cross-referencing of topics. Available from:

FLAMBEAUX SOFTWARE
1147 Broadway, Suite 56
Glendale, CA 91205
Phone: (818) 500-0044

Turbo C Tools A collection of useful functions that make life easier if you are developing any application in Turbo C. (Other toolkits are also available for other C compilers.) The functions are especially useful for creating hypertext programs and programs that are memory resident. Available from Blaise Computing Inc. (See address listed under POWER SEARCH.)

Dr. Dobb's Journal (June 1990) This issue is focused on hypertext and is also available as an electronic hypertext document created with HyperWriter. You can download the issue from the DDJ CompuServe forum (GO DDJ), the Bix hypertext forum (J hypertext/ listings), or from NTERGAID's HyperBoard (203-366-5698). You can also order it direct from NTERGAID for a $15 handling fee. NOTE: There are two versions of the document: an abbreviated one with just the key articles and an unabridged version with all articles, listings, figures, etc.

Node design methodology

Decision tables

A decision table algorithm may serve as a control node from which a user can branch to get detailed advice. Often with some analysis, an expert system can be reduced to a simple decision table with supporting hypertext nodes. For example, outcome cells in the decision table can be buttons that lead the user to a detailed step-by-step procedure to be followed when certain conditions are true.

Decision table algorithms A self-teaching course on how to create and simplify decision table algorithms is available from Pipe Associates. Also available is the Decision Table Algorithm System software that automatically sorts and simplifies decisions tables. Contact:

PIPE ASSOCIATES
Peter Pipe, Senior Associate
962 Chehalis Drive
Sunnyvale, CA 94087
Phone: (408) 733-6885

Logic Gem A software program designed to help you create and simplify decision tables. An added benefit is that once you've completed the decision table, the program can generate source code in a variety of languages. See the discussion of Logic Gem in chapter 6. Logic Gem is available from:

STERLING CASTLE
702 Washington Street, Suite 174
Marina del Rey, CA 90292
Phone: (213) 306-3020

Information mapping

Information Mapping is a comprehensive methodology for organizing information and instructional materials. The approach may be applied to paper documents as well as hypertext networks. The president of Information Mapping has written an excellent, superbly illustrated book on hypertext and Information Mapping called *Mapping Hypertext*. This book as well as formal courses in Information Methodology are available from:

INFORMATION MAPPING
Robert E. Horn, President
80 Marrett Road
Lexington, MA 02173
Phone: (817) 861-7998

The following article is useful for developing a strategy for node design: Jonassen, David (1988). "Designing Structured Hypertext and Structuring Access to Hypertext." Educational Technology, Volume 28, Number 11.

PC hypertext development systems

The following systems run on IBM PCs and compatibles.

AskSam A free-form intuitive information manager. Works with both text and numbers. AskSam is used for storing and retrieving inventory, sales, catalogs, budgets, billings, bibliographies, personnel records, etc. Hypertext feature: Any record in the database can act as a custom menu to select other records containing a common word, symbol or group of words. You can do rapid searches across multiple files. You also can do a "proximity search," in which you look for items that appear near one another. You can store queries that you use often as named programs. Programs can display dialog boxes so you can set different options at run-time. Available from:

AskSam Systems (IBM)
119 South Washington Street
Perry, FL 32347
Phone: (800) 3ASKSAM or (904) 584-6590

BlackMagic A hypertext word processor (IBM). Graphics oriented. Allows you to put hypertext buttons in graphics created with other programs. Includes command buttons, references buttons, note buttons. (IBM) MAGREAD, a shareware program for distributing read-only copies of hypertext networks developed with BlackMagic. Reg-In-A-Box: A text-based read-only hypertext network that presents EPA regulations about underground storage tanks. You can download it from Hyperboard! Note that BlackMagic has been superseded by HyperWriter. Contact:

NTERGAID, Inc.
2490 Black Rock Turnpike, Suite 337
Fairfield, CT 06430
Phone: (203) 368-0632

CLASS HT Hypertext combined with expert systems development capability.

Ist-Class Expert System Inc.
526 Boston Post Road 150 East
Wayland, MA 01778
Phone: (508) 358-7722

Emergency room simulation An impressive instructional simulation of selected emergency room situations. Shows off the PC EGA monitor's ability to display color photographs. This program was developed by Dr. Stephen Reid and his medical students using HyperBase. (See also HyperBase listing.) Requires PC and EGA color graphics monitor. Future versions will support VGA graphics. To request a copy, send a self-addressed, stamped envelope to:

University of Florida
Dept. of Neuro Surgery
P.O. Box J-265
Gainesville, FL 32610

EMPOWERment A personal scheduler and information manager. Features hypertext "date buttons," an automatic calendar, automatic linking, automatic MCI Mail uploading and downloading, and an intelligent planning node. You can easily launch other application programs from within various nodes. Available from:

TAB Books
Blue Ridge Summit, PA 17294-0850
(See order card in this book.)
Phone (800) 822-8138

MKSCRN A courseware authoring tool for the IBM PS/2. The Instructional Technology Lab at the U.C. Davis developed MKSCRN, an object-oriented authoring system to simplify and automate courseware development. Finished courseware modules may contain hypertext jumps, graphics, animations, and many kinds of interactive activities like crossword puzzles, matching answers, fill-in-the-blank, etc. In addition, all modules have these features: glossary, search function, retrace function, complete on-line help, menu system, and a goto function. Using MKSCRN a computer novice can quickly make interactive tutorials with all this functionality. MKSCRN gives educators the freedom to experiment with pedagogical aspects of courseware development without worrying about the mechanics. MKSCRN was developed for Dr. G. Phillip Cartright by Lorri S. Fisher, Ken Kelley, and Jon Gorono. Contributors include U.C. Davis students: Kristina Seyer, Scott Woods, and Stacey Palacki. For more information, contact:

UNIVERSITY OF CALIFORNIA, DAVIS
Division of Education
Davis, CA 95616

Guide A flexible, comprehensive, graphics-oriented hypertext system. Good for developing hypertext instructional materials as well as other hypertext networks requiring graphics. Requires a mouse. Has a Macintosh-like feel. Nodes can be contained within one file and expanded or retracted as desired. Supports several kinds of buttons: expansion, reference, note, and command buttons. Runs on the IBM PC and Macintosh. On the IBM, Guide runs on Microsoft Windows 2.03 or higher or Windows/386. A run-time version of Windows is included in the package. A conversion system is being developed so systems developed on one machine may be run on another. Guide is available from:

OWL INTERNATIONAL
14218 NE 21st Street
Bellevue, WA 98007
Phone: (206) 747-3203 or (800) 344-9737

Harvard Graphics A software package designed for preparing presentation graphics that now has hypertext capability. Using Harvard Graphics, you can create "HyperShows." A HyperShow is a desktop presentation that uses a network of Harvard Graphics charts. Each chart can contain buttons; if you click on a button, a new chart will appear. To create a HyperShow, you first create a regular linear Harvard Graphics slide show. To create a regular linear show, you choose Slide Show Menu from the Main menu and then Create Slide Show from the Slide Show menu. Next, you give the linear slide show a name and select the files that correspond to the slides you want in the show.

Once you have a linear slide show, you can add buttons to individual charts. These buttons enable users to navigate among the slides in a nonlinear way. Here are the steps needed for creating buttons:

1. Get the Chart using the Get/Save/Remove option from the Main menu.
2. Select Draw/Annotate from the Main menu.
3. Select Add.

4. Select Button.
5. Enter the number of the button you want to create.
6. Move the mouse pointer to where you want the upper right corner of the button and click the mouse.
7. Move the mouse pointer to the lower left corner of the desired button area and click the mouse again.
8. Press Esc repeatedly to return to the Main menu.
9. Save the chart.
10. Bring up the HyperShow menu. Go to the Slide Show menu and choose Add ScreenShow effects. Move the cursor down (any column) so it is in the same row as the file name you want and press F8 to bring up the HyperShow menu.
11. A chart appears in which you can define the buttons on the chart. You can specify which other chart you want to jump to if the user presses a specific button. As well as defining a jump location for each button, you must also define a hotkey. This allows the user to activate a button either by clicking on it or by pressing the hotkey.

As well as creating buttons by using the main Harvard Graphics program, you can create buttons while using the Harvard Graphics Draw Partner. This program lets you create drawings (not just charts), which you can add to your HyperShow. You can also import charts files and fine tune them. With a digitizing tablet you can capture printed drawings as well. In addition, Draw Partner will import Lotus .PIC files and import and export Computer Graphics Metafiles (CGM) metafiles. Harvard Graphics is available from:

SPC SOFTWARE PUBLISHING CORPORATION
1901 Landings Drive
P.O. Box 7210
Mountain View, CA 94039-7210
Phone: (415) 962-8910

HyperRez   A memory-resident hypertext system that can be used concurrently with other application programs. See chapter 7 for a discussion of HyperRez. Available from:

MAXTHINK
Niel Larsen
44 Rincon Road
Kensington, CA 94707
Phone: (415) 540-5508 Hypertext BBS: (415) 540-6114

HyperBase developer   ($249.00) This is a developer's version of HyperBase that allows you to create run-time hypertext documents that you can distribute freely without paying royalties to Cogent Software. For example, Dr. Stephen Reid of the University of Florida has developed a sophisticated training simulation of emergency room situations and is distributing it as freeware. (See Emergency Room Simulation.)

Cogent Prolog   ($199.00) A full Edinberg Prolog compiler that allows you to write self-modifying code so that a program can learn and change its own behavior. With Prolog there is no distinction between data and code. With Cogent Prolog you can easily pass predicates as arguments to other predicates. Available from:

COGENT SOFTWARE
21 William J Heights
Framingham, MA 01701
Phone: (508) 875-6553
Contact: Alan Littleford

Hyperdoc   (costs around $995) An industrial strength hypertext system. Any pixel on the screen may be a hot zone for a hypertext button. Hyperdoc provides a built-in graphics editor and a powerful scripting language. Commands are included for interacting directly with dBASE files and AutoCAD. Users have the impression they are working with one application. Included is a command for interfacing with a videodisc player via a Video-Logics board. By using Hyperdoc along with a VideoLogics board you can do *incrustation*, that is, display a video image along with a computer-generated graphic. Hyperdoc proved useful at the 37th annual meeting of the International Technical Communication Conference. An application was developed to help conference attendees decide which presentations to attend. The application offered a complete list of presentations in alphabetical order (or in order by date). A user could then get details on a presentation by selecting it. For more information on Hyperdoc, contact:

HYPERDOC INC.
1 Almaden, Suite 620
San Jose, CA 95113
Phone: (408) 292-7970
FAX: (408) 292-7617

HyperNotes   A hypertext tool that brings order to random notes. You can group notes into categories and assign priorities, due dates or to-do dates to notes. You can browse and edit notes by group, by priority, or by date. Recommended system is a 386; will work OK on a 286; requires a hard disk, and 640K RAM. ($360) Available from:

SAUCER COMPUTER SYSTEMS
1750 S. Brentwood Boulevard
St. Louis, MO 63144-1365

HyperPAD   A hypertext system good for setting up one standard start-up screen for accessing spreadsheets, word processing or database programs. HyperPAD is similar to HyperCard, but it is text-based. Graphics are possible using character graphics. Has a script language, PADtalk, that you can use to customize actions that will occur when a user selects a button. Nodes can have fields, pages and backgrounds. There are different levels of usage: browsing, typing, "painting," authoring, and scripting. ("Painting" involves creating character graphics—detail graphics are not supported.) A conversion program is being developed to allow HyperCard stacks to be used by HyperPAD. See also

Inside HyperPAD. HyperPAD is available from:

BRIGHTBILL-ROBERTS & COMPANY, LTD.
120 E. Washington Street, Suite 421
Syracuse, NY 13202
Phone: (315) 474-3400

HyperSprint   A hypertext interface for Sprint. Sprint is a full-featured word processor available from Borland International. HyperSprint is an interface that transforms Sprint into a customizable hypertext system—works with Borland's Advanced User Interface. HyperSprint is especially suitable for writing books, and other long documents, as well as hypertext-based help systems. Nodes of any size can be loaded. Hypertext jumps within the same file or between files are possible. You can launch external programs of any size from command buttons. You can have multiple nodes on-screen at once and easily switch between them. Includes many hypertext functions; you can customize it to your liking using Sprint's macro programming language. (Sprint is required to use the HyperSprint interface.) All features of Sprint are available, for example: PostScript Printing, automatic table of contents, block sorting, spelling checking, thesaurus, and automatic backup if you stop typing for 3 seconds! Refer to the book *Mastering Sprint Macro Programming*. HyperSprint is available from:

SEYER ASSOCIATES
1015 Cadillac Way, #5-201
Burlingame, CA 94010
Phone: (415) 347-4711

Hypertext on Hypertext   An inexpensive read-only hypertext network that has scholarly articles on hypertext by computer scientists. Includes text and graphic nodes. There is minimal cross-referencing of nodes. The articles are also available in conventional printed format. Available on both Macintosh and IBM-compatible systems. Available from:

ASSOCIATION FOR COMPUTING MACHINERY
11 East 42nd Street
New York, NY 10036
Phone: (212) 869-7440

HyperTIES   A hypertext development system that runs on almost any configuration with at least 256K monochrome or color monitor. The system is conceived of as a hyperbook or electronic encyclopedia. Nodes are articles, which can contain text, graphics, or videodisc sequences. Consists of two subsystems, one for development and one for browsing. Both subsystems are easy to use. Includes alphabetical index, manually constructed Table of Contents, content search, and path history. It does not have a script language. You can download a free demo from the company's BBS (609) 275-6555 or write for a copy. Hypertext Hands On! and Hypertext on Hypertext were developed with HyperTIES. Also see chapter 7 for a discussion of HyperTIES and the Jewish Museum Project. Contact information:

COGNETICS CORPORATION
Charlie Kreitzberg, President
55 Princeton-Hightstown Road
Princeton Jct, NJ 08550
Phone: (609) 799-5005

HyperTSR   An easy-to-use hypertext help system for making on-line hypertext help for other text-based application programs like Lotus 1-2-3, dBASE, WordPerfect. EMPOW-ERment and HyperTSR are available from:

TAB BOOKS
Blue Ridge Summit, PA 17294-0850
Phone: (800) 822-8138
(See the order form in this book.)

HyperWriter   A greatly enhanced version of BlackMagic. Supports graphical hypertext networks on IBM PCs. It is very easy to develop hypertext documents with this system. Graphical nodes can have hot spots that lead you to other nodes, pop-up windows, graphics, external programs. The June issue of *Dr. Dobb's Journal* was distributed as a HyperWriter document. HyperWriter does not require any special graphical interface such as MicroSoft Windows. Many different link types are supported as well as autotours, a linkmap, command buttons, etc. One limitation is that If statements are not supported. You cannot branch to different nodes by checking the data entered by the user. This can be handled in most cases, however, by using multiple-choice questions. Available from:

NTERGAID INC.
2490 Black Rock Turnpike, Suite 337
Fairfield, CT 06430
Phone: (203) 368-0632

IBM LinkWay   A flexible hypertext system that comes with a text editor, a picture editor, desktop tools, and teacher tools. Teacher tools include a homework designer, flash card maker, and lesson planner. Like HyperPAD, IBM LinkWay has its own built-in script language. You can use this language to control the actions that occur when a user selects a hypertext button. LinkWay is useful for developing tutorials that combine video, text, sound and graphics. Available from authorized IBM dealers. Amazingly enough, once you purchase IBM LinkWay, toll free technical support and a LinkWay bulletin board is available from IBM! For information contact:

IBM LINKWAY
IBM Corporation
Boca Raton, FL 33431
Phone: (404) 238-3245

LinkWay Toolkit   This is a set of routines for developers that extends LinkWay's capabilities. It includes device drivers, extra fonts, and special routines for graphics, animation and speech, a 360-page technical reference manual, which is much more extensive than the manual that comes with LinkWay. The kit also includes: an extern command that gives you vector graphics from within a script, precision math (floating), answer analysis and pattern matching functions for developing computer-based training modules, utilities to create MCGA animation sequences, double-length character fonts, and message templates to link LW to foreign languages, different support buttons for videodisc players: Pioneer 4200, Sony 1200, IBM's info window, support for Dynamics Inc. Touch Tablet and the IBM Music feature, global change of access levels, forced color palette changes, low-level mouse driver, and support for HP LaserJet printer. Cost: $300 for single license for developer. $2000 for site. (Run-time programs can still be distributed at no cost.) For more information, contact:

WASHINGTON COMPUTER SERVICES
Elaine Kheriaty
LinkWay Toolkit
2601 North Shore Road
Bellingham, WA 98226
Phone: (206) 734-8248

Ize   An information manager that has its own unique style of hypertext. With Ize you store all information in nodes called *texts*. A text can be just one word or it can be up to 30K in size. You can store many texts (up to 32,000!) in a network, which Ize calls a *textbase*. You retrieve texts by their keywords. When you save a node (a text) in Ize you must assign at least one keyword. Texts in Ize are stored in a special Ize format. If you have ASCII files or files in special word processing formats, you need to import them into Ize. A powerful feature of Ize is its ability to "automatically" create keywords for each text that you import into it. Ize then uses the keywords as the basis for a hypertext-like access system. Available from:

PERSOFT, INC.
465 Science Drive
Madison, WI 53711
Phone: (608) 273-6000

Knowledge Acquisition System (KAS)   On-line (memory-resident) dictionaries with hypertext capability. When using any text-based application program, put cursor on a word and press Alt-M. Then press Return to get a full definition of the word—not just a spelling check. Several dictionaries are available including: Funk & Wagnall's Standard Desk Dictionary, and McGraw-Hill Technical Dictionaries of: Computers, Electrical and Electronic Engineering, Mechanical and Design Engineering, Chemical Terms, Physics, Biology. Also available: a Concise Dictionary of 26 Languages. While reading a definition you can highlight another word of interest and jump to its definition. Available from:

INDUCTEL INC.
Order Dept.
18661 McCoy Avenue
Saratoga, CA 95070
Phone: Outside of CA, (800) 367-4497. In CA, (408) 866-8016

KnowledgePro An expert system that has hypertext capabilities. (A version called KPWIN is also available that runs under Microsoft Windows 2.0 or 3.0.) It allows you to create intelligent hypertext that can provide structure and guidance to users as they explore a hypertext network. The problem with many hypertext systems is that users get lost and don't know what nodes they have and have not seen. With KnowledgePro you can avoid this problem by structuring an intelligent hypertext that can carry on a dialogue with the user. For example, the system might say: "You looked at nodes A, X, L, and M, but it seems you might have missed the main idea that connects these nodes. You might want to see node Q for further information." or "You have been reviewing nodes about (say) computer music. Which particular aspect of this computer music do you want to consider next?" KnowledgePro helps you structure and control hypertext presentations. You can download KnowledgePro's run-time system and a few simple knowledge bases, including a simple hypertext authoring tool from BIX, the Byte Information Exchange. See also Interactive Video Disk Toolkit. Contact:

KNOWLEDGE GARDEN INC.
John Slade, President
473A Malden Bridge Road
Nassau, NY 12123
Phone: (518) 766-3000

CompuServe: Go PCVEN, user options, subtopic #8 BIX—JOIN GARDEN

OPUS I A drawing program with hypertext capability. Just point and click to instantly display a related drawing or bring up the information you need. Also has command buttons to, say, bring up a spreadsheet program. Contact:

ROYKORE SOFTWARE INC.
749 Brunswick Street
San Francisco, CA 94112
Phone: (800) 227-0847

PC-Browse A RAM-resident shareware system that lets you search for an ASCII test document while using another program. You can search for a file name using wildcards or search within files using keywords. Once you find a file, you can paste it (or a part of it) into another application, print it or save it under a different name. Hypertext-style linking is also possible. You can hotkey all functions. Available from:

QUICKSOFT
219 First N. #224
Seattle, WA 98109
Phone: (206) 282-0452

PC-Key Draw This program started off purely as a graphics package for drawing but now it has hypertext capability. Some users like to use it strictly as a graphics program, others make more use of its hypertext capabilities. You can create graphics screens by drawing or by capturing screens created with other programs. You can embed up to 18 buttons in each screen. The buttons link to other screens or to macros. Macros are stored in separate files. Macros can do animation, draw something while you watch, underline a word and so on. Anything the program can do the macro can do. You can also do command buttons. Keeps only 100 bytes in memory for reloading. Links are hidden. It is up to the user to draw a button—you can use clip art. Files are in BSAVE (BLOAD) format. Can export to GEM format (readable by Ventura). Oedware is continuing to work on it and improve it, especially the hypertext aspects. Can handle images larger than the screen. Can import ASCII files. There are 26 fonts available. Available from:

> OEDWARE
> Ed Kidera, President
> P.O. Box 595
> Columbia, MD 21045
> Phone: (301) 997-9333

Personal HyperBase ($99) A development system that allows you to create hypertext documents with dynamic buttons. The buttons can do different things depending upon the unique history of the user. For example, if the user has skill X and has read chapter Y, then do action Z. Buttons can contain Prolog code, which is read and interpreted when a button is activated. When the user goes to a node, the system reads and analyzes the text in the node, so nodes may contain "latent code"—code that gets executed each time the user reads the node. Graphics nodes with buttons embedded in them are possible. Different buttons may appear at different times depending on the user and the history of the user's performance with the system. Comes with a graphics capture utility and a graphics editor. (See note below about a sample application developed by Stephen Reid.) Available from:

> COGENT SOFTWARE
> 21 William J Heights
> Framingham, MA 01701
> Phone: (508) 875-6553
> Contact: Alan Littleford

Plus A HyperCard-like product that runs on the Macintosh and IBM PCs and PC compatibles under Windows 3.0 and the OS/2 Presentation Manager. Note that you need at least a 286 machine with a high-density drive and two megabytes of hard disk space. Plus uses objects such as fields, graphics, and hypertext buttons. Fields may be for word processing or database applications. You put the objects into nodes or "cards," which you can also treat as objects. Plus might be a good choice if you want to write hypertext applications that run on both the Macintosh and IBM PC. The Macintosh version of Plus features a conversion program that changes HyperCard stacks into IBM stacks. Available from:

> SPINNAKER SOFTWARE
> 201 Broadway 6th Floor
> Cambridge, MA 02139-1901
>
> Customer inquiries: (617) 494-1200 or (800) 826-0706
> FAX ordering: (617) 494-1219
> Dealer Inquiries: (800) 323-8088

PLUS Development Partner Program: (612) 942-3303

ToolBook   A powerful graphics hypertext system for Microsoft Windows 3.0 or higher. Requires at least a PC AT with 640K standard memory plus 256K extended memory. (1.5 megabytes of memory is recommended.) Also, you need from two to eight megabytes of disk space, a mouse and a VGA, EGA, or Hercules monitor. ToolBook has a powerful scripting language called OpenScript with hundreds of command words. Some developers with HyperCard applications on the Macintosh are considering converting them to Tool-Book on the PC. ToolBook is available from:

ASYMETRIX CORPORATION
110 − 110th Avenue N.E., Suite 717
Bellevue, WA 98004

Transtext   A hypertext word processor based on the same source code used to create Sprint. Comes with several utilities. For example, the utility REFALL shows all hypertext jumps from a file. INVERT shows all hypertext jumps to a file. SREF collects ideas into hypertext categories. MARKER makes hypertext jumps to key ideas in files. Available from:

MAXTHINK
Niel Larson
44 Rincon Road
Kensington, MA 94707
Phone: (415) 428-0104

PC-hypertext   A shareware hypertext system for use with ASCII files. Features automatic backpath tracking and recording of paths chosen in a network. Displays PC Paintbrush graphics (Hercules, CGA, EGA, VGA modes). Available from MaxThink. (See address above.)

PDC Prolog   A powerful extension of Turbo Prolog. Comes with a built-in extensible editor and many new built-in predicates. DOS and OS/2 versions are source code-compatible with minor exceptions. Also available are a Professional Developer's manual and a Prolog Toolkit. A hypertext programmer's toolkit is under development. See the discussion in chapter 8 for details. Contact:

PROLOG DEVELOPMENT CENTER/ATLANTA
568 14th Street N.W.
Atlanta, GA 30318
Phone: (404) 873-1366
FAX: (404) 872-5243
BBS: (404) 872-5358

Turbo Prolog   An inexpensive yet powerful Prolog compiler with many built-in predicates. Includes a built-in editor, and several predicates that interface effectively with MS-DOS. This makes it easy to create a hypertext system in Turbo Prolog. (See chapter 8, which includes the source code for a complete hypertext editor.) Prolog is especially good for developing intelligent hypertext applications. Includes special graphics predicates, an external database system, and many sample programs. Also includes a description of how to write a Prolog interpreter which enables meta-programming, a type of programming in which you can pass predicates as arguments to other predicates. (See also PDC Prolog.) Turbo Prolog is available from:

BORLAND INTERNATIONAL
4585 Scotts Valley Drive
P.O. Box 660001
Scotts Valley, CA 95066-0001
Phone: (408) 438-8400

Window Book Technology   Perhaps the first PC hypertext development system for publishers, software developers and organizations who need on-line documentation. Run-time "Window Books" may be compiled and distributed. A table of contents helps readers keep a sense of context. Runs fast on an IBM PC and needs only 128K. Boston Documentation Development, Inc. in Newton, MA has used the system to develop documentation for Lotus 1-2-3, dBASE and other application programs. The writers claim that using Window Book technology they need one-third fewer words to document something than would be required with conventional paper documentation. This may be true because with hypertext-style (associative) writing you don't need to repeat yourself, you just refer the reader to the appropriate text with a button. Available from:

BOX COMPANY INC.
56 Howard Street
Cambridge, MA 02139
Phone: (617) 576-0892

Xanadu   An "industrial strength" hypertext server designed to run on a local area network controlled by a Sun Workstation. Any computer, such as an IBM PC or Macintosh that can communicate with a Sun can be used to develop and run front-end applications. Xanadu frees up the front-end application program to handle a specific interface, similar to the way SQL can be enabled on a network by dBASE IV. Xanadu customers will probably be large corporations whose MIS group wants to implement an information system in a local area network. Also, third-party developers will be developing front-end applications.

Xanadu supports all kinds of nodes stored in digital format: text, sound, video, and graphics. Multiple back-end servers can be connected to each other via LAN connections, but to the end user it will look like one network. The developer claims that the information pool can grow in an unbounded fashion with little performance degradation. Unlimited link typing is supported and a link can point to a document or to any byte within a document. Links are automatically bidirectional (that is, there is automatic hypertext backtracking). In addition to a type name, a link may contain other information: the creator of the link, when it was created, and a comment.

You can filter a hypertext network in various ways to create a web of the major network. For example, you can specify that you want to see only nodes of type X created by person Y after last October. You can put sensors and alert on documents. A *sensor* senses when an event happens. An *alert* notifies you in some way that the event has taken place. For example, you can put a sensor on a document so that if the document is modified in any way, the system will send you an alert, perhaps an E-mail message of some sort. How the alert is enabled depends on how the front-end application is programmed.

Xanadu also supports version control and history tracking. That is, it can display to author or reader how one document was transformed into another. An exact copy of each document is not stored, but rather information about the changes that were made to the original document. Yet documents are said to appear very quickly due to the proprietary algorithms used by the system.

NOTE: The vision for Xanadu came from Ted Nelson, who continues to be an adviser to the Xanadu Operating Co. Xanadu is funded by Autodesk. Available from:

XANADU OPERATION COMPANY
550 California Avenue, Suite 101
Palo Alto, CA 94306
Phone: (415) 856-4112

Xhelp   An on-line information manager with hypertext capability. It may be memory-resident so you can pop up the information when required. Written entirely in assembly language so it is extremely fast and requires little memory. Runs fine on a plain PC. Available from:

EXWELLS SOFTWARE COMPANY
P.O. Box 8387
Berkeley, CA 94707
Phone: (415) 657-9300

Macintosh hypertext systems and related programs

CLR HyperArrays   External routines that speed up numerical calculations on arrays. Available from:

CLEAR LAKE RESEARCH
2476 Bolsover, Suite 343
Houston, TX 77005
Phone: (713) 523-7842

HyperBASIC   A system for creating external commands (XCMDs) for HyperCard. Available from:

TEKNOSYS, INC.
3923 Coconut Palm Drive, Suite 111
Tampa, FL 33619
Phone: (800) 873-3494 or (813) 620-3494
FAX: (813) 620-4039
CompuServe: 73237,2370

AppleLink: D3375
MacNET: TEKNOSYS

Eyecons! 301 icons ready for use. Available from:

HEIZER SOFTWARE
P.O. Box 232019
Pleasant Hill, CA 94523
Phone: (800) 888-7667

Guide A hypertext system that allows multiple, scrollable nodes on-screen; it has expansion buttons, reference buttons, and command buttons. Easier to use than systems requiring programming. Conversion programs are being developed so that hypertext documents "guidelines" can run on either the Macintosh or IBM PCs and compatibles. Available from:

OWL INTERNATIONAL
14218 NE 21st Street
Bellevue, WA 98007
Phone: (206) 747-3203 or (800) 344-9737

Hyperbook Maker Prints your HyperCard stack as a collated ready-to-staple book. Also lets you create a new stack from cards that are in different stacks. Available from:
IDEAFORM
P.O. Box 1540
Fairfield, IA 52556
Phone: (515) 472-7256

HyperCard Comes bundled with the Macintosh. Allows hypertext-links if programmed explicitly. Good for linking to Video and CD-ROM. Many educational and entertaining software programs (stacks) are becoming available for HyperCard.

HyperEasy training Tutorials on audio tape—how to use and program HyperCard. From:

COGNITION TECHNOLOGY CORPORATION
55 Wheeler Street
Cambridge, MA
Phone: (800) 622-2829 or (617) 492-0246

Hypergate Hypertext development system (Macintosh). The developer of Hypergate is distributing an educational simulation entitled "The Election of 1912." See chapter 7. Available from:

EASTGATE SYSTEMS, INC.
P.O. Box 1307
Cambridge, MA 02238
Phone: (617) 782-9044

MacSmarts Professional An expert system tool that can link to databases and spreadsheets, HyperCard stacks, MacPaint and PICT images, and text files. Available from:

COGNITION TECHNOLOGY CORPORATION
55 Wheeler Street
Cambridge, MA 02138
Phone: (800) 622-2829 or (617) 492-0246

Icon Factory   A large library of icons and an editor you can use to build and install icons in your own HyperCard stacks. Available from:

HYPERPRESS
P.O. Box 8243
Foster City, CA 94404
Phone: (415) 345-4620

SuperCard   A hypertext system that takes advantage of the MAC II features: color screens and resizable screens. SuperCard also has better print functions than HyperCard. Can link to video, CD-ROM, Stereo, and even DOS applications with Macintosh SE or MAC II. Available through local dealers or contact:

SILICON BEACH SOFTWARE
P.O. Box 261430
San Diego, CA 92126
Phone: (619) 695-6956

ScriptEdit   An editor for working with multiple scripts simultaneously. All card objects may be indexed. Available from:

SOMAK SOFTWARE, INC.
535 Encinitas Boulevard, Suite 113
Encinitas, CA 92024
Phone: (800) 842-5020 or (619) 942-2556

The "HyperCard" for the Apple II

Tutor-tech   A hypermedia toolkit for the Apple II computer. Especially good for teachers and trainers. You can create graphic nodes with buttons that link to graphic nodes. You can import clip-art from Print Shop, Newsroom, or Mousepaint pictures. No programming required. Gives the Apple II the feel of a Macintosh. Supports videodisc players Pioneer LD-V2000 and LD-V4200 with extra videodisc interface and cables. Available from:

TECHWARE CORPORATION
P.O. Box 151085
Altamonte Springs, FL 32715-1085
Phone: (407) 695-9000

Hypertext for the Amiga

The Thinker is a hierarchical text processor with hypertext. Any word in a Thinker document is a potential hypertext button. Also buttons can be in this form:

    < Thinker:goals,target income >

Here, Thinker is the disk name, goals is the file name and target income is the node name. A useful feature of the Thinker is the ability to display only the first line of each node. This lets you see a large part of the document all at once. If you move blocks of text while the document is in "outline form" all of the text associated with a single line of text gets moved also.

The Thinker has an interesting and quite useful "see-thru button" (referred to as a "see-thru link" in the Thinker documentation). If a button consists of a string surrounded by angle brackets, you can select a menu option so that the Thinker displays the contents of the node pointed to. Notice, here, that you are not going to the remote link. Rather you are "peeking," as it were through a window. You can enable and disable a see-thru button. When you disable see-thru, only the button is visible. If you move the button to a new location in the document and then enable "see-thru" the text will again become visible, but in its new location. The Thinker is available from:

POOR PERSON SOFTWARE
3721 Starr King Circle
Palo Alto, CA 94306
Phone: (415) 493-7234

HyperCard on the Atari

Spectre 128 Enables an Atari ST computer to emulate a Macintosh. Spectre is a cartridge you plug into an Atari. You use it along with emulation software. In addition to Spectre, to run HyperCard on an Atari, you need 128K Macintosh ROM (read only memory) chips, which you plug into the Spectre cartridge. Using Spectre you can format an Atari Hard Disk so that one partition is for MS-DOS, one for Macintosh, and one for Atari. You also need to move Macintosh software on Macintosh diskettes to the Atari hard disk "Spectre" format. You can do this by hooking up a Mac to an Atari via a null modem cable (a special cable that allows two micros to communicate directly). Or you can download Macintosh software from bulletin boards. You also need a Macintosh telecommunications program in Spectre format. For this you might want to visit your local Atari or users group. Sounds like a lot of work, but it can be fun to "teach" different computers to work together. I find it helps to avoid giving unwarranted loyalty to one computer. (We're all here to help each other.) Spectre is available from:

GADGETS BY SMALL, INC.
40 W. Littleton Boulevard, #210−211
Littleton, CO 80120
Phone: (303) 791-6098

Hypertext applications

Hypertext on PCs

DOS Help! is a hypertext PC-DOS tutorial and reference guide. It was developed with xText, a hypertext compiler and toolkit, which is also available if you want to create your own memory-resident hypertext help systems. A more technical hypertext manual called

Tech Help! can also be purchased. Contact:

FLAMBEAUX SOFTWARE
1147 Broadway, Suite 56
Glendale, CA 91205
Phone: (818) 500-0044

ComputorEdge   San Diego's computer magazine. Available in paper and in hypertext format for Macintosh and IBM PC computers. See description of *ComputorEdge* in chapter 7. For a free copy, send a formatted diskette, and a self-addressed stamped envelope to:

COMPUTOREDGE
P.O. Box 83086
San Diego, CA 92138
Phone: (619) 573-0315
BBS: (619) 573-1675

Foreign language instruction   (French and Spanish) Pronunciation tutors with native speaker voice reproduction. Developed with HyperPAD, which is not required. Voice output comes from the SPEECH THING, an inexpensive device that adds speech capability to PCs. (NOTE: Macintosh versions also available, see below.) Available from:

HYPERGLOT SOFTWARE COMPANY
505 Forest Hills Boulevard
Knoxville, TN 37919
Phone: (800) 726-5087

What makes music work   A self-teach guide on music theory for nonmusic majors. Teaches musical notation, chords, scales, musical structure, musical composition. Based on the book with the same title. (See also Katakana.) Available from:

SEYER ASSOCIATES
1015 Cadillac Way, #5-201
Burlingame, CA 94010

HyperCard applications on the Macintosh

MacAtlas   Maps of the world, all continents by country, the USA by state, and each state by county. You can click on a map to zoom in on a more detailed map. For more information contact:

MICROMAPS
P.O. Box 757
Lambertville, NJ 08530
Phone: (800) 334-4291 or (609) 397-1611

Miscellaneous HyperCard stacks are available from:

TELEGRAPHICS
936 Sir Francis Drake Boulevard #R
Kentfield, CA 94904
Phone: (415) 454-7519

BMUG
1442A Walnut Street #62
Berkeley, CA 94709-1496
Phone: (415) 549-2684

The Hypertext 1987 Digest   A self-contained hypertext document (on diskette). Contains 150 articles by hypertext authorities. Research from elementary education to the space station. Contributors include: Ted Nelson, K. Eric Drexler, and Nicole Yankelovich. Available from:

EASTGATE SYSTEMS, INC.
P.O. Box 1307
Cambridge, MA 02238
Phone: (617) 782-9044

HyperTutor   A tutorial that teaches you how to program in HyperTalk. Written as a HyperCard stack. Available from:

CHANNELMARK CORPORATION
2929 Campus Drive
San Mateo, CA 94403

AmandaStories   HyperCard stacks for fun and education. Available from:

AMANDA GOODENOUGH
AmandaStories
1025 Martin Road
Santa Cruz, CA 95060-9721

Focal Point   A HyperCard stack designed to help you increase productivity. Available from:

TRITON PRODUCTS
1159 Triton Drive
Foster City, CA 94404
Phone: (800) 227-6900

Executive Life   Another HyperCard stack designed to help you increase productivity. Available from:

NEW WEST SOFTWARE
5462 Oceanus, Suite "B"
Huntington Beach, CA 92649
Phone: (714) 898-1039

The 20th Century Navigator   A HyperCard guidance program for use with The Video Encyclopedia of the 20th Century, a videodisc-based collection of historical material maintained in primary-source format. The Navigator can conduct searches of all 2,278 video units and can create presentations by interfacing with videodisc players and VCRs.

Available from:

CEL EDUCATIONAL RESOURCES
477 Madison Avenue, 4th Floor
New York, NY 10022
Phone: (800) 235-3339

Japanese Language Instruction   Hiragana/Katakana and Kanji Exercises for use with HyperCard. See chapter 7. This is a rich learning environment for studying the Japanese writing system. Includes animation of correct stroke order and digital recording of native speaker of Japanese. (See also Traveler's Guild: Japanese.) Available from:

ANONAE SOFTWARE
P.O. Box 7629
Berkeley, CA 94707
Phone: (415) 845-8292

Traveler's Guide: Japanese   A computerized language course with hypertext capability. When you start the course you can choose from a number of subject areas such as "Useful phrases," "Making Friends," "Eating Out" and so on. Once you choose a topic, you can choose different kinds of learning activities: flash cards, matching exercises, fill-in's, sentences, and conversations. When you are working on an exercise you can click on any Japanese word if you need help. Then a translation node will pop up at the bottom of the screen. Then if you want more help you can click on an Info button to get more detailed information on the word. Figure 10-2 shows a sample exercise with the mouse pointer on the word taizai.

Because I wanted to know the meaning of taizai I clicked on that word and the translation appeared at the bottom of the screen. Then I clicked on Info and a more detailed screen appeared as you can see in Fig. 10-3. After clicking the Continue button I was returned to the Making Friends exercise in Fig. 10-2.

Besides the exercises, the program has a hypertext Language reference section, which you can access at any time by pressing F1. You can explore various topics in this reference section and backtrack when desired to the task you were working on previously. A mouse is not required to use the system, but I found it more fun with a mouse. In addition to the software, the package comes with a pronunciation tape with native speakers, a tape script and a user's manual. For more information, contact:

TRAVELER'S GUILD
A Division of GuildWare Inc.
315 West Washington
Marquette, MI 49855
Phone: (906) 228-5030

Chinese Language Instruction!   "The Hanzi Assistant" is a HyperCard stack that creates computerized flash cards. Each card includes traditional calligraphic image of the character, stroke-by-stroke animation as well as digitized pronunciation in male and

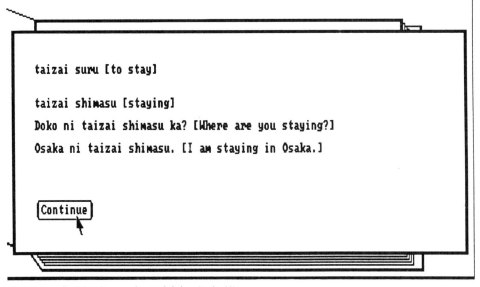

Making Friends

Dono gurai koko ni taizai shimasu ka?

☐ When are (you) leaving?

☐ Where are (you) staying?

☐ About how long are (you) staying here?

Select the best translation for the sentence above.
Click-on any Japanese word to check its meaning.

Fig. 10-2 Exercise from Traveler's Guide: Japanese.

taizai suru [to stay]

taizai shimasu [staying]

Doko ni taizai shimasu ka? [Where are you staying?]

Osaka ni taizai shimasu. [I am staying in Osaka.]

Continue

Fig. 10-3 Destination node explaining "taisai."

female voices. Requires Macintosh with CD-ROM drive. Available from:

PANDA SOFTWARE
101 Bartlett Hall
Dartmouth College
Hanover, NH
Phone: (603) 646-2176

HyperCard Foreign-Language Instruction Pronunciation tutors, vocabulary tutors, verb tutors, grammar drills, etc. Spanish, French, German, Russian, Japanese, Italian, Chinese. Prices from $29.95 to $249.95. (Also available on IBM PCs.) Available from:

HYPERGLOT SOFTWARE COMPANY
505 Forest Hills Boulevard
Knoxville, TN 37919
Phone: (800) 726-5087

StackPaks A variety of HyperCard stacks, education, personal management, entertainment. Available from:

EDUCORP
531 Stevens Avenue, Suite B
Solana Beach, CA 92075
Phone: (800) 843-9497

Articles, magazines, newsletters

Binder, C. (April 1988, Vol. 1, No. 9) "Hypertext: Features and Benefits." *Managing End User Computing*. Auerbach Publishers Inc., A Warren, Gorham & Lamont company.

Binder, C. (Spring, 1987) "The Promise of a Paperless Workplace." *Optical Insights*. Boston Computer Society, One Center Plaza, Boston, MA 02108.

Binder, C. (Spring, 1988) "The Emerging Industry." *Optical Insights*. The BCS CD-ROM/Optical Disc Group newsletter.

Bush, Vannevar (August 1945) "As We May Think." *Atlantic Monthly*. 8 Arlington Street, Boston, MA 02116.

Byte (Several articles on hypertext) Volume 13, Number 10, October 1988. To order, call or write:

BYTE Back Issues
One Phoenix Mill Lane
Peterborough, NH 03458
Phone: (603) 924-9281

Communications of the ACM—An entire journal issue devoted to Hypertext: Volume 31, Number 7, July 1988. NOTE: This issue is also available in hypertext format: "Hypertext on Hypertext" (IBM and Macintosh). Available from:

ACM ORDER DEPARTMENT
P.O. Box 64145
Baltimore, MD 21264
Phone: (800) 342-6626 for credit card orders 8:15 to 4:45 PM EST.

ComputorEdge   San Diego's computer magazine. Available in paper and in hypertext format for Macintosh and IBM PC computers. See description of *ComputorEdge* in chapter 7. For a free copy, send a formatted disk, and a self-addressed stamped envelope to:

COMPUTOREDGE
P.O. Box 83086
San Diego, CA 92138

Computer Currents   Lists new innovative software, often mentions new hypertext products. Contact:

COMPUTER CURRENTS PUBLISHING, INC.
5720 Hollis Street
Emeryville, CA 94608
Phone: (800) 365-7773 or (415) 547-6800

Conklin, Jeff (September 1987). "Hypertext: An Introduction and Survey." *COMPUTER*, an IEEE publication. This is a comprehensive introduction to hypertext and includes a good bibliography of scholarly sources. Mainly oriented toward mainframe computers. Jeff Conklin's research focuses on developing information systems for capturing and using design rationale. Cost for a back issue is $6.00, which includes postage and handling. Jeff can be reached at:

MCC
9390 Research Boulevard
Austin, TX 78759

HyperAge Magazine   Two excellent issues were published. However, the magazine appears to have ceased publication. For back issues contact:

HYPERAGE COMMUNICATIONS INC.
108 East Fremont Avenue
Sunnyvale, CA 94987
MCI Mail: hyperage

HyperMedia was a prototype publication from Mix Publications (Summer 1988). It has been superseded by *MacMedia*, which is available from:

HYPERMEDIA COMMUNICATIONS
501 2nd Street, Suite 414
San Francisco, CA 94107
Phone: (415) 243-9885

HyperNews   A newsletter on hypertext products available from NTERGAID (makers of HyperWriter). Available from:

NTERGAID INC.
2490 Black Rock Turnpike, Suite 337
Fairfield, CT 06430
Phone: (203) 368-0632

MaxThink Newsletter An update on MaxThink hypertext products. Available from:

MAXTHINK
Niel Larson
44 Rincon Road
Kensington, CA 94707
Phone: (415) 540-5508
PC-Hypertext BBS: (415) 540-6114 (contains hypertext shareware)

Multimedia Update A newsletter available from:

MULTIMEDIA COMPUTING CORPORATION
2900 Gordon Avenue, Suite 100
Santa Clara, CA 95051
Phone: (408) 245-4750, (800) 229-4750
FAX: (408) 739-5712

The Node Four issues a year of mind-expanding, futuristic possibilities. Frequently has articles on HyperCard stacks. Available from:

THE NODE
P.O. Box 1174
San Francisco, CA 94101

HyperLink This was a magazine for people interested in learning more about Hyper-Card, Plus, IBM LinkWay and other hypertext products. *HyperLink* described itself as a toolkit, an information reference, valuable software, and a friend. Software presented in the magazine was also available on a disk called StackSolutions. This magazine might not be currently available, but you might be able to get back issues. Contact:

HYPERLINK
P.O. Box 7723
Eugene, OR 97401

Inside HyperPAD A magazine containing tips and techniques for HyperPAD users. See HyperPAD. Contact:

THE COBB GROUP
P.O. BOX 24444
Louisville, KY 40224-9957

Inside ToolBook A 16-page journal with tips and techniques for ToolBook users. Sample topics: how to create graphics, customize menu bars, program with OpenScript, link information with hypertext. Contact:

INSIDE TOOLBOOK
The Cobb Group
P.O. Box 35160
Louisville, KY 40232-9719

MacSMARTS Hypercard software from:

COGNITION TECHNOLOGY CORPORATION
55 Wheeler Street
Cambridge, MA 02138
Phone: (800) 622-2829 or (617) 492-0246

Marchionini and Schneiderman (January 1988), "Finding Facts vs. Browsing Knowledge." *Hypertext Systems Computer* (an IEEE publication).

Microtimes A San Francisco Bay Area computer magazine. Contains a good balance of articles on Atari, Macintosh, and PC computers and software. Features a column by Jim Warren who has worked closely with hypertext guru Doug Engelbart. *Microtimes* is distributed free in the San Francisco Bay area, but you can subscribe. For sample copy, send $2 for shipping cost. Contact:

BAM PUBLICATIONS INC.
Microtimes Subscription Department
5951 Canning Street
Oakland, CA 94609
Phone: (415) 652-3810

Multimedia Computing & Presentations A monthly report on the latest developments in the hypermedia. Available for $375 ($150 education/nonprofit) from:

CREATIVE STRATEGIES RESEARCH INTERNATIONAL
2900 Gordon Avenue, Suite 100
Santa Clara, CA 95051
Phone: (408) 245-4750

NOTE: Creative Strategies has been a high-technology consulting and research company in Silicon Valley since 1969.

PC Magazine A Review of Personal Information Managers, many of which support hypertext. (Volume 7, Number 21, December 13, 1988.)

PC AI The Artificial Intelligence Magazine for Personal Computing. Often features articles on hypertext and expert systems. Gives comprehensive listings of new software products. Available from:

PC AI
3310 West Bell Road, Suite 119
Phoenix, AZ 85023
Phone: (602) 439-3253

Seyer, Philip C. (February 1989) "Performance Improvement with Hypertext." *Performance and Instruction* is the journal of the National Society for Performance and Instruction. (See NSPI under Organizations.) Available from:

PERFORMANCE AND INSTRUCTION
4423 East Trailridge Road
Bloomington, IN 47408-9653
Phone: (202) 408-7969

Books

Book and diskette: *Hypertext Hands-On!* (Diskette 0-201-15171-5) by Ben Shneiderman, University of Maryland and Greg P. Kearsley. The diskette contains the same material as the book, only in hypertext format. A run-time version of HyperTIES is used to enable hypertext on the diskette. Discusses basic concepts of hypertext, typical applications, and design issues. Available from:

ADDISON-WESLEY PUBLISHING COMPANY
Reading, MA 01867
Phone: (617) 944-3700 CS Marketing, Ext. 2396

Book and Diskette: *Mastering Sprint Macro Programming*, by Eddy Conway. Publisher: Scott, Foresman and Company. This book shows you how you can customize Sprint with its macro programming language. Several sample programs show you how to enable hypertext functions.

Computer Lib by Ted Nelson. Originally published in 1974. Recently updated. Published by Tempus Books (an imprint of Microsoft Press).

Computer Supported Collaborative Work: A book of readings. Edited by Irene Greif. Available from Morgan-Kaufmann Press, San Mateo, CA (1988). Articles by Doug Engelbart (an early hypertext guru) and others. Includes discussions on hypertext as well as other computing issues.

Designing & Writing Online Documentation by William K. Horton. Published by John Wiley & Sons, 1990.

D.C. Engelbart, "A Conceptual Framework for the Augmentation of Man's Intellect," in *Vistas in Information Handling*, Vol 1, Spartan Books, London, 1963.

Exploring Hypertext Programming: Writing Knowledge Representation and Problem-Solving Programs by Safaa Hashim. Contains source code for MicroIBIS—an issue-based information management system. Discusses the theory of problem solving by argumentation using hypertext. Available from:

TAB BOOKS
13311 Monterey Lane
Blue Ridge Summit, PA 17294-0850
Phone: (800) 822-8138

HyperPAD Companion. Available from:

THE COBB GROUP
P.O. Box 24444
Louisville, KY 40224-9957

HyperTalk Programming by Dan Shafer. Available from:

HAYDEN BOOKS
A Division of Macmillan Publishing Company
4300 West 62nd Street
Indianapolis, IN 46268
Phone: (800) 257-5755

Hypertext/Hypermedia by Jonassen, David H. Educational Technology Publications: Englewood Cliffs, New Jersey 07632, 1989. A creative paper version of a hypertext network originally created using HyperCard. The book consists of many text fragments (nodes) organized in hypertext fashion. At the beginning of the book there is a "hypermap" that simulates a hypertext control node. Each page in the book contains either a hypermap or a structured node. Each node contains labeled information blocks in the Information Mapping-style of writing. (See Information Mapping under Node Design Methodology in this chapter.) Typical information lock types are: Description, Links to Other Texts, Links to Other Documents.

Hyperdocuments & How to Create Them by James Martin, Prentice Hall, Englewood Cliffs, New Jersey 07632, 1990. Contains a lot of good general tips on developing hypertext networks. No specifics on available hypertext systems.

Interactive Multimedia by Sue Ambron and Kristina Hooper. This book offers an overview of several systems. Available from Microsoft Press.

Literary Machines by Ted Nelson. One of the first books about hypertext. Available from:

XANADU OPERATING COMPANY
550 California Ave., Suite 101
Palo Alto, CA 94301
Phone: (415) 856-4112 or (415) 332-2344

Mapping Hypertext by Robert E. Horn. An introduction to Information Mapping and how it can be used to organize hypertext. This book looks like hypertext in paper form. Available from:

THE LEXINGTON INSTITUTE
80 Marriett Road
Lexington, MA 02173
Phone: (617) 890-7003

Text, Context and HyperText available from MIT Press.

Turbo Prolog Advanced Programming Techniques (No. 3008) by Safaa Hashim and Philip Seyer. Appendix A of this book contains many predicates useful for programming hypertext in Turbo Prolog. Chapter 7 shows how to develop an editor that can automatically search a knowledge base. The knowledge base may contain names of all files on a hard disk. Contains an expert system and a machine learning program. Available from TAB Books. See also *Exploring Hypertext Programming* by Safaa Hashim (No. 3208).

Turning Text into Hypertext This is a workbook that shows how to take advantage of hypertext systems on personal computers. Teaches practical skills for designing hypertext solutions to paper overload. This is by Robert Glushko, Search Technology, Inc. Available from:

MULTIMEDIA COMPUTING CORPORATION
2900 Gordon Avenue, Suite 100
Santa Clara, CA 95051
Phone: (408) 245-4750 or (800) 229-4750
FAX: (408) 739-5712

Organizations and individuals

If you need help in developing a hypertext system, you might want to contact one of these organizations. They might be able to refer you to a hypertext specialist or perhaps accept a contracting assignment themselves.

AI RESOURCES
324 Rossiter Avenue
Baltimore, MD 21212

Works with hypertext, expert systems, and CD-ROM technologies; helps companies that need to process huge amounts of text.

AMERICAN INTERACTIVE MEDIA
11111 Santa Monica Boulevard
Los Angeles, CA 90025
Phone: (213) 473-4136

This organization is working on Compact Disc Interactive projects, especially elastic music. See chapter 9.

AMERICAN EXPOSITIONS, INC.
110 Greene Street, Suite 703
New York, NY 10012
Phone: (212) 226-4141

American Expositions hosts Multimedia Expositions. At these expositions, there are usually several seminars on hypertext/hypermedia, as well as companies who are exhibiting hypertext/hypermedia products.

ASSOCIATION FOR COMPUTING MACHINERY
11 East 42nd Street
New York, NY 10036
Phone: (212) 869-7440

This group publishes *Communications of the ACM* and other publications that often include scholarly articles on hypertext/hypermedia.

AUTODESK INC.
22320 Marinship Way
Sausalito, CA 94965
Phone: (415) 332-2344 or (415) 331-8093

Ted Nelson works for Autodesk. Autodesk is supporting the Xanadu Project.

WM. "KELLY" BALTHROP
5659 Glacier Drive
Springfield, OR 97478
Phone: (503) 741-2225

Develops hypertext networks with HyperCard, SuperCard, and IBM LinkWay.

BMUG MAILING ADDRESS:
    1442A Walnut Street, #62
    Berkeley, CA 94709-1496

OFFICE ADDRESS:
    2150 Kittridge Street, #3A/B
    Berkeley, CA 94704-1414
    Recorded Announcements: (415) 849-9114
    Business Phone: (415) 549-2684
    FAX: (415) 849-9026
    Helpline: (415) 849-HELP or (415) 849-4357 (limited use for nonmembers)

BMUG is an educational nonprofit corporation dedicated to collecting, evaluating and disseminating information about graphical interface computers. BMUG is primarily, though not exclusively, oriented toward Macintosh users. Several special interest groups have formed on topics such as HyperCard Scripting and Multimedia. The organization distributes an extensive collection of HyperCard stackware as well as a newsletter. Note that there is a BBS and Helpline for members. Meetings are held every Thursday.

BOSTON DOCUMENTATION DEVELOPMENT
125 Adams Street
Newton, MA 02158
Phone: (617) 965-5300

This organization develops hypertext applications.

BIX, McGraw-Hill, Inc.
One Phoenix Mill Lane
Peterborough, NH 03458
Phone: (603) 924-9281

With BIX (Byte Information Exchange) you can get the latest information on hypertext from BIX's on-line hypertext forum. Link up with hypertext developers and users!

Cole-Gilburne Fund
2560 Ninth Street, Suite 320A
Berkeley, CA 94710
Phone: (415) 841-4267

Venture capitalist that funds hypermedia projects and projects involving groupware, which enables groups of people to work together interactively on computer systems.

DLS Group, Inc.
Deborah Lee Stone
3003 East Third Avenue, Suite 307
Denver, CO 80206
Phone: (303) 333-4513
FAX: (303) 393-6320

Computer-based training, interactive instructor-led and self-paced training, hypermedia, job aids.

Haight-Ashbury HyperCard Club, SIG 0007
University of Utopia
543 Frederick Street
San Francisco, CA 94117
Phone: (415) 759-2455

This club is interested in inquiries from people who would like to get together and brainstorm ways to use HyperCard as a tool for showcasing ideas. They want to have stack-creating socials and study groups.

HyperCard Forum, SIG 0028
University of Utopia
543 Frederick Street
San Francisco, CA 94117
Phone: (415) 759-2455

This groups wants to use HyperCard for social evolution and information navigation. Lots of discussion about idealistic and futuristic applications are all part of this network.

HYPERMEDIA
1334 East 21st Street
Eugene, OR 97405
Phone: (503) 484-5450

HyperMedia develops customized hypermedia application programs.

HYPERPRESS PUBLISHING CORPORATION
P.O. Box 8243
Foster City, CA 94404
Phone: (415) 345-4620 (HyperCard stacks)

HYPERVIEW SYSTEMS CORPORATION
28 Jacome Way
Middletown, RI 02840
Phone: (800) 842-6758

INFORMANIA, INC.
Anne Derryberry
3305 Upas Street
San Diego, CA 92104

Dedicated to improving human performance through designing and developing custom training solutions.

INTERACTIVE DESIGN ASSOCIATES
Steve Walker
205 Oak Villa Road
Dallas, OR 97338
Phone: (503) 623-9037

Video and hypermedia-based training programs in educational and industrial environments.

KNOWLEDGE SUPPORT SYSTEMS
Barry Raybould
30 Spruce Hill Drive
Northboro, MA 01532
Phone: (508) 393-5342

CBT, Hypertext, Electronic Job Aids, Expert Systems, Information Retrieval, CD-ROM and Performance Technology.

KNOWLEDGE WORKSHOP
Attention: Elise Yoder
4750 Old William Penn Highway
Murryville, PA 15668

KNOWLEDGE SUPPORT SYSTEMS
Barry Raybould, President
30 Spruce Hill Drive
Northboro, MA 01532
Phone: (508) 393-5342

Knowledge Support Systems focuses on planning, designing, developing, and implementing hypermedia-based Performance Support Systems. These systems enable employees to immediate-access individualized on-line help—software guidance, advice and assistance, data, images, tools, monitoring systems, etc.—so they can perform their jobs with a minimum of support and intervention by others.

OMNICOM ASSOCIATES
Diane Gayeski
407 Coddington Road
Ithaca, NY 14850
Phone: (607) 272-7700

Custom video, CBT, interactive video, desktop publishing.

MOTOMEDIA
Peter Yamaguchi
157 South Boulevard
San Mateo, CA 94402
Phone: (415) 573-0907

Motomedia does interactive multimedia, interactive video, CD-ROM, HyperCard applications, and instructional design.

MCC SOFTWARE TECHNOLOGY PROGRAM
P.O. Box 200195
Austin, TX 78720
Phone: (512) 343-0978

NSPI
1126 Sixteenth Street, N.W., Suite 102
Washington, DC 20036
Phone: (202) 861-0777

National Society for Performance and Instruction (NSPI) is a society of educators, writers, trainers, psychologists, instructors, professors, and other professionals interested in improving human performance. For more information, contact the address given above. NSPI publishes a journal called *Performance and Instruction*, which occasionally has articles on how hypertext can be used to boost human performance. Also, see the listing for "Emerging Technology Committee of NSPI."

New Era Video
5894 S.W. 42nd Street
Miami, FL 33155
Phone: (305) 663-9451

Emerging Technology Committee of NSPI
Attention: Carl Binder
Precision Teaching and Management Systems, Inc.
P.O. Box 169
Nonantum, MA 02195
Phone: (617) 332-2656

This NSPI committee is researching new unfolding technologies that will help people work better, faster, and more effectively with more enjoyment. See description on page 248 of NSPI, the National Society for Performance and Instruction.

P.B. Smith and Associates
Harvey G. Ottovich, Chief Engineer
Desktop Publishing Specialists
660 Market Street, Suite 215
San Francisco, CA 94104
Phone: (415) 391-1333
FAX: (415) 391-4562

This group distributes the VIMAGER discussed elsewhere in this chapter. The VIMAGER allows you to incorporate still images into a hypertext program from any video source such as a camcorder or the Canon still-video camera RC-250, XAP Shot.

PDR Information Services
Monica Mefferet
2901 Tasman Drive, #215
Santa Clara, CA 95054
Phone: (408) 727-7607
FAX: (408) 986-8820

Specializes in computer based training and hypermedia applications in training.

Precision Teaching and Management Systems, Inc.
Carl Binder, President
P.O. Box 169
Nonantum, MA 02195
Phone: (617) 332-2656

Precision Teaching and Management Systems focuses on fluency-building instructional technology—a system instruction that involves time-based mastery criteria. Carl Binder,

President of Precision Teaching and Management Systems is also interested in on-line hypertext and authored "Hypertext Design Issues" in the Fall, 1989 issue of *Performance Improvement Quarterly* published by NSPI.

SEYER ASSOCIATES
1015 Cadillac Way, #5-201
Burlingame, CA 94010
Phone: (415) 347-4711

Develops customized AI software, job performance tools, hypertext networks and expert systems for IBM PCs and compatibles and Macintosh computers. Services include front-end analysis, instructional design and writing, as well as programming and scripting. Uses a variety of software including HyperCard, Prolog, HyperWriter, IBM LinkWay, HyperSprint, HyperTSR, Turbo C++, KnowledgePro, and Guide.

SHADOWLIGHT DESIGNS
Alan Weiler
484 Lake Park Avenue, #206
Oakland, CA 94610
Phone: (415) 531-8329

ShadowLight Designs develops interactive training, promotions and reference systems using HyperCard and other similar development systems on both the Macintosh and PC-DOS OS/2 personal computers. Provides complete software development, including instructional design, content development, copywriting, graphic design, animations, programming, testing and final delivery. The company can also work with in-house subject-matter experts, writers, designers or programmers according to the needs of the project and the resources of the client organization. ShadowLight Designs sometimes provides HyperCard stacks to prospective clients.

ST. MARGARET MEMORIAL HOSPITAL
Sandra K. Arjona, MLS
815 Freeport Road
Pittsburgh, PA 15215

Ms. Arjona is exploring the feasibility of using hypertext to publish medical journals in hypermedia format with reference, graphics, and audiovisual links.

TAGUS PIPS LTD.
Ian Hopkins Technology Centre
Epinal Way
Loughborough, Leics LE11 OQE
ENGLAND
Phone: (509) 611123
FAX: (509) 23495

CAD/CAM, Industrial robots, EPOS Equipment and Network Management Systems,

Performance Aids; distributor for Peter Pipe's Decision Table Algorithm System software.

TEKNOWLEDGY SOURCES INC.
Louis E. Frenzel
6050 NW 68th Street
Parkland, FL 33067
Phone: (305) 341-0727

Programmed instruction, job aids, information mapping, expert systems, audio tutorial, hypermedia.

TEXAS INSTRUMENTS HYPERMEDIA SYSTEMS & SERVICES
P.O. Box 655474, MS238
Dallas, TX 75265
Phone: (214) 680-5012

THE DUBLIN GROUP, INC.
100 First Street, Suite 350
San Francisco, CA 94105
Phone: (415) 227-4777

Develops courseware using a wide variety of systems. Calls upon a network of performance technologists.

THE HYPERMEDIA GROUP
1832 Woodhaven Way
Oakland, CA 94611
Phone: (415) 339-3322
MCI Mail: KTI

THE INTERNATIONAL INTERACTIVE COMMUNICATIONS SOCIETY
San Francisco Bay Area Chapter
P.O. Box 1372
San Carlos, CA 94070
Hotline: (415) 328-7318

Weekly meeting in San Francisco with educational presentations, for example: "Authoring Tools for CDI." Excellent place to network. This chapter has over 400 members.

THE INTERNATIONAL INTERACTIVE COMMUNICATIONS SOCIETY
International Headquarters
Deborah Palm, Mgr.
2298 Valerie Court
Campbell, CA 95008-3723
Phone: (418) 866-7941

THE OXKO CORPORATION
P.O. Box 6674
Annapolis, MD 21401
Phone: (301) 266-1671

Provides AI strategies and planning; expert systems, neural networks, hypertext, dynamic simulation, technology and tool evaluation.

THE PACIFIC GROUP
Sam Shmikler
13101 Washington Boulevard
Los Angeles, CA 90066
Phone: (213) 306-1779
FAX: (213) 827-5141

Draws upon a network of performance technologists, instructional developers, multimedia professionals, evaluation specialists and management consultants.

VANTAGE DESIGNS
Ellen Lichtig, President
322 Montevista Avenue, #204
Oakland, CA 94611
Phone: (415) 652-2434

Develops interactive educational tools: tutorials, job aids, reference systems using Macintosh products such as HyperCard and SuperCard.

VIDEOLOGIC INC.
245 First Street
Cambridge, MA 02142
Phone: (617) 494-0530

VideoLogic develops multimedia technologies. An important product from VideoLogic is the Multimedia Interactive Control System software (MIC). This software works with a PC digital video adapter called the DVA-4000 also made by VideoLogic. It also supports other display technologies including IBM InfoWindow, Sony View and Matrox. Using this technology you can have hypertext buttons that jump the user to live video segments displayed in separate windows. VideoLogic and Owl International are working together to develop a Guide Video Toolkit. Other hypertext system developers are working with VideoLogic as well. For example, Hyperdoc has a special script command called "VIDEO" that passes commands directly to the DVA-4000 video adapter. Users of VideoLogic products include Brigham Young University, American Interactive Media, and IBM. (See chapter 8 and if you want more details on the DVA-4000 see also the February 27, 1990 issue of *PC Magazine*.)

XANADU OPERATION COMPANY
550 California Avenue, Suite 101
Palo Alto, CA 94306
Phone: (415) 856-4112

ZOG
Carnegie-Mellon University
Computer Science and English Depts.
Pittsburgh, PA 15213

Graphics video, sound, and animation

These products are useful for creating graphics, video, sound and animation nodes.

Animator A PC program for creating animated nodes. A VGA monitor is required. Animation data may be stored on hard disk so that long animation sequences are possible. Editing can also be done from hard disk files. Available from:

AUTODESK INC.
22320 Marinship Way
Sausalito, CA 94965
Phone: (415) 332-2344 or (415) 331-8093

Audio Visual Connection (AVC) A system that lets you capture and edit images and sounds. Includes PS/2 boards and software. Available from IBM dealers.

ColorCard An add-on for HyperCard that allows movable windows and color on models that support color. Available from:

MACLABORATORY
314 Exeter Road
Devon, PA 19339
Phone: (215) 688-3114

FANTAVISION An inexpensive program for creating simple, but eye-catching animated nodes with sound effects. For PCs and Macintosh computers (about $49.95). Available from:

BRODERBUND SOFTWARE, INC.
17 Paul Drive
San Rafael, CA 94903-2101
Phone: (415) 492-3200

Interactive Video Disk Toolkit For the PC KnowledgePro system. Lets you control the Sony LDP2000 laser disk play from inside a KnowledgePro knowledge base. Provides intelligent use of video media from hypertext. That is, the system can trigger a video session or a sequence of frames based on its AI evaluation of the user's progress through the hypertext information. An inference mechanism in KnowledgePro can help to guide the user through a hypertext network. Available from:

KNOWLEDGE GARDEN INC.
John Slade, President
473A Malden Bridge Road
Nassau, NY 12123
Phone: (518) 766-3000

HotShot Graphics   A graphics editor for IBM PCs. Useful for capturing, editing, cataloging, and printing text and graphics images (even Microsoft Windows screens). You will find this program valuable if you are preparing graphic images for inclusion in hypertext programs on IBM PCs or for desktop publishing. Most of the illustrations in this book were prepared with HotShot Graphics. Available from:

SYMSOFT
924 Incline Way
Incline Village, NV 89450
Phone: (702) 832-4300

IntroVoice V   A PC circuit board, software manual, mike and speaker. A complete voice input/output system 500-word voice recognition with 98% + accuracy. **IntroVoice VI**   A speech recognition and synthesis system. **Micro IntroVoice**   A stand-alone voice recognition and synthesis system. It has a 1,000 word vocabulary and an unlimited text-to-speech. **HAL**   Home automation link-environmental control. Also has a 500-word vocabulary. Differs from IntroVoice V in that IntroVoice VI has speech synthesis and Introvoice V doesn't. **MicroTalker**   Just synthesis. **PTVC-756**   A hand-held computer that has bar coding, voice recognition, and synthesis. It has a 500-word vocabulary and is a complete voice input/output system. Available from:

VOICE CONNEXION
17835 Skypark Circle, Suite C
Irvine, CA 92714
Phone: (714) 261-2366

Sound Blaster   Stereo music/voice/MIDI/game PORT. Developed by:

CREATIVE LABS, INC.
131 S. Maple Avenue, #6
30-D Knowles Drive
Los Gatos, CA 95030
Phone: (800) 451-0900

Sound Blaster is distributed by:
BROWN-WAGH PUBLISHING
30-D Knowles Drive
Los Gatos, CA 95030
Phone: (800) 451-0900

PC-Key Draw   See earlier entry under "PC Hypertext Development Systems."

SPEECH THING   An inexpensive device that enables you to create digitized or synthesized speech nodes with an IBM PC or compatible. It plugs in line with the parallel printer and enables clear speech or music. Also included is SmoothTalker software that reads ordinary ASCII text files and produces synthesized speech. Input may also come directly from the keyboard. A related product is the **VOICE MASTER KEY SYSTEM,** a card that plugs into a PC. Along with software, it enables interactive voice recognition with speech response. Works with most MS-DOS applications. Speech recording and editing is also supported. See also Talking Turbo Expert. Available from:

COVOX INC.
675 Conger Street
Eugene, OR 97402
Phone: (503) 343-1271

Talking Turbo Expert   A PC system that lets you develop rule-based backward chaining expert systems that speak clearly in English. A menu-driven system. Uses the SPEECH THING from COVOX, Inc. Final solution is also spoken. Available from:

THINKING SOFTWARE INC.
46-16 Sixty-fifth Place
Woodside, NY 11377

Tutor-tech   A hypermedia toolkit for the Apple II computer. Especially good for teachers and trainers. You can create graphic nodes with buttons that link to graphic nodes. You can import clip-art from Print Shop, Newsroom, or Mousepaint pictures. No programming required. Gives the Apple II the feel of a Macintosh. Supports videodisc player Pioneer LD-V2000 and LD-V4200 with extra videodisc interface and cables. Available from:

TECHWARE CORPORATION
P.O. Box 151085
Altamonte Springs, FL 32715-1085
Phone: (407) 695-9000

Video Lesson Writer 42   Interactive video authoring system for Apple II and IBM PCs. **Video Disk Writer**   A video authoring system for Macintosh. **Video Lesson Writer 2000**   An interactive video authoring system for Apple II computers. (Interactive videotape systems are also available for Apple IIs and IBM PCs.) Contact:

WHITNEY EDUCATIONAL SERVICES
415 South Eldorado Street
San Mateo, CA 94402
Phone: (415) 340-9822

VIDEO HARDWARE SONY COMPONENTS PRODUCTS COMPANY
655 River Oaks Parkway
San Jose, CA 95134
Phone: (408) 423-0190

VIMAGER   A real-time video image capture and processing system. You can capture vido images from standard video cameras and import them into your hypertext/hypermedia applications. VIMAGER is being used, for example, to develop tutorials for nurses on how to operate hospital machinery. Contact:

AITECH INTERNATIONAL CORPORATION
William P. Lutz
Director of Marketing & Sales
1574 Centre Point Drive
Milpitas, CA 95035
Phone: (408) 946-3291
FAX: (408) 946-6901

LASERLINK   A set of videodisc player drivers for use with IBM LinkWay. Over 30 player functions. Available from:

MONKEY TREE COMPUTER SERVICES
2707 Jefferson Street
Bellingham, WA 98225
Phone: (206) 671-2545

Studio/1   A Macintosh paint program that enables animation. Works with HyperCard. Available from:

1820 Gateway Drive
San Mateo, CA 94404
Phone: (800) 245-4525

Fig. 10-4   A ClickArt cartoon.

ClickArt business cartoons   If you are developing a hypertext network and want to incorporate graphics, prescanned cartoons might come in handy. Cartoonist Phil Frank has put together a collection of more than 100 images showing humorous business-related subjects in bit-mapped format. Subject categories include computers, employment events, finance, headers, hijinks, monsters, overwork, symbols, taxes and more. Available for PCs and Macintosh. See Fig. 10-4. Available from:

T/MAKER
1390 Villa Street
Mountain View, CA 94041
Phone: (415) 962-0195

Index

A

access speed, 91, 118
action links, 63
advertising in hypermedia, 211-212
AmandaStories, 235
Amiga hypertext systems, 232-233
Analyzing Performance Problems, 159
Anderson, Scott, 40
ANIANIMAT animation, 40
animation, 38-41, 253-257
  ANIANIMAT, 40
  Animator, 253
  ANSIANIM, 37
  FantaVision, 40
  HyperCard, 38
  PC-KEY-DRAW, 40
  scripts, 38
Animator, 253
ANSIANIM character graphics, 35-37
APA mode, 33, 34
Apple II, hypertext systems, 232
applications and uses for hypertext, 2,
  83-92, 121-141,
  233-234
  access speed, 91
  advertising, 211-212
  annotation of work, 91
  book development, 124-125
  ComputorEdge magazine, 130-132
  continuity vs. diversity issues, 83-
  84
  cross-referenced documents, 128
  decision-making, 91
  Dr. Dobb's Journal, 129-130
  entertainment, 211
  expert systems, 135-136
  help systems, 89-91
  Hunger Project, 213
  inspiration-capturing ability, 84-85
  Knowledge Acquisition System
    (KAS), 126-128
  media labs, 211
  museum cross-referencing, 134-135
  networking, 91
  on-line help, 133-134
  organizational abilities, 86-88
  Oxford English Dictionary (OED),
    125-126
  productivity improvements, 121-124
  project management, 88-89
  simulations, 135
  telecommunications, 211
  tutorials, 90, 136-140
  updating information, 91
  writing tool uses, 85-86
arguments, 18, 20
article-based systems, 32, 118, 119
articles, magazines, newsletters, 238-
  242
artificial intelligence (AI), 20
ASCII graphics, 112-113
askSam, 10, 218
Atari, hypertext systems, 233
Audio Visual Connection (AVC), 253
Augment system development, 5
authoring guidelines, network development, 105-117
automatic linking, 75-79, 204-206
  build-your-own system, POWER
    SEARCH, 76
  EMPOWERment, 75-76
  Ize, 77-79
autotours, 118

B

Begeman, Michael L., 21
bit-mapped graphics, 33-34, 118
BlackMagic, 10, 21-24, 32, 52, 57,
  58, 124-125, 128, 219
book development programs, 124-125
bookmarks, 27-28, 113
books, 242-244
Boxer hypertext system, 7
Brand, Steward, 211
*British Journal of Educational Psy-
  chology*, 114
browsers, 23
buffers, disk, 36
Bush, Vannevar, 4-5
buttons, 18, 49-58, 21, 118
  command, 64-73, 118
  date, 74
  expansion, 50-51
  graphics, 36
  guide, 50-55
  HyperWriter links, 58-62
  insertion-type, 198
  lexical, 126, 127
  LinkWay objects, 56-58
  note, 51-53
  reference, 54-56, 118
  see-thru, 50
  video displays, 43
  wildcard, 192
Byte, 8

C

C language, programming hypertext,
  175, 201-206
card scripts, 147
card-based systems, 32, 118, 119
cards, 144
character graphics, 34-36
Chinese Language Instruction, 236-
  237
chunk-style hypertext, 6
CLASS HT, 219
ClickArt Business Cartoons, 257
CLR HyperArrays, 230
Cogent Prolog, 221-222

ColorCard, 253
command buttons, 64-73, 118
  advantages, 73-74
  command tail, 68
  EMPOWERment, 64-66
  external program control, 68-69
  Guide, 66
  KEY-FAKE, 69-71
  LinkWay external, 66-68
  scripts files, 71-73
command tail, 68
Communications of the ACM, 8, 23
compact disk interaction (CDI), 210
CompuServe, 48, 73
Computer Language, 124
computer-animated nodes, 38-41
ComputorEdge, 92, 130-132, 234
*Concise Dictionary of 26 Languages,
The*, 126
Conklin, Jeff, 8, 21
control nodes, 13, 29
control structures, programming
  hypertext, 148
copy-protected software, 118
Crossland, Sigurd P., 72

D

date buttons, 74
Decision Table Algorithm System,
  100-102
decision tables, 99-102, 217-218
decision-making, 91
definition blocks, 107
Design Journal system, 21
*Designing and Writing Online Docu-
mentation*, 21
development systems, PC, 218-230
digitized voice nodes, 47
directories and subdirectories, 15
disk buffers, 36
"distance" education, 9
Document Examiner hypertext system,
  7
documentation, network development,
  115-117
DOS Help!, 233
DOS links, 63
DOS utilities, 15-18
DR utility, 15-16
Dr. Dobb's Journal, 129-130, 206,
  217

E

editor, hypertext (HE.PRO), 23, 178-
  190
  commented code, 178
  editing features, 181
  exiting files, 180-181
  filenames, 179
  hypertext jumps, 180

list of files, directory, 179
  loading program, 178
  saving trails, 181
  source code, 182-190
elastic music, 210
Election of 1912 simulation, 135
Emergency Room simulation, 219
empirical approach, network development, 103
EMPOWERment, 10, 13, 15, 32, 45,
  48, 49,
  58, 72, 121-124, 175, 219
  automatic linking, 75-76
  command buttons, 64-66
  reference buttons, 56
Engelbart, Doug, 5, 7
entertainment hypermedia, 211
example blocks, 107
Executive Life, 235
expansion buttons, 50-51
expert systems, 30, 135-136, 160
Exploring Hypertext Programming, 8,
  18, 196
Eyecons!, 231

F

4C, 215
FantaVision animation, 40-41, 253
faxable nodes, 48
field scripts, 147-148
fields, 57, 119, 144, 148
filenames, 14, 191
Find command, programming hypertext, 148
fixed nodes, 31
Focal Point, 235
folders, LinkWay, 57
Foreign Language Instruction, 234
future developments, 209-213

G

Go command, programming hypertext, 148
Goodenough, Amanda, 39
Gookin, Dan, 131
GRAB, 34
GRABIT, 34, 63
graphics, 118, 253-257
  APA mode, 33-34
  ASCII-type, 112-113
  bit-mapped, 33-34, 118
  button embed-able, 36
  captions placement, 111
  character-type, 34-36
  GRABIT, 63
  holographic images, 209-210
  HotShot, 64
  HyperCard, 37
  importing, 62
  links creation, 62-64

network development, 111-113
  graphics links, 61-62
  graphics nodes, 33-37, 63
Guide, 9, 10, 32, 37, 45, 57, 58, 94,
  220, 231
  command buttons, 66
  programming hypertext, 155-158
guide buttons, 50-55
guided tour approach, network development, 98-99

H

handlers, 144
handles, programming hypertext, 158
hardware requirements, 118
Harley, 114
Harvard Graphics, 220-221
Hashim, Safaa, 8, 18, 80, 196
help systems (*see also* tutorials), 89-
  91, 133-134
Help! Engine, xText, 171-172
hierarchical approach, network development, 95-97
hierarchical browsers, 23
holographic images, 209-210
Horn, Leonard, 87-88
Horn, Robert E., 88, 114
"hot spots," 21, 118
hotlinks, 68
HotShot, 34, 64, 254
Hunger Project, The, 213
HyperBase Developer, 10, 221
HyperBASIC, 230
Hyperbook, 231
HyperCard, 8-9, 13, 32, 33, 136, 231
  animation, 38
  browse mode, 40
  graphics nodes, 37
  HyperTalk scripting language, 39
  scripting, 143-150
  selection mode, 39
  voice nodes, 47
HyperCard Foreign-Language Instruction, 238
Hyperdoc, 10, 37, 42, 43, 57, 58,
  150, 154-155, 175, 222
HyperEasy Training, 231
Hypergate, 9, 135, 231
hypermaps, 87-88, 97-98
hypermedia, 1, 8, 86, 212
HyperNotes, 222
HyperPAD, 10, 13, 30, 32, 150-153,
  212, 222-223
HyperRez, 10, 131, 132, 221
HyperSprint (*see also* Sprint), 27, 55-
  56, 83, 90, 97, 175, 223
HyperTalk, 30, 39
Hypertext 1987 Digest, The, 235
hypertext development, 1-12
  applications and uses, 2

Augment system development, 5
chunk-style, 6
memex development, 5
personal-computer systems, 9-12
Xanadu system, 7-8
hypertext editor (HE.PRO), 178-190
Hypertext Editor, The (HE), 10, 26
Hypertext Hypermedia, 87, 114
Hypertext on Hypertext, 223
HyperTIES, 10, 58, 135, 223-224
HyperTSR, 10, 133-134, 172-175,
    202, 224
HyperTutor, 235
HyperVision, 256
hyperware, 8
HyperWriter, 2-3, 13, 23, 24, 26, 32,
    34, 37, 42, 45,
    57, 100, 104, 150, 175, 206, 224
    action links, 63
    buttons and links, 58-62
    DOS links, 63
    graphics links, 61-62
    importing graphics, 62
    text links, 59-61

I

IBM Link Way (*see* Link Way)
Icon Factory, 232
IF-THEN=IF-THEN-ELSE, 148
importing graphics, 62
index approach, network develop-
    ment, 103-104
INDUCTEL, 126
information blocks, 107
information mapping, 87-89, 113-114,
    218
insertion buttons, 198
instructions, network development,
    115-117
Interactive Video Disk Tookit, 253
Intermedia hypertext system, 7
IntroVoice VI, 209
IntroVoice V, 254
issue nodes, 18
Issue-Based Information Systems
    (IBIS), 8, 18-21, 80, 196
Ize, 11, 68, 77-79, 225

J

Japanese Language Tutorial, 136-140,
    236
Johnson, Scott, 129
Jonassen, David H., 87, 88, 114, 218

K

Kanji Exercises, 137-140
KEY-FAKE, 68-71
KeyPilot, 216
Knowledge Acquisition System
    (KAS), 11, 126-128, 225

knowledge base, 30
KnowledgePro, 30, 58, 135-136, 158-
    161, 226

L

languages, programming (*see* pro-
    gramming languages)
Larson, Niel, 103
LASERLINK, 256
Levy, Steven, 162
lexical buttons, 126, 127
linear search triggers, 163
links, 18, 21, 88, 118
    action, 63
    automatic linking, 75-79, 204-206
    DOS, 63
    graphics to create, 62-64
    graphics, 61-62
    hotlinks, 68
    HyperWriter buttons, 58-62
    networking computers, 73
    programming hypertext, 193
    see-thru, 50
    text, 59-61
    typed links, 18, 79-80
LinkWay, 11, 30, 32, 34, 37, 40, 150,
    175, 224
    buttons and objects, 56-58
    command buttons, external, 66-68
    document buttons, 58
    fields, 57
    find buttons, 58
    folders, 57
    go buttons, 58
    link buttons, 58
    nodes, 57
    objects, 57
    pages, 57
    picture pop-up buttons, 58
    pictures, 57
    programming hypertext, 153-154
    script buttons, 58
    text pop-up buttons, 58
LinkWay Toolkit, 224-225
Literary Machine, 6, 29
Logic Gem, 100-102, 218
logical operators, programming
    hypertext, 148
LOGiiX script, Guide programming
    hypertext, 156
LWCAPTUR, 34

M

M program, 210
MacAtlas, 234-235
Macintosh hypertext systems, 230-
    232, 234-238
macros, musical nodes, 45-47
MacSmarts Professional, 231
Mager, Robert, 159

mapping, 19, 87-89, 113-114, 218
Mapping Hypertext, 88, 114, 218
Marcus, Dwight, 210
MCI Mail, 48, 73
media developments, 209-210
Media Lab, The, 211
memex development, 5
memory, disk buffers, 36
memory-resident hypertext systems,
    162-175
    PC-Browse, 162-167
    xText, 167-172
MKSCRN, 220
Multimate, 68
Musical Instrument Digital Interface
    (MIDI), 43
musical nodes, 43-45
    elastic music, 210
    macros to refine commands, 45-47
    tutorials, 136

N

National Society for Performance and
    Instruction (NSPI), 3, 40
navigation tools, 23-28
navigational nodes, 14
Nelson, Ted, 5-8, 29, 89, 213
Neptune hypertext system, 7
network browsers, 23
network development, 73, 91, 93-119
    authoring guidelines, 105-117
    bookmarks, 113
    combined approaches, 104-105
    decision tables, 99-102
    documentation's writing style, 115-
        117
    empirical approach, 103
    graphics use, 111-113
    guided tour approach, 98-99
    hierarchical approach, 95-97
    hypermaps, 97-98
    hypertext system selection guide-
        lines, 118-119
    index approach, 103-104
    information mapping techniques,
        113-114
    modified alphabet, 105
    orphan nodes, 107-108
    pop-up network design, 119
    related nodes, branching, 107
    revising, 103, 108-109
    screen design, 109-111
    summary approach, 98
    table of contents approach, 93-95
    testing, 103
nodes, 1, 13-15, 31-48, 119
    cards, 144
    characteristics, 31
    computer-animated, 38-41
    control nodes, 13, 29

creation, programming hypertext, 193
decision tables, 217-218
design methodology, 217-218
digitized voice, 47
faxable, 48
fixed vs. scrollable, 31
graphics, 33-37, 63
intelligence-added, 149-150
issue, 18
LinkWay, 57
musical, 43-45
navigational, 14
orphan, 107-108
parent, 18
people as nodes, 47-48
position, 18
stacks, 38, 144
terminal, 15, 51
text, 31-33
tour points, 26-27
transitional, 14, 103
note buttons, 51-53
Notecards hypertext system, 7
NPSI Journal, 114

O

objects, LinkWay, 57
on-line help systems, 133-134
OPUS I, 226
organizations and user groups, 244-253
orphan nodes, 107-108
Oxford English Dictionary (OED), 125-126

P

pads, 151
PADTalk scripting, 30, 151-153
pages, LinkWay, 57
parent nodes, 18
PC hypertext development systems, 9-12, 218-230
PC Magazine, 15, 72, 206
PC MagNet, 68
PC-Browse, 11, 24-25, 162-167, 175, 226
    hypertext capability, 166
    jump to other files, 166
PC-HyperText, 132, 228
PC-Key Draw, 11, 40, 226-227, 254
PC-Resource, 206
PDC-PROLOG, 194-196, 228
Personal HyperBase, 227
Personal Power, 99
pictures, LinkWay, 57
Pipe, Peter, 100, 159
Plus, 11, 37, 150, 162, 227

pointing devices, 209
points (*see* buttons)
pop-up networks, 119
position node, 18
power failures, 28
POWER SEARCH, 76, 89, 215, 216
ProBAS HyperHelp ToolKit, 216-217
ProComm, 48, 83
productivity enhancement, 121-124
Programmer's Journal, 206
programming hypertext, 143-207
    automatic linking, 204-206
    buttons and button tools, 144-145
    C language, 201-206
    card scripts, 147
    cards, 144
    control structures, 148
    developing original applications, 175-206
    distributing your own help systems, 175
    Dr. Dobb's Journal, 206
    field content modification, 148
    field scripts, 147-148
    fields, 144
    filenames, Turbo Prolog, 191
    Find command, 148
    Go command, 148
    Guide, 155-158
    handlers, 144
    handles, 158
    HyperCard scripting, 143-150
    Hyperdoc, 154-155
    HyperPAD, 151-153
    Hypertext Editor (HE.PRO), 178-190
    IF-THEN and IF-THEN-ELSE, 148
    insertion buttons, 198
    intelligence added to nodes, 148-150
    KnowledgePro, 158-161
    languages, 30, 118
    links, 193
    LinkWay scripting, 153-154
    logical operators, 148
    LOGiiX script, 156
    memory resident systems, 162-175
    node creation, 193
    PADTalk scripting, 151-153
    PDC-PROLOG, 194-196
    Plus, 162
    Sprint, 196-201
    stack scripts, 146-147
    stacks, 144
    ToolBook, 161-162
    tools, 215-217
    topics, 158
    Turbo Prolog, 176-194
    wildcard buttons, 192
project management, 88-89

publications, 238-242

Q

Quattro Pro, 16-18
query systems, 24-25

R

reference buttons, 54-56, 118
    EMPOWERment, 56
    HyperSprint, 55-56
reference materials, hypertext, 238-244
reference points, 54
Reg-In-A-Box, 128-129
Regis, 135-136
Reid, Stephen, 219
Rittle, Horst, 8, 18
RN utility, 15-16
Robbins, Anthony, 99
run-time engines, 118

S

scan codes, PC, 70-71
Schaffer, Eric M., 114
screen design, network development, 109-111
ScriptEdit, 232
scripting   (*see* programming)
scripts files, command buttons, 71-73
scripts, animation, 38
scrollable nodes, 31
see-thru buttons=links, 50
Shaw, Greg, 212
simulations, 135, 219
SmoothTalker voice converter, 47
software, 8, 118
Sound Blaster, 254
sound and speech programs, 209, 210, 253-257
source files, xText, 168-170
sources and resources, 215-257
Spectre 128, 233
SPEECH THING, 47, 210, 254
Sprint (*see also* HyperSprint), 11, 15, 27-28, 124, 175, 196-201
stack scripts, 146-147
StackPaks, 238
stacks, node-networks, 38, 144
Standard Desk Dictionary, 126
storyboards, 8
string searches, 204-206
Studio=1, 256
summary approach, network development, 98
SuperCard, 9, 232
SuperKey, 68
SUPERTEXT, 201
SuperText Toolkit, 217

T

table of contents approach, network development, 93-95
tail, command, 68
Talking Turbo Expert, 255
TechHelp!, 217
telecommunications, 211
terminal nodes, 15, 51
text links, 59-61
text nodes, 31
Thinker, 11, 49, 50, 232-233
ToolBook, 161-162, 228
topics, programming hypertext, 158
tour points, 26-27
tours, 26-27, 118
trails, 26, 118
transitional nodes, 14, 103
Transtext, 58, 228
Traveler's Guide: Japanese, 236
Trigg, Randall, 8
triggers, 163
Trueman, 114
Turbo C programming tools, 217
Turbo C Toolbox, 202

Turbo C++, 18
Turbo Prolog, 175-194, 210, 228-229
Tutor-tech, 232, 255
tutorials, 90, 136-140
Twentieth-Century Navigator, The, 235-236
typed links, 18, 79-80

U

user groups and organizations, 244-253
user nodes, 47-48
utilities, DOS, 15-18

V

Video Lesson Writer 42, 41, 255
video nodes, 41-42
VIMAGER, 34, 255-256
Voice Mastery Key System, 47, 209
voice, digitized, 47, 209-210
Voyetra Technologies, 210

W

Wang, Wally, 131

WATSON, 48, 211
We hypertext system, 7
webs, 28-30
What Makes Music Work, 136, 234
wildcard buttons, Turbo Prolog, 192
Window Book Technology, The, 11, 229
WinSong, 43-45
Word, 15
word processor use, xText, 170-171
WordPerfect, 15, 68
writing tools, 85-86

X

Xanadu system, 7-8, 229-230
Xhelp, 12, 230
xText, 12, 13, 58, 167-172, 175
  Help! Engine launch, 171-172
  source file creation, 168-170
  word processor usage, 170-171

Z

Zog hypertext system, 7

Other Bestsellers of Related Interest

COMPUTER TECHNICIAN'S HANDBOOK

3rd Edition—Art Margolis

"This is a clear book, with concise and sensible language and lots of large diagrams . . . use [it] to cure or prevent problems in [your] own system . . . the [section on trouble-shooting and repair] is worth the price of the book."

—*Science Software Quarterly*

More than just a how-to-manual of do-it-yourself fix-it techniques, this book offers complete instructions on interfacing and modification that will help you get the most of your PC. 579 pages, 97 illustrations. Book No. 3279, $24.95 paperback, $36.95 hardcover

LEARN DOS—GUARANTEED!

—Richard P. Cadway

Use DOS as the tool it was intended to be! This book tells you how to make MS/PC-DOS work for you, without making you digest an encyclopedia of specialized information and technical jargon. Cadway concentrates exclusively on the most important DOS commands and most basic hardware installations—he explains what the major parts of DOS do, how the file system works, and just enough DOS to install and use your applications effectively. 192 pages, 28 illustrations. Book No. 3331, $14.95 paperback only

THE FAX HANDBOOK

—Gerald V. Quinn

This comprehensive guide explores what a fax machine can do for your business's bottom line, and explains all of the elements of owning and operating a fax machine. You will understand how fax machines work, and why they have become as crucial to today's workstation as the photocopier. This book also gives you set up and operation guidelines for your fax. You'll find tips on power supplies, connecting to the telephone, and the best locations for the machine within the workstation. 160 pages, 42 illustrations. Book No. 3341, $8.95 paperback, $16.95 hardcover

WORDPERFECT® 5.1 MACROS

—Donna M. Mosich, Robert Bixby, and Pamela Adams-Regan

Get everything you need to know about macros in any version of WordPerfect through 5.1. Create and use macros to generate form letters, automate mailing list production, index manuscripts, and more! There are more than 300 usable macros covered in this guide (and available on disk), with explanations and illustrations on how the macro command language is used. 480 pages, 162 illustrations. Book No. 3617, $26.95 paperback, $34.95 hardcover

DATA DICTIONARIES FOR DATABASE ADMINISTRATORS—Robin J. Vinden

This straightforward guide shows you, in clear, easy-to-follow language, how to use data dictionaries to manage your database. The emphasis is on establishing procedures for setting up a data dictionary and maintaining basic rules of data control. Graphs and line drawings illustrate key points. You'll discover new and practical ways to manage and ensure the integrity of stored data. 192 pages, 15 illustrations. Book No. 3515, $17.95 paperback, $29.95 hardcover

THE FROZEN KEYBOARD: Living with Bad Software—Boris Beizer

". . . an entertaining, insightful, and wide-ranging computer volume for all collections." —**Booklist**

Now you can learn to "live with" bad software, bad features, poor support, unreadable instruction manuals, and all the other ills that plague the personal computer user. Assuming a reluctant user's viewpoint, the author discusses bugs, user-friendly and other con games, menu-driven versus command-driven software, hostile software, and other key problems. 300 pages, 288 illustrations. Book No. 3146, $17.95 paperback only